W9-ABZ-316

The Letter of Violence: Essays on Narrative and Theory,
  by Idelber Avelar

Intellectual History of the Caribbean,
  by Silvio Torres-Saillant

Forthcoming titles

None of the Above: Contemporary Puerto Rican Cultures and Politics,
  edited by Frances Negrón-Muntaner

Puerto Ricans in America: 30 Years of Activism and Change,
  edited by Xavier F. Totti and Félix Matos Rodríguez

Cosmopolitanisms and Latin America

Against the Destiny of Place

Jacqueline Loss

COSMOPOLITANISMS AND LATIN AMERICA
© Jacqueline Loss, 2005.

First published in 2005 by
PALGRAVE MACMILLAN™
175 Fifth Avenue, New York, N.Y. 10010 and
Houndmills, Basingstoke, Hampshire, England RG21 6XS
Companies and representatives throughout the world.

PALGRAVE MACMILLAN is the global academic imprint of the Palgrave Macmillan division of St. Martin's Press, LLC and of Palgrave Macmillan Ltd. Macmillan® is a registered trademark in the United States, United Kingdom and other countries. Palgrave is a registered trademark in the European Union and other countries.

ISBN 1–4039–7034–3

Library of Congress Cataloging-in-Publication Data

Loss, Jacqueline.
  Cosmopolitanisms and Latin America : against the destiny of place / Jacqueline Loss.
    p. cm.
  Includes bibliographical references and index.
  ISBN 1–4039–7034–3 (alk. paper)
    1. Latin American literature—20th century—History and criticism.
  2. Cosmopolitanism—Latin America. I. Title.

PQ7081.L77 2005
860.9'3552—dc22   2005047610

A catalogue record for this book is available from the British Library.

Design by Newgen Imaging Systems (P) Ltd., Chennai, India.

First edition: November 2005

10 9 8 7 6 5 4 3 2 1

Printed in the United States of America.

To Bobbie and Cal

Contents

Acknowledgments

This project began as a dissertation at the University of Texas at Austin where the guidance of Naomi Lindstrom was indispensable. She was the initial public for my rehearsal of these ideas, and her encouragement, detailed revisions, and organizational insights have been decisive.

At every juncture, I have been lucky enough to know Esther Whitfield, and for that fortuitous encounter I am grateful to Alicia Borinsky and her 1995 seminar on Writing and the Americas. Esther has laboriously read and reread numerous parts of this manuscript. Her generosity, humor, and tolerance have helped me to weave together personal and professional aspects of this writing process.

César Salgado's interventions have contributed to making this manuscript more of what it should be. I appreciate his reading of chapter 1; moreover, his intellectual rigor is to be emulated. Víctor Fowler-Calzada not only collaborated on the translation of chapter 5 into Spanish for the online journal of the Escuela de Cine in Cuba, *Miradas*, but also allowed me to render more fully the significance of many central issues within the Cuban context.

I am also immensely grateful to my colleagues Osvaldo Pardo and Freya Schiwy who, in addition to providing me with all kinds of vast and open support, have been instrumental in helping me communicate my ideas more effectively on this project.

Reina María Rodríguez, Jorge Mirailles, and Antonio José Ponte conversed with me at length about the significance of Reinaldo Arenas on screen in Cuba. I revisit those conversations frequently and continually invent new ones for future meetings. Tomás Fernández Robaina shared with me invaluable insight on this same topic.

I am grateful to Ernesto René Rodríguez on whom I can always count to revitalize my relation to words and ideas. His approach to place, his strategy of survival through defamiliarization, as well as his immense stories and videos discretely mark my theoretical vision. And to Antonio Garza, on whom I've bounced ideas off for years because he understands what I mean sometimes before I do. Furthermore, he has read the entire manuscript likely more than once and possesses a tenacity for listening and interrogating to which I am indebted. As Nikola Petkovic and I translated each other for each other, we actively debated villages and cities, provincialism and cosmopolitanism, among many other things with pertinence to this manuscript.

Donna Bagdasarian is exceptional; she took my manuscript for a test drive a long time ago, when she did me the dear favor of copy-editing it.

Really, I have internalized a motley assortment of dialogues that are elaborated in and beyond these pages. My resistance to and insistence upon their commonalities could at least form an annotated bibliography. It is my hope that all these people are able to recognize traces of our connections within: Mauricio Almonte, Susan Briante, Madeline Buchsbaum, Mia Carter, Tanya Cecarrelli, Ileana Corbelle, Philippe Essomé, Alessandro Fornazzari, Isabel Garayta, Andrew Hurley, Daniel Loss, Barbara Loss, Calvin Loss, Emily Lundin, Florence Preiser, Ronald Reeser, Richard Reyes-Gavilán, Fernando Rosenberg, Armando Suárez-Cobián, Caridad Tamayo, and Roberto Tejada.

I feel that Alexander Martin went beyond the call of duty when he worked with me on a section of chapter 4 for *Nepantla*. Aaron Walker and I played "name that book" one afternoon, and we almost got it right—at least a subtitle emerged. Michael Mejías's persistent tips on publicity are most appreciated. I thank Kerry Stefancyk for her assistance with the bibliography, endnotes, and formatting, and Barbara Lindsey for her technological expertise. I could not ask for more from my colleagues in Modern and Classical Languages at the University of Connecticut who have created an environment that is so conducive to thinking and carrying out investigations.

The book's cover is the fruit of dear friendships: Joseph Michael López's photograph and Francisco López's design were certainly not conceptualized together and I thank them both for their willingness to combine these nonfamiliar entities.

Thank you to my editor Ella Pearce, without whom this process could not be realized.

Cosmopolitanisms between the Americas

For almost a week in November 2002, Diamela Eltit was in the "house"—in the Casa de las Américas, the Cuban Revolution's beacon to cultures resistant to U.S. domination within the Americas. Along with other artists, Eltit founded the *CADA* (Colectivo de Acciones de Arte—Art Actions Collective) in Santiago, Chile in 1979. However, she gained international attention, primarily from academics in the United States, only after the publication of her first novel, *Lumpérica*, in 1983. The Casa de las Américas is located near Havana's Malecón, far from the scenarios of the Chilean neo-avant-garde where Eltit debuted. It announces itself as "a meeting place of all cultures of the Americas," and it has indeed successfully linked elements of cultures not only throughout Latin America but also with the other parts of the world. It has gone a long way toward fulfilling what it set out to do in 1959 under the direction of Haydee Santamaría, not only to help make Havana the principal meeting place for Latin American writers and artists, but also to be a repository and showcase for their works.

Within the revolution's elaborate network of cultural institutions, Casa de las Américas is especially internationally oriented, but undoubtedly selectively so, keeping in mind Cuba's shifting criteria for the role of art within society.[1] As Eltit is temporarily housed there, we may question the degree to which Casa's very patrimony is challenged by trends constitutive of scholarly disciplines that are geographically distant from the actual site of artistic production. It is certain that, at the outset, Casa has depended on such challenges to patrimony, cultural convergences, and active engagement with texts from distant places in solidarity with the revolution's struggle, but their significance is altered in the aftermath of the disintegration of the Soviet Union and the dollarization of the Cuban economy.[2] Authors and their texts may travel to Cuba, but the idea of a cosmopolitan Cuba—that has sustained intellectuals across the globe—has transformed. Eltit "en la Casa" reflects the more global scramble for artistic and intellectual alternatives to neoliberalism.

Eltit's aesthetic renditions of the *testimonio*, for instance, are central within Latin American cultural and literary studies as conceived within the United States because of the way in which they dramatize the relationship between the theoretical self and the corporeal other. The more traditional *testimonio*, in much of Latin America, conveys the marginal perspectives of the oppressed—those who have suffered the fate of collective tragedy, war, or political repression. Cuba is unique with respect to this genre, since beginning in the 1970s, the *testimonio* has been vindicated by an official category of a prize awarded by Casa de las Américas. Eltit's difficult-to-classify text, *El padre mío* (1989), is almost a parody of *testimonio* in the sense that its fragmented speech communicates nothing that could possibly unify the collective sphere, as a comprehensible and explicit political act. Her novel *Por la patria* (1986) fictionalizes the process of creating effective political speech. When these two works are considered within the context of a state institution that several decades before officially cast that genre as the individual's testament to a collective struggle and revolutionary triumph, their meaning, as well as that of Casa, shifts.

Frequently paired with the renowned publication of Casa, the magazine *Review* of the Rockefeller-sponsored Center for Inter-American Relations emerged in 1968 after the demise of Emir Rodríguez Monegal's Paris-based and CIA-financed *Mundo Nuevo* to disseminate Latin American literature in the United States. Eltit's first novel, *Lumpérica*, was actually translated by an ex-director of the *Review*, Ronald Christ, and the journal has published her writings on more than one occasion. Although the intricacies of cultural traveling are elaborate, we can trace a general pattern of movement wherein: (1) what in Chile was initially cast as marginal and provocative (2) is canonized in the United States and (3) enters Cuba as both "canonical elsewhere" and innovative.

As this instance suggests, the importance of Cuba in reconceptualizing cosmopolitanism in and vis-à-vis Latin America cannot be overlooked.[3] Situated in a comparative context, with a focus on Latin America, this book examines the rubric of discrepant cosmopolitanisms as opposed to those that are merely and more limitedly consumerist or universalist. The discrepancy to which I refer is almost tautological in the sense that the very concept of cosmopolitanism without the descriptive "discrepant" already implies a negotiation between the city and the world. By virtue of dominant history's disregard for the previous economies of translation and exchange that sustained particular communities, certain subjects are codified as cosmopolitan; others as merely local. In the aftermath of these historical experiences, the tendency in cultural studies has been to vindicate the local sphere. The discrepancy that interests me calls attention to the historical, political, and aesthetic connections among critics and writers who were suppressed by those dynamics of power. The local spheres are frequently more cosmopolitan—interactive, porous, and translational—than these histories concede. While this book questions how Reinaldo Arenas's and Eltit's writing confront other previous and contemporary cosmopolitanisms, it also reveals the intersections of theoretical and authorial preoccupations regarding worldly affiliations.

It is fair to ask what justifies the juxtaposition of a Chilean writer and a Cuban one, other than language, in a broad sense, a degree of overlapping in the years that they produce, and different but comparable experiences of living in an authoritarian regime. The somewhat more traditional textual dependence in chapters 2 and 3 are paralleled by studies in visual cultures in chapters 4 and 5. This symmetry allows me to explore these two writers' articulation of their experiences of creating under adverse conditions as well as the drawing attention of critics to particular aspects of the authors' framing as sustenance for their own work. In addition, the structure of this book illustrates the powerful residues of a flirtation between socialism and neoliberalism within an examination of complicated processes of commodification. The politics of the Cold War and the policies of the United States toward Latin America, in general, and Cuba and Chile, in particular, lurk in the background. We may recall that the coup of Salvador Allende was realized with the support of the United States whose actions were promulgated by the characteristic Cold War fear of communism in the Americas. The U.S. involvement in Batista's Cuba is well documented; this is to say that in the cases of both Castro's Cuba and Pinochet's Chile, various "outside" spaces have been periodically called upon as unofficial jurors on internal affairs. These experiences bear on our discussions of cosmopolitanism in the respective contexts. The Pinochet case—spearheaded by the Spanish Judge Baltasar Garzón, beginning with the campaign to extradite the military ruler from London to Spain on account of human rights abuses—clearly confounds the terms for defining the internal sphere and elicits a critical negotiation between cosmopolitanism and nationalism. The very core of Pinochet's dictatorship already problematized those terms. The free-market economic policies of Pinochet's extremely nationalistic government were established by a group of Chilean economists, known as the Chicago Boys, who had been trained abroad at the University of Chicago between 1956 and 1961. In March 1975, the well-known Milton Friedman even gave a series of lectures in Santiago, and soon after debates concerning the efficacy of the shock-like treatment of inflation, drastic free-market measures were put into practice.[4] The drastic nature of the times, as is by now well documented, was not only economic. During the 1970s and 1980s, a paradigm of patriotism and order composed the other face of these neoliberal economic policies, thus illustrating that the relationships between apparently free-flowing globalizing strategies and absolutist limits, cosmopolitanism, and nationalism are complex.

What culture and capital from the outside has meant for Cuban artists living in Castro's Cuba, under a U.S. blockade and restrictive policies of cultural exchange, presents a very different set of problems for a discussion on cosmopolitanism, but one that possesses points of contact with the United States and Chile, making it fascinating to pose together these artists' stories. Our initial allegory begins to model the complexity of this game, as revolutionary Cuba's Casa de las Américas' stake on poetics not absorbable by the capitalist market and its fluctuations principally in terms of taste and demand legitimizes Diamela Eltit's "avant-garde" aesthetic. My contention is that this process cannot be isolated, rather it can be explicated through other episodes of consumption. In chapter 4, we see how Hollywood has managed to sanitize Reinaldo Arenas's similarly critical practice, and in chapter 5, how largely U.S. disciplinary challenges are involved in inverted, yet similar processes.

Arenas and Eltit are not brought together for the purposes of comparison, but rather as a means to consider the degree that they posit that their experiences of repression may be communicated to others, some of whom have not undergone such experiences of regime. To a large extent, chapters 2 and 3 consider how the authors and the writer-characters that they create acknowledge their own affiliations with the world. As a counterpart, chapter 5 scrutinizes the narratives of subjects that push the limits of conceptualizations of the *literary*; the categorically insane are not customarily thought of as capable of conveying anything true or valid about the actual place they live in. The invention of worlds described in an unlikely and "unwriterly" publication, for example, that is produced by the multinational fashion house Benetton, as we shall soon see, surprisingly brings us back to place.

The very crux of this book is the different valences of cosmopolitanism. Rather than retreat into a singular geographical region as a strategy of challenging the superficial grouping together of writing under the Spanish American rubric, this book enacts what it theorizes and insists that, without abandoning crucial precepts of postcolonialism, it is possible to continue to juxtapose the motley groups of cultural objects. Special attention is paid to the consequences of framing cultural production as local, regional, national, and transnational whether this framing takes place within the writers' more personal accounts of their affiliations or within their more traditionally literary contributions. By considering these more personal accounts that appear in the form of interviews and essays, I emphasize how these writers circulate as cultural commodities within critical texts and within industries. The skillful self-awareness of their maneuvers is a crucial element of my investigation into the process of "labeling." A conversation between an archeology of cosmopolitanism and an embodied cosmopolitanism renders a sort of double vision; as this very conversation deconstructs the notion that the concept in the past circulated in the absence of migratory bodies.

To engage the conceptual term *cosmopolitismo* in relation to the questionable conglomerate of "Latin American" literature, however, requires examining its historical genealogy. The idea of a "cosmopolitan" Latin American literature, in its most pejorative incarnations, is associated with betrayal and debility while, in its most affirmative ones, as rebellion and even anticolonialism. In this way, the engagement functions as a self-critical appropriation of a term whose relation to a nineteenth-century Latin American tradition of cultural pluralisms, Timothy Brennan argues in "Cosmo-Theory," has been obscured by U.S. Americans who identify themselves as exceptional on account of their pluralism, which is nevertheless exportable. Brennan's point here, in fact, is reminiscent of George Yúdice's caution in "We are Not the World." A U.S. depiction of multiculturalism is all too often mistaken to be universal and used toward normative ends. The practice of incorporating others into a U.S. American version of diversity shares with colonizing tactics the propensity for possession and unequal methods of exchange. All too often an Arab or a Chinese is included to satisfy an aspiration for multiplicity that unfortunately resembles the replication of sameness wherein these others are exotics or locals within a unified U.S. American sphere. To react to such good intentions without giving in to the tendency of eradicating difference requires attention to how distinct a migrant's attachment to new and old places is, why he or she migrates, what is the relation between the migrant's homeland and the host country, as well as what are the diverse commitments of the individual and the community in rear- ranging their lives according to distinct geographical and historical frameworks. The cosmopolitanism advocated through the present approach verifies context and specificity at the same time that it is driven toward archiving those cultural objects that uniquely portray un-homely and decontextualized sites.

Casa de las Américas' homage to a renowned Chilean writer, with participants from Chile, the United States, and Venezuela, had been pre- ceded by a "Semana del autor" in 2000 with Argentine Ricardo Piglia and another in 2001 with his compatriot Luisa Valenzuela. Following Eltit was Nicaraguan Ernesto Cardenal in 2003, and Brazilian Rubem Fonseca in 2004. The selection process, alluded to before, is not unique to revolutionary Cuba or to the "Semana de autor." It is not surprising that Casa de las Américas, like most cultural institutions, invites people with whom some of its members have already had personal contact and that may stimulate an audience without destroying the latter's system of values. Because Cuba is the premier leftist state in the Americas, the implications of such basic invitational practices merit closer examina- tion. For instance, Irene Rostagno describes the first decade of Casa as one that promoted the " 'Cubanization' of Latin American culture" (1997, 95). This happened in part because the director of Casa's magazine at that time, Roberto Fernández Retamar, traveled to make contacts with writers outside of the country, whom he later invited to "happenings" in Havana (Rostagno 1997, 95). To see how such encounters affected the dissemination of Latin American literature, we need look no further than José Donoso's *La historia personal del Boom* (1972) where he recounts Casa de las Américas' importance for the international commodification of Latin American literature. Still, one of the goals of Casa has been to ensure that the capitalist market is not the driving force behind its promotions and publications. This purpose is evident on the frontpage of Casa's bulletin on Eltit:

Dedicar a Diamela Eltit esta Semana implica—aparte de honrarnos con la presencia de una de las(os) escritoras(es) más importantes de la actual literatura latinoamericana—"apostar" por una poética que marcha a contrapelo del mainstream, y que se empeña en sacudir nuestras más enraizadas convicciones.

[Dedicating this week to Diamela Eltit implies—apart from honoring us with the presence of one of the most important writers of contemporary Latin American literature—"betting" on a poetics that goes against the mainstream and that insists on shaking up our most rooted convictions.]

The "mainstream" referred to in this text relates to a publishing circuit difficult to pinpoint geographically. It must allude to the marketing of Latin American women writers, such as Isabel Allende, Angeles Mastretta, and Laura Esquivel, who speak to large audiences in Latin America and the United States, writers that Gisela Norat describes as having been "catapulted" by trade publishers (Norat 1991, 21). That Eltit's own writing has been said to resist such market's forces has had very real effects on the circulation of Eltit's works within Chile, on its resonance within *crítica cultural*, and in the scholarship about the discipline of Latin Americanism largely generated in the United States. *Crítica cultural* (cultural critique), as conceptualized by Nelly Richard especially in *Revista de Crítica Cultural*, the journal she has directed in Chile since 1990, is conceived, in part, as the theoretical component of the 1980s' "marginal," "neo-avant-garde," and "extrasystematic" artistic resistance to a very particular experience of authoritarianism: Pinochet's neoliberalism.

The set of confluences among artistry, politics, and commodity are central to my bringing together Eltit and the late Cuban writer Reinaldo Arenas in this discussion. Eltit straddles continents as a Chilean neo-avant-garde "minoritarian" writer and object of fascination for Latin Americanists that, much like Casa, pride themselves on attending to that which is ignored by the mainstream. Arenas has recently become a more massive figure, upon entering into a distinct network of circulation emblematized by the image on the cover of Javier Bardem on the last edition of his autobiography. The Spanish film star, described by Chris Perriam as "probably the nearest to being the physically dominant screen male of twentieth-century Hollywood type," plays the "pájaro" Reinaldo (Perriam 2003, 13). When Hollywood captures this dissident so central in Cuban letters, he is at least momentarily released from the confines of various niches that lie primarily under the domain of particular intellectual and homosexual readerships within and outside of Cuba.

The failure as well as the success of the market depends, in part, on "betting" as well as on the speed of consumers to adjust their tastes from one product to another. In response to María Teresa Cárdenas's efforts to get Eltit to explain what she really meant by the failure of the market in "hypertechnological" times, she said,

> Esta hipertecnología tan corta, en el sentido de que todo es desechable, hace que el apego al objeto sea muy alto, pero no a la memoria del objeto. Es el objeto sin memoria, porque va desechándose por una nueva tecnología o por el surgimiento de otro producto que lo discontinúa y lo hace anacrónico. Está el deseo del objeto, pero ese objeto de antemano porta el fracaso.

> [This hyper-technology, so short, in the sense that all is disposable, makes the interest in a commodity to be very high, but not in the memory of the commodity. It is the object without memory, because it has been disposed of for a new technology or for the emergence of another product that discontinues it and makes it anachronistic.] (Eltit 2002b)[5]

Recalling Walter Benjamin's analyses of commodification, Eltit's insight rationalizes not only the more distant processes in Hollywood, but also those dynamics closer to our homes—our perhaps more critically cosmopolitan ones as theorists. Judging solely by the *Modern Language Association*'s database, Arenas (1943–1990) and Eltit (1949–) receive roughly the same amount of attention by critics, but surely one can expect shifts in supply and demand.

Two persistent points of focus in this book are the authors Arenas and Eltit, whose rejection of the comfort of regimented constituencies results in their writing being perceived as raw, vindictive, even alienating, and as such, ripe for critiquing. Key to the working of this discomfort lies in the unsteady relationship that their writing establishes with the family, the nation, the market, the readers, and their inherited artistic traditions. Not only is "place" at the forefront of the worlds scripted by Arenas and Eltit, but their visions also transform its predominance. Taking its lead from these artistic narratives, *Cosmopolitanisms and Latin America: Against the Destiny of Place* formulates an archive of such gestures. It examines cosmopolitanisms and cosmopolitans in three distinct, yet corresponding ways: (1) as conceptual terms that function within an intellectual and poetic tradition of late-nineteenth- and early-twentieth-century Latin American letters; (2) as a discourse that emerges from or is embedded in the writing of particular contemporary authors; and (3) as a mode of negotiating the discipline of Latin Americanism. Possessing undertones of resistance and coalescence to colonialism, imperialism, and globalization, the term *cosmopolita* circulates in Latin American cultural studies from the early nineteenth century onward, but it was during the period of *modernismo* that it acquired a singular intensity. We continue to be challenged by the centuries-old question of unity and diversity and at the same time are perplexed by the degree to which cosmopolitanism can be justified in light of uneven material and historical factors resulting in unrequited and unsolicited partial unions. The shadows of colonialist and neo-imperial projects within enlightenment programs and ideals render most propositions dubious that attempt to go beyond particulars. Still, what seems to be the most positive aspect of the diverse positions on cosmopolitanism is the emerging discourse of self-fashioning that accounts for but is not based solely on facile and reductive politics of identity.

In recent years, as much despite as because of the long and complex history of the term *cosmopolitan*, much critical attention has been paid to it, especially within cultural studies in North America, as well as in gender studies, political theory, and philosophy. Cosmopolitanism as a conceptual method of analysis continues to be seductive, partly because of its weighty inheritance and relevance, its durability and resilience, its qualities that are not as apparent in concepts that may at first seem to have similar undertones such as hybridity and globalization. Among many other important participants, the key players in this discussion are Timothy Brennan, Bruce Robbins, Pheng Cheah, Walter Mignolo, Martha Nussbaum, and Amanda Anderson.[6] Numerous journals including *Theory, Culture, and Society*; *Boston Review*; and *Public Culture* have invested in the social and cultural ramifications of globalization and cosmopolitanism.[7] One particular angle focusing on this subject reached odd heights—not as might be expected with Bruce Robbins's exquisitely articulated 1995 "The Weird Heights: On Cosmopolitanism, Feeling, and Power," but a year earlier, in the *Boston Review*—with Martha Nussbaum's defense of humanist cosmopolitanism in the face of Richard Rorty's vision of U.S. patriotism based on "traditional American pluralism" (Nussbaum et al. 1996, 15). As Brennan has already suggested in "Cosmo-Theory," a false binary emerged out of this debate. Neither was the pluralism as "American" as Rorty claimed, nor was the cosmopolitanism as detached from local particulars as Nussbaum argued.

With scarce direct interaction with one another due to discrepant methodological approaches, scholars in the humanities and in the social sciences have returned to the sociopolitical and cultural platform on cosmopolitanism. In the social sciences, *World Poverty and Human Rights: Cosmopolitan Responsibilities and Reforms* (2002) by Thomas W. Pogge, confronts in moralistic and legal terms, the degree to which cosmopolitanism, as a program, can be relied on to address the world's injustices. In *Nations without Nationalisms* (1993), Julia Kristeva forays into cosmopolitanisms for a wider public unaccustomed to complex semiotic analysis, contending with France's xenophobic policies in the 1980s and 1990s. Likened to Kristeva's effort for his watered-down stylistic approach geared toward a wider audience, Jacques Derrida, in *On Cosmopolitanism and Forgiveness* (2001, published in French in 1997), draws on Immanuel Kant's *Perpetual Peace* (1983, published in German in 1795) in its discussion of hospitality and a world-city of refugees. No list could possibly account for the diverse motivating factors that are behind this renewed cross-disciplinary interest in cosmopolitanism.

While the focus on the subaltern in postcolonial and Latin American studies is in itself a cosmopolitan venture of recuperation, we have yet to exhaust the benefits of reclaiming a cosmopolitan framework with the potential to address both the lack of attention to aesthetic issues of which cultural studies have been accused and the limits of being grounded. Writers may position themselves or critics may position writers as more local or cosmopolitan in order to convey authority. This authority could serve more than just one function: to help writers and critics secure their places within constricted registers of national culture and/or to disrupt those existing constructions either by grounding their marginal narratives of sexual and national identity in local traditions or by encountering for them transnational links. Reengaging distinct historical and contemporary *cosmopolitanisms* in the Spanish American context provides alternatives to the categorization of cultural studies as yet another North American instance of imperialist nostalgia and cultural critique as the South's almost autochthonous contestation. By imperialist nostalgia, I mean the sort of congratulatory gestures that attempt to inextricably unite the eclectic theorist with the hybrid other. While the terms *autochthonous* and *contestation* present an aporia that cannot be so easily resolved if conceived in binary or essentialist terms that are characteristic of some simplistic identity politics, here cosmopolitanisms are invoked as a strategy for dealing with the apparent schisms between U.S. and Latin American realizations of cultural theory and critique. Their complicated multidimensionality makes them a convenient tool to consider writers' relation to cultural patrimony, gender, identitarian, and national politics. More modest cosmopolitanisms might disassociate from the elitism of world citizenry and embrace multiple affiliations, yet still be invested in comparative contexts of identity formation, aesthetics, and the circulation of art objects on more than one level.[8] Locating discrepant cosmopolitanisms within the poetics of late-nineteenth and early-twentieth-century *modernismo* challenges the perception that this distinct and less exclusive cosmopolitanism is only contemporary. That they have been resurrected in a given time in the United States with the goal of fulfilling particular local purposes need not be justification for relegating it to the sidelines. They elucidate Arenas and Eltit as traveling subjects who are self-conscious about the manner in which place figures in their public personas as writers and about its cultural capital vis-à-vis diversely positioned readers—a cultural capital that is based on readers' own professional affiliations.

As Bruce Robbins has emphasized in his important contributions to cosmopolitan studies, being grounded does not necessarily mean being parochial, nor does being cosmopolitan signify being rootless. This is to say "struggles for social justice that simply begin at home, within a given nation-state, do not demand to be described as nationalist or to be dismissed as parochial" (Robbins 1998, 9). In the process of reclaiming these politicized *cosmopolitanisms*, my readings of fictions and "allegories of vocation" written in diverse cultural contexts articulate the dissonance between these commonly associated terms—grounded and parochial, cosmopolitan and rootless. The theoretical underpinnings of this argument are intricately tied to my engagement with particular texts by authors who, colloquially speaking, would unlikely be deemed as cosmopolitan. Preoccupied at once with the rights of national subjects, the authors also show the weaknesses of investing entirely in this constructed discourse.

While it would be a mistake to characterize Reinaldo Arenas's writing as parochial, most of it, even that which was conceived in exile, is grounded in a specific Cuban geography and literary history, so much so that many of his international reviewers point to the difficulty that non-Cubans face upon reading it. Nonetheless, whereas Arenas's writing predicates itself on its readers' familiarity with the land and revolutionary and exilic canons, it also articulates a space "beyond" this knowledge—it follows that critics make room for this creative simultaneity. The stories that these authors tell about themselves oblige us to a critique of insularisms, provincialisms, and globalizations. These authors do not always imagine themselves to be citizens of the world or even go so far as to uphold this category. Diamela Eltit grew up in the lower middle-class neighborhoods of Santiago. She wrote her first novel while teaching and raising children. She calls herself a "vieja de barrio," which when loosely translated means "an old woman from the block," the "old" referring not so much to age, but rather to the history that she shares with the place. It connotes her membership within this economic and social class and her busybody-like knowledge of the neighborhood. Taken with Eltit's other writing, this framing suggests that Eltit is far from abandoning the nation-state and the rights of citizenry it may provide. The analysis of such "allegories of vocation," or rather—those critical works that, in addition to performing the proposed task, construe a narrative and justification for their intellectual vocation—is an integral part of arriving at this sort of "willfully provocative" cosmopolitanism (Robbins 1993, 182–83).

Influential within cosmopolitanism studies, as a whole, and specifically within Robbins's contributions, are James Clifford's conceptualization of "discrepant" cosmopolitanisms and his investigation into the flexibility of professional affiliations developed in *The Predicament of Culture* (1988) and in "Traveling Cultures" (republished in 1997). As an outcome of his refiguration of the encounter between ethnographer and object of study into one in which both are involved in multiple cosmopolitan affiliations, the *cosmopolitanism* that emerges from Clifford's transformation, "recognizes something important: worldly, productive sites of crossing; complex, unfinished paths between local and global attachments. Cosmopolitanism, viewed without universalist nostalgia, seems to hold a promise" (Clifford 1998, 362). Because this statement is open-ended, it is difficult to imagine its consequences for engaging literary texts, but Clifford's conceptualization of the term has served as a point of departure for several critical inquiries, including this one.

By reading contemporary discrepant cosmopolitanisms with the nuances of the term's late-nineteenth and early-twentieth-century usage within Spanish American letters in mind, commonly held assumptions about the provincialism of political struggles and the cosmopolitanism of culture capital are cast aside. Cosmopolitanism is then sundered from its more colloquial and regressive associations. This book examines cosmopolitan impulses embedded in prose and links these revelations to the processes by which the diverse commercial and intellectual investments conceive of place and difference. Following Román de la Campa's lead, the discipline of Latin Americanism needs to be envisioned as a "transnational discursive community with a significant market for research and sales in the industrial capitals of the world" that is, to a large degree, determined by Latin American migrants whose meager salaries in their "native" countries do not support their research aims (de la Campa 1999, 1). Relating the contours of this community to the shifts in the market, as articulated by Eltit, elucidates the varying functions of transnational critics. They may be vendors, archivists, conservationists, and even elegists. In the post–cold war era that is frequently cast as suffering a dearth of secular ideologies other than neoliberalism, determining who we are, where we are, and by what global economic forces we are constituted is complicated.

Engaged in a process of evaluating disciplines, some critics are wary about overvalorizing terms such as marginality, decentering, heterogeneity, difference, subalternness, and hybridity in so far that they empty Latin American culture of aesthetics, its own symbols and historical references. It is not so much a preoccupation with preserving aesthetics, per se, that motivates their critique, but rather a consideration for a more radical critique of power and coloniality that these categories may circumvent. Mabel Moraña's *boom subalterno* specifically relates to the utilization of Latin America by transnational, postcolonial critics as another symbol of the hybrid other, to valorize their own postcolonial criticism and maintain Latin America "en el lugar del otro, un lugar preteórico, calibanesco y marginal, con respecto a los discursos metropolitanos" (in the place of the other, a pre-theoretical, Calibanesque, and marginal place, with respect to metropolitan discourses) (Moraña 1998, 236). When and how should resistance to these forms of marginalization and colonialist exploitation be enunciated? In "Leones, cazadores e historiadores: A propósito de las políticas de la memoria y del conocimiento," an essay that itself resonates with a canonical text of the past—José Martí's 1891 "Nuestra América"—Hugo Achugar argues for the continuous implementation of Latin American cultural references within literary histories in order to combat U.S. cultural imperialism. After signaling that "las culturas de las varias América Latina no forman parte del Commonwealth a pesar de la globalización" (the cultures of various Latin Americas do not form a part of the Commonwealth despite globalization), Achugar reflects on whether "estemos simplemente en una reedición del panamericanismo que intenta obliterar el 'nuestro americanismo' de Martí" (we are simply in a re-edition of Pan-Americanism that tries to obliterate Martí's "our-Americanism") (Achugar 1998, 284). Alarmed by the U.S. multilateral influence on Latin American intellectuals, Achugar invokes previous cultural imperialisms delineated by Martí and José Enrique Rodó in efforts to uphold the continuity of an intellectual history that may ward off the historical amnesia that is brought on by narratives of globalization. The erosion of the traditional role of the intellectual and of aesthetics by cultural studies on account of transdisciplinary practices is particularly vexing to Beatriz Sarlo who urges critics not to cave into eclecticism and to respect particular traditions. Echoing Aijaz Ahmad's response to Fredrick Jameson about the allegorical nature of third world texts, Sarlo rejects the persistent reduction of contemporary Latin American art to political allegory. Rather than focus on the deficiency inherent within the categorization of the third world, Sarlo insists, in a manner not unlike Achugar's, that intellectuals hold on to something that cultural studies often neglect—aesthetics. Still, flexibility of meaning and attention to form can be as detrimental as they are liberating in the sense that they, like cosmopolitanism studies, may avoid the teleological narrative of redemption.

Nelly Richard's critique of the way in which a standard academic version of cultural studies has normalized multidisciplinary knowledge by focusing on utilitarian values and by casting aside the "posibles zigzags de la fantasía que larguen el sujeto hacia errancias de sentidos" (possible zigzags of fantasy that release the subject toward wanderings of meanings) is central to the present recuperation of cosmopolitan zones (Richard 1998, 262). Considering feminism to be the discourse that has most forcefully tried to reconcile a collective and individually pluralistic approach, Richard suggests that distinct peripheral lived experiences be interwoven in discourses of postmodernism. Theorizing such "microexperiences" is crucial to combating the binary logic of "international" cultural studies known to frame the third world as body and experience to its own theory. Richard claims in her suggestively entitled article, "Intersectando Latinoamérica con el latinoamericanismo" (Intersecting Latin America with Latin Americanism), that

la autoridad conceptual implicada en el hablar sobre Latinoamérica desde la academia internacional se ejerce a través de una división del trabajo que, en el inconsciente de muchos de los discursos del latinoamericanismo, suele oponer teoría y práctica: razón y materia, conocimiento y realidad, discurso y experiencia, mediación e inmediatez. (Richard 1998, 251)

[the conceptual authority implied in speaking about Latin America from the international academy, is exerted through a division of work that, in the unconscious of many of the discourses on Latin Americanism, is used to opposing theory and practice: reason and matter, knowledge and reality, discourse and experience, mediation and immediacy.]

The passage ends with an invocation of Jean Franco's even more severe observation that the North frequently allocates itself to the position of thought as opposed to the South allocating itself to the body. These divisions necessitate recalling that the meaning of nationalism varies according to its instrumentalization. One mode of challenging such binaries as North, South: thought, body would be to call into question the notions that nationalisms are ipso facto chauvinist and that there is no way to effectively critique the sociopolitical and cultural effects of globalization.

Approaching cosmopolitanism historically is one way to deflect the characteristic acceleration that exploits unity and difference. Must we return, as Martha Nussbaum has suggested, to the cynics? How about returning to the brief anecdote but embracing something other than Nussbaum's moralistic universalism? As recalled by Diogenes of Laertius, in Corinth, when Alexander the Great asked Diogenes of Sinope, the cynic who died in 320 BC and lived in a barrel in the streets of Athens, where he was from, he answered, *Kosmopolites* (*polites*— citizen, *kosmos*—world). To Alexander's question of how he could assist him one day when Diogenes was sunning himself, Diogenes requested that Alexander move away as he was blocking the sun. The ludic moment that the event retains is interesting in a discussion of cultural studies, which frequently assumes identity categories constructed through scientific means to explain being and culture, leaving out their more nebulous, but equally important, aspects. The misanthrope, known as the dog, lived in the streets and searched for an honest man while asserting his position as a citizen of the world. The allegorical value of this tale of eccentricities and imperialisms lies in its ability to orient cosmopolitanism toward the body, a link that this anecdote makes detectable almost immediately. Upon turning to contemporary anecdotes in the present context, the experiences of the body with itself as well as that of merging bodies with other bodies become an alternative to hierarchical unions. While the usage and implications of *cosmopolitan* vary dramatically according to diverse contexts, it is the ideal of becoming a citizen of the world, and not the bodily oriented cosmopolitanism, that is often emphasized. By bodily oriented cosmopolitanism, I mean one that would take into account that philosophies are enveloped in bodies; theory and matter are essential to the Diogenes anecdote. On the one hand, cosmopolitanism as an aspiration entails often exclusionary "normative" dimensions. On the other, in different sectors and with varied agenda, more repressive governments and identity-oriented critics often exclude "actual" cosmopolitans.

The story of *jineteros* in Cuba is a case in point. Economic despair within Cuba, among many other factors, influences women and men alike to hustle. *Jinetear* (to ride, as in to ride a horse) is an ambiguous term whose definition is more apparent when it is time to punish, but nevertheless, successful *jineteros*—meaning those who adequately mount a foreigner—are rewarded with migration, and these days, if one is lucky, it can also suggest going back and forth to and from Cuba, using the legal paraphernalia acquired through marriage. In this process, the roles of *jineteros* as cultural interpreters and negotiators can only be compared with that of artists and intellectuals who, if they are lucky, sometimes possess similar rights. Esteemed and frowned upon for their contributions to the nation's wealth and their proximity to the rest of the world, these *jineteros* are cosmopolitans. Though they may not identify themselves as such, their experiences negotiate between local and global attachments that the guardians of the nation may find threatening to their legal and belief systems.

Because of cosmopolitanism's nuanced history and presence as a polemical concept in a variety of disciplines, it is useful to relate aesthetic and ethical issues that include intellectual positioning and formation, insiders and outsiders, the city and the country, as well as the metropolis and the colony. Bringing out a discussion of the cosmopolitan realm may seem to run somewhat counter, however, to the discussions delineated above among mostly Latin American scholars on globalization and the subaltern. Take, for example, Alberto Moreiras's account of a Brazilian Comparative Literature conference, in which ensued a debate that firmly placed the nation and literature, on one side, and transnationalizing cosmopolitanism and cultural studies, on the other (Moreiras 1998, 69). This binary makes the misleading assumption that cosmopolitanism is only identifiable with a singular metropolis and ignores its different functions within Latin American literary and cultural critique. The present approach pays attention to literariness and nationalism without disentangling from transnationalizing networks. By avoiding consolidating arguments on the topic of writers' roles in the national and transnational spheres according to predetermined identity schemes, we can enter an alternative archival project that involves restoring the complexity of the mise en scène.

These recent reevaluations often juxtapose an adjective to *cosmopolitanism* that attempts to narrow or humble its scope. Such a desire to interpret flexibly, expand, and limit cosmopolitanism is not new. For instance, in a 1965 analysis of the term entitled "Local Attachment and Cosmopolitanism—The Eighteenth-Century Pattern,"

Alan D. McKillop calls an "exclusive and rigorous cosmopolitanism" that which "belittles national vanity" and local attachments (McKillop 1965, 197). As an example of the exclusive cosmopolitanism, McKillop cites Viscount Henry St. John Bolingbroke's 1752 *Letters on the Study and Use of History* in which "a wise man looks on himself as a citizen of the world: and, when you ask him where his country lies, points, like ANAXAGORAS, with his finger to the heavens" (quoted in McKillop 1965, 196). A more inclusive cosmopolitanism, for McKillop, places value on national and regional differences and sees "love of home or country as part of an infinitely varied scheme" (McKillop 1965, 196). While McKillop's "exclusive" and "inclusive" are not frequently encountered in current investigations on *cosmopolitanisms*, the contemporary "nuanced," "discrepant," and "vernacular" do imply a similar focus on inclusiveness.

For instance, Gustavo Pérez Firmat's "nuanced" cosmopolitanism describes *criollo* culture's translations of foreign elements.[9] Contesting "countless essays and manuals" in which "criollism is a nativist reaction to the cosmopolitan excesses of *modernismo*," Pérez Firmat's *The Cuban Condition* (1989) argues for the " 'cosmopolitanism' of criollist literature" (Pérez Firmat 1989, 8). Beyond this definition of a movement within literature in the first half of the twentieth century that is more complicated than it is typically considered, Pérez Firmat relies on Rufino Blanco Fombona's definition of criollism, "tener dentro del pecho un corazón americano y no un libro extranjero" (having in your breast an American heart and not a foreign book) (quoted in Pérez Firmat 1989, 8). Such an apparently dated explanation still resonates with the current clash of "Pan-American" and "Our American" discourses. My analyses (in chapter 2) of Reinaldo Arenas, in part, explores the limits of Pérez Firmat's understanding of criollism and "nuanced" cosmopolitanism for explaining affiliation, gender construction, and the translations of epithets into powerful signifiers of belonging to alternative communities.

Apart from the critical grammar of "nuanced," the adjective "discrepant" present in James Clifford's work, is another mode of describing the expansive tendencies of a resurgent cosmopolitanism and their relation to conflicting histories of displacement.

> Such cultures of displacement and transplantation are inseparable from specific, often violent, histories of economic, political and cultural interaction—histories that generate what might be called discrepant cosmopolitans . . . I'm not saying there are no locales or homes, that

everyone is—or should be—traveling, or cosmopolitan, or deterritorialized. This is not nomadology. Rather, what is at stake is a comparative cultural studies approach to specific histories, tactics, everyday practices of dwelling and traveling: traveling-in-dwelling, dwelling-in-traveling . . .

How are national, ethnic, community "insides" and "outsides" sustained, policed, subverted, crossed—by distinct historical subjects—for their own ends, with different degrees of power and freedom? (Clifford 1997, 36)

By bringing to the surface the notion that cosmopolitan perspectives can be the result of a painful process of exclusion from a rigid community and displacement, Clifford's understanding of cosmopolitanism makes his work suitable for studying contesting histories. The way Arenas and Eltit unify a discussion of the body, pain, gender, travel, and intellectual self-positioning can be elaborated through Bruce Robbins's study of discrepant cosmopolitanism and intellectual self-fashioning, which is itself engaged with Clifford's ethnographic and cultural studies.

Like Clifford and Pérez Firmat, Homi K. Bhabha foregrounds the cosmopolitanism of the vernacular realm and the coincidence of attachments to local and global spheres in his exploration of "vernacular cosmopolitanism." These different foci converge in their ability to imagine a means, other than parochial nationalism, to contradict globalization. This cosmopolitan realm is more actual than normative; it is opposed to exclusive sorts of belonging; it envisions underprivileged and marginal experiences to be capable of rendering cosmopolitan perspectives; it is attached to various places or positions; it is often employed in discussions of intellectual vocation and the manner in which intellectuals orient themselves vis-à-vis their objects of study.

Although the contemporary reevaluation of *cosmopolitan* is closely linked to the sociopolitical and cultural mappings of postcolonial subjects, with the exception of Walter Mignolo's systematic approach to what he calls dialogic ethics and the modern/colonial world system and of Camilla Fojas's most recent reflection (2005) on *cosmopolitanism* and *modernista* cultural production, little critical theory has focused on the context of Latin America. With respect to the ideological weight that is exerted on my work by the cultural studies situated in the North American academy, I think it helpful to recall Moreiras's critique of Domingo Milliani's naïve participation in the process of universalization and developmentalism, and especially, his notion that *general literature* is the end product of an endogenous search within the history of Latin American literature. Moreiras points to the fact that what has been chauvinistically cast as *general literature* "borrows" extensively from extraterritorial, that is, foreign, traditions. Nevertheless, the insult of derivatism plagues the criticism of "less" general literatures. Evidence of this line of thinking that erroneously privileges the unified products of Latin America is located in Roberto Fernández Retamar's "Calibán: Apuntes sobre la cultura de nuestra América" (Calibán: Notes Toward a Discussion of Culture in Our America).

First published in 1971 in the journal *Casa de las Américas*, Fernández Retamar's crucial study is an important construction of the boundaries of Latin Americanism, imagining one side to be populated with those virile Calibans and the other to be scattered with those cosmopolitan Ariels. Although Fernández Retamar insists on their interdependency, his determined vision concerning the influence of the outside on Latin American discourse helped to justify a radical division of intellectuals in the late 1960s and early 1970s. The Padilla case serves as a structural backdrop of Fernández Retamar's argument, which, although it entails a complex analysis of "our American" intellectuals, turns out to increasingly point fingers at those more unsavory political characters.[10] Officials interpreted Heberto Padilla's poetry as counterrevolutionary and his personal associations abroad as betraying his nation. Padilla's brief imprisonment and haunting confession caused an international uproar, and it was at this juncture that Fernández Retamar analyzes "our American" intellectuals.[11] Less than a month before Fernández Retamar wrote "Calibán," many international intellectuals, including Simone de Beauvoir, Carlos Fuentes, Juan Goytisolo, Jean Paul Sartre, and Susan Sontag, who once supported the revolution, denounced its treatment of Padilla and compared the revolution's tactics of repression with the "most sordid moments of the Stalinist era" in a letter to Fidel Castro dated May 20, 1971.[12] Even under these severely politically divisive circumstances where very high stakes were already established, Fernández Retamar acknowledges the impossibility of someone from his own generation being formed primarily on national literature. Regarding this somewhat paradoxical situation, Ricardo Castells argues: "Although Fernández Retamar repeatedly insists in Calibán on the autochthonous character of the Cuban revolution, in reality his intellectual formation also has a strictly European orientation" (Castells 1995, 174). In a manner that echoes Rufino Blanco-Fombona's early-twentieth-century critique of the French for considering Latin American "others" "rastaquouères" and themselves "cosmopolitans" for the possession of similar behavioral characteristics, Fernández Retamar targets the French writer Péguy for disingenuously imagining himself as a cosmopolitan when he primarily focuses on the French tradition (Fernández Retamar 1979, 28). In contrast, a writer from the "periphery" is forced into a cosmopolitan perspective because of not only qualitative but also psychological limits. Fernández Retamar actually pathologizes the condition when he diagnoses Jorge Luis Borges with a case of "phagocytosis," a process through which the foreign is assimilated, consumed, and even devoured (Fernández Retamar 1979, 28). Fernández Retamar's version of Cuban nationalism and intellectual positioning has been particularly fascinating to Timothy Brennan. Echoes of Fernández Retamar's argument can be heard in Brennan's return to the negative implications of cosmopolitanism—a "convenient noplace"—in the process of categorizing Cuban Alejo Carpentier as a "worldly Cuban" and definitively not as a cosmopolitan on the basis that Carpentier's impulse was to work toward a continuum for his literary creations with popular cultures (Brennan 1997, 306).[13]

Fernández Retamar's far-reaching essay is a point of departure for exploring the archive of this conceptual term in nineteenth- and twentieth-century Latin American thought. Literary historians tend to agree that *modernismo* spans approximately three and one-half decades, from the early 1880s with the publication of José Martí's *Ismaelillo* in 1882 to Rubén Darío's death in 1916. It is often said that the movement's practitioners had in common the desires to be modern and to be cosmopolitan. To a large degree, in the 1890s, the Hispanic Cuban North American War (1898) contributed to a frenzied questioning of affiliations and as a result, by 1900, cosmopolitan thought was viewed in a very different light.[14] Around the same time in France, *cosmopolitanism* was similarly subjected to reevaluation in the face of the Dreyfus Affair, wherein a Jewish captain in the French army was falsely accused of betraying the nation. The consequences of multiple affiliations were burdensome. In the Spanish American context, cosmopolitanism's practitioners of the late nineteenth century are often perceived as men of economic privilege, capable of traveling and adopting cultural codes of these locations, and thereby of standing in for the nebulous category of "citizens of the world." It is also important to remember that their tendency to embrace France is related to their experience of colonization by Spain. After 1898, there was a general movement toward establishing Hispanism, in the wake of years of antagonism toward Spain.

Prologues and author's notes in Rubén Darío's works, José Enrique Rodó's influential book-length essay of 1900 *Ariel*, as well as the novel *De sobremesa*, written by Colombian José Asunción Silva in 1896, and first published in 1925 can textually ground an interrogation into the sometimes deficient equation of cosmopolitanism with Europeanization. Some *modernista* writers use *cosmopolitismo* as a means of holding onto singularity, as in an ideal of harmony or unity, but there are also those who intellectually align themselves with the discordance and diversity of actual cosmopolitans. Turn-of-the-century battles over the sovereignty of Cuba brought to the fore the principal role of this national entity among intellectuals of the Americas. In light of the persistent weight that Cuba exerts on geopolitics, exemplified by the imprisonment of different brands of so-called threats to national and international safety and order—from drug addicts and dissidents to Taliban and their sympathizers—across the island today, it is impossible to consider Latin American cosmopolitanisms without linking them to the *modernistas'* reflections on a similar topic. Cosmopolitanisms can offer intellectuals a way to confront epochal crises. They may link them to an ideal aesthetic realm to which their own place in the world denies them access. What are often identified as cosmopolitanisms' more seemingly regressive qualities must be put into a global context of increased modernization, the Hispanic Cuban North American War, and the U.S. acquisition of the Panama isthmus (1903).

In one of the most noted prologues of the *modernista* period, Spanish critic Juan Valera admires Rubén Darío's *Azul* (Azure) for its cosmopolitan spirit:

El libro está impregnado de espíritu cosmopolita. Hasta el nombre y apellido del autor, verdaderos o contrahechos y fingidos, hacen que el cosmopolitismo resalte más. Rubén es judaico, y persa es Darío; de suerte que por los nombres no parece sino que usted quiere ser o es de todos los países, castas y tribus. (Valera, 1994, 10)

[The book is impregnated with a cosmopolitan spirit. The author's first and last names, be they true or feigned, make that cosmopolitanism stand out even more. Rubén is Jewish, and Darío is Persian; in this way, on account of your names you don't just seem—you want to be or you are from every country, breed, and tribe.]

Recalling the weight of biological ties, the word "impregnado" and the phrase "es de todos los países" form metaphors for miscegenation and reproduction that emphasize the symbolic power of bloodlines in the construction of an autochthonous literature. However, the degree to which Darío's cosmopolitanism compares with that of the compatriots of the Spanish critic requires looking at another part of this letter-prologue, dated October 22, 1888.

> Ninguno de los hombres de letras de la Península, que he conocido yo, con más espíritu cosmopolita, y que más largo tiempo han residido en Francia y que han hablado mejor el francés y otras lenguas extranjeras, me ha parecido nunca tan compenetrado del espíritu de Francia como usted me parece. (Valera 1994, 11)

> [None of the men of letters of the Peninsula whom I have known, with more cosmopolitan spirit, who have resided in France for a longer time, who have spoken better French, in addition to other foreign languages, has ever seemed to me to have such an affinity with the spirit of France as you.]

It is apparent that, at first, an authoritative voice lends legitimacy to the cosmopolitan-ness of the non-European subject. For Valera to be so astounded by the Nicaraguan's spirit that he suggests peninsular artists pale in comparison reveals what he thinks about artists' susceptibility to cosmopolitanism. The closer to Paris they are and the less that they appear to mediate between more than one world, the easier it is for them to be cosmopolitan. While Valera casts cosmopolitanism primarily as a spirit, upon closer investigation, cosmopolitanism's relevance to material matters hinges on the recognition that may be attained by being in proximity to a cultural center where critics, writers, and publishers converge. It may seem that Valera suggests that the more Gallic the spirit, the better the art, but his attention to the conditions of postcolonial production complicates this hierarchy.

> Veo, pues, que no hay autor en castellano más francés que usted, y lo digo para afirmar un hecho sin elogio y sin censura. En todo caso, más bien lo digo como elogio. Yo no quiero que los autores no tengan carácter nacional; pero yo no puedo exigir de usted que sea nicaragüense, porque no hay ni puede haber aún historia literaria, escuela y tradiciones literarias en Nicaragua . . . Estando así disculpando el galicismo de la mente, es fuerza dar a usted alabanzas a manos llenas por lo perfecto y profundo de este galicismo; porque el lenguaje persiste español legítimo y de buena ley, y porque si no tiene usted carácter nacional, posee carácter individual. (Valera 1994, 12)

[I see, then, that there is no other author more French in Castilian than you, and I say this to affirm a fact, without praise or censor. In any case, I say it more as praise. I do not want authors to lack a national character; but I do not demand you to be Nicaraguan either, because there are not any nor could there be any literary traditions in Nicaragua . . . Considering this, pardoning your mental Gallicism, it is hard to give you whole-hearted praise for the perfection and profundity of this Gallicism; because the language remains legitimate Spanish of a good standard, and because if you do not have a national character, you possess an individual character.]

Darío's innovative verse interrupts the flow of the critic's own language, impelling him into imprecision, hemming and hawing, and stumbling over words. It is as if Valera's attempt to thoroughly dominate the production of an ex-subject of the mother country requires him to add detail upon detail and revise his own critical language. He employs a strange type of backdoor condescension: "Yes, you are more 'French' than I am, but you have no tradition: you cannot help it." Is Darío's cosmopolitanism perceived by Valera to be a last resort in the absence of a national culture? Not exclusively, at least, since, even Spaniards, with full access to an autonomous literary tradition, still aspire to such heights of cosmopolitanism. This process by which cosmopolitanism acquires multiple nuances culminates in Valera's advising Darío to open up his mind to more diverse absorption that would include other colors besides the blue of French letters.

Unlike in *Azul*, in *Prosas profanas* (1993/1896), Darío's own words in the preface ("Palabras liminares") complicate our understanding of his positionality. In the process of downplaying the importance of his words—they are "neither fruitful nor opportune"—Darío explains himself and his production through a series of negations.

Por la absoluta falta de elevación mental de la mayoría pensante de nuestro continente, en la cual impera el universal personaje clasificado por Remy de Gourmont con el nombre *Celui-qui-ne-comprend-pas*. *Celui-qui-ne-comprend-pas* es, entre nosotros, profesor, académico correspondiente de la Real Academia Española, periodista, abogado, poeta *rastaquoère*. (Darío 1993, 9)

[For the absolute lack of mental elevation of the thinking majority of our continent, in which reigns the universal character classified by Remy de Gourmont as a *Celui-qui-ne-comprend-pas*. *Celui-qui-ne-comprend-pas*, is among us, professor, academic, official member of the Real Academia Española, journalist, lawyer, poet, *rastaquoère*.]

More than any other textual category, these introductory words fall into the allegories of vocation, which, as previously invoked, are those critical works that, in addition to performing the proposed task, compose a narrative and justification for their intellectual pursuit. In this allegory of vocation, the poet's position vis-à-vis French letters remains central; however, this time, Darío questions the postcolonial's dependence on Spanish institutions and French cultural models while he invokes "universal" classifications to do so.

Upon considering the above quotation in light of the French epithet *rastaquouère*, "Nombre que dan en Francia a los hispanoamericanos muy ostentosos cuyos recursos no se conocen a ciencia cierta" [A name given in France to very ostentatious Spanish Americans whose means are not known for sure], the interwoven issues of profession and class that Darío straddles become apparent (Silva 1968, 44).[15] Both Valera's and Darío's words depict a cultural situation whereby Latin Americans are limited to the category of *rastaquouère* while the French are practically born cosmopolitan. Not until 1927 did the word "rastacuero" appear in the dictionary of the Real Academia Española. *Le Grand Robert de la Langue Française* (2001) suggests that *rastaquouère* (the contemporary spelling) came into Spanish from the word "rastracuero" and appeared in French around 1880, employed by authors such as Maupassant and Goron. A variation of its etymology narrated by Venezuelan critic Ángel Rosenblat actually suggests that the word came into French from the early-nineteenth-century Venezuelan "arrastacuero," which is used to describe one who pretends to have power or wealth (Rosenblat 1960, 43). As early as 1908, however, in "Notículas: ¿Qué es el rastacuerismo?" Venezuelan critic Rufino Blanco-Fombona expresses a frustration with the term's usage in France through a series of fictitious interviews. Though conducted in a light anecdotal tone, they manifest a sound theoretical imperative to illustrate that, although to a large degree, the act of being is a construction that resembles the act of pretending, the two are customarily thought of as disparate except when it is the "other," in this case, the South American "other," who is under scrutiny. Preoccupied mostly by the way the epithet gets applied to a whole "racial" group that is then associated with trickery, Blanco-Fombona attempts to provide a new set of connotations. Wondering whether *rastacuero* can be used to refer to peoples other than South Americans, Blanco-Fombona surmises that the "rastaquouère" (the accepted spelling) must be the sort of person who seeks out foreign opinions to form his own and thus looks much like a snob. However, he goes on to say the term *snob* is applied universally; in fact, France teems with snobs (Blanco-Fombona 1908, 299). By twisting around the terms in the colonial imaginary, Blanco-Fombona comes to the conclusion that "rastacuero," must mean "cosmopolita," and so, the "rastacuero" must be a free and practical man of the future (Blanco-Fombona 1908, 300).

Given that the notion of pretending or posing is charged, it is interesting to consider the French appropriation of a Venezuelan expression to reflect upon the continental fascination with the other's supposed manipulation of origins in his or her apparent desire to be someone else. Much in the way that Judith Butler views drag to be capable of destabilizing gender constructions, Sylvia Molloy warns against equating the act of posing with the frivolity of dressing up as another. Doing so ignores that posing "proposes new modes of identification based on recognition of desire more than on cultural pacts, and offers (and plays at) new sexual identities" (Molloy 1998, 149). This definition of posing in which the body is seen to reconfigure its relations to the world resonates with the meaning of *cosmos*, that is, "order" or "adornment" as in "cosmetics."[16] By associating the process by which different spatial entities adorn or make up the world through posing, the focus turns once again to *modernistas'* implementation of the French *rastaquoère* whereby adornment suggests trickery and the neutering or erasure of a local reality.

In "Palabras liminares," Darío momentarily and ironically links the poet, a manipulator of language, to the *rastaquoère*, a manipulator of origins, only to later disassociate himself from this subversive field by retreating into the faraway past. Alienated by the increasing professionalization of the poetic realm, Darío's questioning of the professor, academic, correspondent of the Real Academia Española, journalist, lawyer, poet, and *rastaquoère* leads to a curious assertion of a nonprofessional and nonambiguously gendered identity: "Hombre soy" (I am a man).

¿Hay en mi sangre alguna gota de sangre de África, o de indio chorotega o nagrandano? Pudiera ser, a despecho de mis manos de márques; mas he aquí que veréis en mis versos princesas, reyes, cosas imperiales, visiones de países lejanos o imposibles; ¡qué queréis!, yo detesto la vida y el tiempo en que me tocó nacer . . .

(Si hay poesía en nuestra América ella está en las cosas viejas; en Palenke y Utatlan, en el indio legendario, y en el inca sensual y fino, y en el gran Moctezuma de la silla de oro. Lo demás es tuyo, demócrata Walt Whitman.)

Buenos Aires: Cosmópolis.
¡Y mañana! (Darío 1993, 11)

[Is there in my blood any drop of African, Chorotegan or Nagrandan Indian blood? It could be, despite my hands of a marquis; but I have here apparent in my verses princesses, kings, imperial things, visions of faraway or impossible lands. What do you want? detest the life and time in which I happened to have been born . . .

(If there is poetry in our America' it is in old things; in Palenke and Utatlan, in the legendary Indian, and in the sensual and refined Inca, and in the great Montezuma of the gold chair. The rest is yours, democratic Walt Whitman.)

Buenos Aires: Cosmópolis

And the future!]

As Darío hypothesizes whether there is poetry in our America, the ambiguous tone of the passage intensifies. There is doubt as to whether the phrase "Buenos Aires: Cosmópolis" is really a response to the critical preoccupation with the absence of an autochthonous literature of the Americas or whether, in reality, it refers to yet another alienating terrain composed of multiethnic immigrants that, in the vein of Rodó's *Ariel*, threaten to diminish the exceptionality of Latin America. The cosmopolitan realm, as Darío presents it here, likely involves all of these conflicted possibilities. Through an association with poetry, Darío affirms a connection with indigenous people of a Romantic past, in a manner that smoothes out all racial disparities. Beneath such "hands of a marquis," the individual parts, the racial groups, their histories and present politicized situations are barely visible. In the poetic realm, far from the cosmopolitan and heterogeneous Buenos Aires of the 1890s, Darío's marquis hands homogenize and romanticize, but still refuse to respect in full the diversity of their contemporaries.

Evident in Darío's discussion of an indigenous past and present heterogeneity is a tension between actual demographic cosmopolitanisms and romanticized visions of universality described by distinct critics. Noël Salomon refers to the difference between "cosmopolitismo demográfico" (demographic cosmopolitanism) and "cosmopolitismo cultural" (cultural cosmopolitanism) (Salomon 1978, 30), while Mihai Grünfeld more evidently focuses on class by using the terms "aristocratic cosmopolitanisms" and "actual cosmopolitanisms." Cosmopolitanism can refer to an artistic retreat into a past that is critical of a society in which global economic shifts necessitate poets to sell their wares to a market and in the process be taken for less-than-real objects, posers, *rastaquouères*. However, it can also stand for the very demographic promiscuity that threatens artists' unique societal position.

Proximity to Paris does not guarantee a cosmopolitan status to modernist writers or to the characters they create. The extent to which those with more power than American cultural and geographical travelers impose their versions of cosmopolitanism is especially evident in Silva's *De sobremesa*.[17] As Benigno Trigo (1994) has argued, the protagonist of this novel-diary, José Fernández, appears as if he were a receptacle of diverse theories, especially those of the Austrian writer and physician Max Nordau, whose *Degeneration* (1892) privileges traditional literature over modernist literature for its clarity in meaning and unity achieved through form and discipline, as well as for its concern for the audience. Fernández's interpretations of what he reads are recorded in his diaries of his travels that he speaks aloud to a group of friends—they are expressions of a postcolonial migrant who goes to the so-called cosmopolitan capitals and then returns home. The novel begins with Fernández's companions seated, surrounded by collectibles from all over the world, listening to Fernández's contemplations about himself and contemporary international thought. The fact that many of these works had yet to become available in Spanish contributes to Fernández's conceptualization of himself as both part of the modern world, anchored in Europe, and at a distance from it; it is this distance that prevents him from commenting about the specificities of such topics as Nietzsche's *eternal return* and the Frenchman B.A. Morel's category of degeneration, but which also means that, unlike the student in José Enrique Rodó's *Ariel* (1900), he is less burdened by the presence of the source texts.

The initial scene is set in a luxurious salon located in the American continent at the end of the nineteenth century. The interior, with its excess of exotic sounds, sundries, and flavors from all over the world, attests to what in the novel's code would be José Fernández's cosmopolitan nature; for, within it, is

> el comedor iluminado *a giorno* . . . los jarrones de cristal de Murano . . . las frágiles porcelanas decoradas a mano por artistas insignes; los cubiertos que parecen joyas; los manjares delicados, el rubio jerez añejo, el johanissberg seco, los burdeos y las borgañas . . . los sorbetes helados a la rusa, el tokay con sabores de miel (Silva 1968, 11)

> [the illuminated dining room *a giorno*, . . . the crystal jars from Murano . . . the fragile porcelains decorated by hand by renowned

artists; the covers that look like jewels; the delicate food, the blond aged
jerez, the dry Johannesberg, the Bordeaux and the Burgandy . . . the
frozen Russian-like sorbets, the Tokay with flavors of honey.]

The plenitude of this setting corresponds to the levels of excess in
which José Fernández indulges through sensual and intellectual experiences. He is a prisoner of his and his friend's circular reflections on
amorous relations, travel, writing, and sport. Fernández's memories of
numerous females who form a part of the quest for the ideal Helena
are blurred together as are the distinct cities inhabited by nearly identical bourgeois city dwellers. The grand hotels that Fernández enters
are all characterized by the same absurd "conjunto cosmopolita de
estas mesas redondas" (cosmopolitan ensemble of roundtables) that
he too has in his own salon and their gastronomic offerings and other
commodities that one finds at these hotels around the globe are
similarly unanimous (Silva 1968, 75). However, although Fernández
critiques the collapse of specificity in modern life, he lives in a manner
that is emblematic of modernity.

That the protagonist does not systematically record the dates of his
travel throughout Europe reflects the novel's overall defiance of linear
norms of time and spatial specificity. Be it China or Danzig, Paris or
Interlaken, the bourgeoisie drinks the same "té tibio" (lukewarm tea)
(Silva 1968, 76). The simultaneity of time and place in *De sobremesa*,
characteristic of literary cosmopolitanism, is also the aesthetic counterpoint to the changes within national societies posed by the movement of international capital.[18] Pulled by many different ideological,
cultural, and psychological forces, the novel's protagonist is nearly
impossible to place on any one side of any binary formula. For
instance, the beginning of this fictional *sobremesa*—this over-the-table
ritualistic discussion—is taken up by the protagonist's fascination with
the Russian diarist Marie Bashkirtseff. José Fernández explains that,
while he reads Bashkirtseff, he is also reading Nordau's *Degeneration*
that casts her as a principal example of the *mal de siglo*, degeneration.
The protagonist's citation of entire passages from Bashkirtseff's diary
points to his consumption with as well as repulsion by her. The more
Fernández attempts to clarify his identification with her, the more he is
self-deprecating, in part, because he cannot help his reading being
overdetermined by other more dominant readings of the Russian
writer: whether they be those of the "doctór alemán" (German doctor)
or of Mauricio Barrés in "La leyenda de una cosmopolita" (The Legend
of a Cosmopolitan) (Silva 1968, 28).

His experience of double consciousness is staggering and he is aware of "convertirme en el rastaquoere ridículo, en el *snob* grotesco . . ." (becoming the ridiculous rastaquoere, the grotesque snob) (Silva, 1968, 44). José Fernandez even verbalizes that *rastaquoere* and *cosmopolita* are two faces of the same entity. After Fernández's friend assures him that his experience at a sumptuous party was enjoyable, Fernández wonders why it even matters if parties are successful if social relations are dictated solely by partygoers' predictable assessments' of origins.

> Si mi lucidez de analista me hizo ver que para mis elegantes amigos europeos no dejaré de ser nunca el *rastaquoere*, que trata de codearse con ellos . . . y para mis compatriotas no dejaré de ser un farolón que quería mostrarles hasta donde ha logrado insinuarse en el gran mundo parisiense y en la *high life* cosmopolita? (Silva 1968, 184)

> [If my wiz of an analyst made me see that for my elegant European friends I'll never stop being the *rastaquoere* that tries to hobnob with them . . . and for my compatriots I'll never stop being a big fluff who wants to show them the extent to which he has achieved working his way into the great Parisian world and into the cosmopolitan *high life*.]

The "double subject" condition of the Latin American is a principal cause of José Fernández's consternation throughout the entire novel. That Fernández sees himself as less than whole and always as he is imagined by others prevents him from taking any action. For Juan Gustavo Cobo-Borda, the protagonist is neither "el rastaquoere ridículo" [*sic*] (the ridiculous rastaquoere) nor "el snob grotesco" (the grotesque snob), but rather someone who tries to maintain different aspects of his subject position "a través de la holgura de su posición económica, saborear todo lo que el viejo mundo le ofrece sin por ello perder sus raíces muy metidas en el barro infantil de su tierra natal (through enjoyment of his economic position, to savor all the old world offers him without losing his roots deeply embedded in the childhood mud of his birth land) (1988, 110). Cobo-Borda brings to the surface how Fernández forms his identity abroad as a snob who is always made to recognize his otherness to such a degree that he appropriates the epithet "rastaquoere" to describe himself. Like an artist unable to produce sonnets, a political thinker unable to realize any plan, a lover unable to reach his Ideal, José Fernández epitomizes the modernist "feminized" man described by Nordau as well as Pedro Henríquez Ureña in a different context, who succumbs not only to his infertile production, but also to his own delusions. Fernández looks at the closely linked personal and social realms of his own life as if he were an outsider to them. He records not merely his perceptions of the woman he regards but also what he suspects that woman to imagine him to be thinking when he observes her. Critical and participatory, affirmative and renouncing, the ideology that supports Fernández, like the meaning of *cosmopolitismo* within *De sobremesa* and in *modernismo*, as a whole, resists easy facile categorization. Even when seduced by the overpowering and internalized critical gaze of science, Fernández is unable to properly convert to its conceptualizations of normalcy.

With the encroaching U.S. imperialism as a point of reference, conversion is a frequent topos of studies of *modernismo*. The process considers intellectuals and artists who were considered to be more aesthetically driven and located in European letters to those politically engaged as well as anchored in the American soil. Whether we comply with this progressive narrative or not, it is fascinating to observe how particular writers dealt with accusations in a manner distinct from Silva's protagonist. In response to Rodó's accusation that he had not been a poet of America, Darío's preface to the 1905 *Cantos de vida y esperanza* concedes that a bard ought to approach the masses in America. In that book's much-noted first poem entitled "Yo soy aquel que ayer no más decía" (I am that one that yesterday said only), Darío continues to make reference to a cosmopolitan identity,

y muy siglo diez y ocho y muy antiguo
y muy moderno; audaz, cosmopolita. (Darío 1971, 25)

[And very eighteenth-century and very ancient,
And very modern; bold, cosmopolitan.]

while appearing more political than he did in his previous works. This is a coincidence that illustrates the impossibility of construing superficial exclusionary binaries when it comes to thinking about the term *cosmopolita*. As Darío explains in the preface, the universal does not necessarily preclude political or historical issues: "Si en estos cantos hay política, es porque aparece universal" (If in these cantos there are politics, it is because they appear universal) (Darío 1971, 21). The ambiguity and aesthetics of Silva's novel revolves around a cosmopolitan realm that may be useful to at least recall, if not uphold, in the face of critical desires of mastery and complicity.

In José Enrique Rodó's work, these divergent cosmopolitanisms similarly emerge in a manner that continues to elucidate the complicated history of this concept in *modernista* writings.[19] Under the stated influence of Joseph Ernest Renan's play *Caliban* (1878) and unstated yet no less important influence of Darío's "El triunfo de Calibán" (1981/1898), Rodó upholds the character of Ariel from Shakespeare's *The Tempest* as an exemplary cultural symbol of the Latin American intellectual. The imperialist doctrines and actions linked to the Hispanic Cuban North American War and U.S. annexation of the Panama isthmus threatened to absorb Latin America into the United States where democracy and mediocrity prevailed. Rodó understood this threat to be linked to Latin Americans' imitation of North American utilitarianism. Through Rodó's essay, the figure of Ariel comes to be impressed in American thought as an "airy" intellectual who favors reflection free from the practicalities of the public life.[20] As in Darío's "Palabras liminares," Rodó's *Ariel* is characterized by a regression into a cultural past under the threat that even more drastic change is imminent. Its retrospective and prescriptive tone have made it a model for intellectuals' complicated negotiation of resistance to neo-imperialistic gestures throughout the twentieth and now even into the twenty-first century.

The authorial voice of *Ariel* is, however, highly mediated; that is, Rodó does not reveal these prejudices in his own voice, but rather through the voice of the teacher figure named Próspero. Rodó's use of classical rhetorical and generic devices, explored at length by Roberto González Echevarría in *The Voice of the Masters*, is part of an overall attempt to reconfigure a modern world that lives simultaneously with a classical tradition. González Echevarría's observation that Rodó's rhetoric is rooted in the classical dialog of a paternalistic Socrates and a student who is actually silenced is key to seeing how the essay elides the "other" in order to assert one voice, referred to, in *Ariel*, as both universal and cosmopolitan.

Speaking through the teacher Próspero, Rodó instructs the youth of America to create their young society out of the virtues of ancient Greece and Christianity, characterized by elegance and charity.[21] Próspero encourages treasuring *otium* and dissuades the youth from imitating the barbarity of the North. Through leisure time, the young can ponder topics that focus on ideals, rather than on material or practical ends. In addition, this leisure time, to be filled with selfless contemplation, prevents the vulgar elements from taking over society through a process of natural selectivity that ensures Latin Americans stay clear from Northern utilitarianism. By concentrating on spirituality rather than on the contemporary material and historical forces, *Ariel* affirms, Latin American youth would be able to realize the glory of Greece, considered by Rodó, as a newly emerging culture. The trope of encountering the specificity of one's culture in what is considered the universal sphere is maintained through envisioning youthful American civilization in terms of "Ancient" Greece, at its prime.[22]

Although this location of the particular in the universal provides rigid modes of action whose goal is to afford a stable space for identity construction, by privileging universality, taken as a necessary dimension of cosmopolitanism, over particularity, the American continent along with its ancient, nearly extinct indigenous American peoples is bypassed.[23] In a manner similar to Darío's Romantic fantasies of the grandeur of passed away Indians, Rodó construes a direct kinship with a long ago and faraway part of the world that can then justify the particular's need to ignore the present state of indigenous life in "our America" as he confronts U.S. imperialism. Rodó contrasts that harmonic timeless model with the contemporary situation of the Southern Cone, to whose physicality, however, we would be hard-pressed to find any concrete literary reference.[24] As in Darío's "Palabras liminares," Rodó's approach to the contemporary world reflects a *modernista* nativist or antinativist anxiety that compels him to trot the globe in search of universals with whom he can establish affiliations and help him to conceptualize a more accommodating modernity. To this end, he employs the French writer and founder of positivism, Auguste Comte (1798–1858) who had denounced the degree of specialization within advanced societies.

Un alto estado de perfeccionamiento social tiene para él un grave inconveniente en la facilidad con que suscita la aparición de espíritus deformados y estrechos . . .

La belleza incomparable de Atenas, lo imperecedero del modelo legado por manos de diosa a la admiración y encanto de la humanidad, nacen de que aquella ciudad de prodigios fundó su concepción de la vida en el concierto de todas las facultades humanas, en la libre y acordada expansión de todas las energías capaces de contribuir a la gloria y al poder de los hombres. (Rodó 1994, 48)

[In his view, the most serious flaw in a state of high social perfection lies in the frequency with which it produces deformed spirits, spirits extremely adept in one aspect of life but monstrously inept in all others . . .

The incomparable beauty of Athens, the longevity of the model this goddess of a city bequeathed to us, were owing to a concept of life based on the total harmony of all human faculties and the mutual agreement that all energies should be directed toward the glory and power of mankind.] (Rodó 1988, 43, trans. Sayers Peden)

Having diagnosed Latin American societies to be increasingly afflicted by specialization, Rodó attempts to stall this process and forge a distinct Latin American future that, unlike the North American one, takes its material from ancient Greece. We may see Rodó's emphasis on universality and harmony as a defensive gesture intended to resist the diversification that immigration and imitation posed on a culture that he conceived to be coherent.[25]

The contradictions in Rodó's essay around *cosmopolitismo* are extensive and contribute to our interest in reconsidering its feasibility in the present. As in Valera's account where cosmopolitanism is entwined with Gallicism in the project of autochthonous cultures, Rodó suggests how, in the absence of autochthony, cosmopolitanism—here, read as ties to ancient Greece—is seen to represent liberation from a colonized cultural mind.

> Pero en ausencia de esa índole perfectamente diferenciada y autónomica, tenemos—los americanos latinos—una herencia de raza, una gran tradición étnica que mantener, un vínculo sagrado que nos une a inmortales páginas de la historia, confiando a nuestro honor su continuación en lo futuro. El cosmopolitismo, que hemos de acatar como una irresistible necesidad de nuestra formación, no excluye ni ese sentimiento de fidelidad a lo pasado ni la fuerza directriz plasmante con que debe el genio de la raza imponerse en la refundición de los elementos que constituirán el americano definitivo del futuro. (Rodó 1994/1900, 105–06)

> [But in lieu of an absolutely distinct and autonomous particularity, we Latin Americans have a heritage of race, a great ethnic tradition, to maintain, a sacred place in the pages of history that depends upon us for its continuation. Cosmopolitanism, which we must respect as a compelling requisite in our formation, includes fidelity both to the past and to the formative role that the genius of our race must play in recasting the American of tomorrow.] (Rodó 1988, 73, trans. Sayers Peden)

This description of a prophetic fidelity to the past is detached from the "real" memories of the masses of "cosmopolitans" with many particular pasts whose presence is threatening to Rodó. Understanding the phrase "herencia de raza" in light of Gerard Aching's explanation of nineteenth-century Spanish American conceptions of "raza," whereby ethnic difference, dissent, or difference are ignored in favor of "the concretization of a pure and unchallengeable meaning and identity," helps to explain both Rodó's and Varela's approximate equation of race and cosmopolitanism (Aching 1997, 156). Rodó's cosmopolitanism is, in other words, this racial manifest destiny, which, in its concretization, distances itself from the conditions of modernity. Tradition, in the sense of a particular continuity that ignores mixing, is upheld in the face of the heterogeneity of the present.

In fact, at the same time that Rodó praises cosmopolitanism, he also complains about the working-class immigrants who flock from Mediterranean countries to the Southern Cone. Although Rodó was himself a child of immigrants, he reacted to the onslaught of immigrants with intense elitism:

> El presuroso crecimiento de nuestras democracias por la incesante agregación de una enorme multitud cosmopolita; por la afluencia inmigratoria, que se incorpora a un núcleo aún débil para verificar un activo trabajo de asimilación y encauzar el torrente humano con los medios que ofrecen la solidez secular de la estructura social, el orden político seguro y los elementos de una cultura que haya arraigado íntimamente, nos expone en el porvenir a los peligros de la degeneración democrática. (Rodó 1994/1900, 80–81)

> [Large numbers of immigrants have added to a nucleus still too weak to assimilate and channel properly this flood of humanity in ways that can be provided by a solid secular social structure, a secure political system, and deeply rooted personal values. This situation conjures up the future dangers of a democratic deterioration.] (Rodó 1988, 99, trans. Sayers Peden)

That the very first part of this extract in which the adjective "cosmopolitan" appears ("The rapid increase of our democracies by the incessant accumulation of an enormous cosmopolitan multitude") is left out of Margaret Sayers Peden's translation could suggest she did not think its content substantial enough to support a lengthy English explanation of what Rodó meant by "democracies" and "cosmopolitan." Rodó's vision of cosmopolitan masses, in the case above, is primarily that they disrupt unity and quality, an association important to remember with respect to future valorizations of the cosmopolitan experiences of the masses, as in the "discrepant" cosmopolitanism conceived by James Clifford.

If we are to examine intellectual self-positioning in twentieth- and twenty-first-century letters, we may not overlook the multiple significations of *cosmopolita* and *cosmopolitismo* in the turn-of-the-twentieth-century *Ariel*. Attachment to the past, as an almost mythical category, displaying particular racial qualifications is only present in the form of parodic traces in Arenas's and Eltit's writing. In both cases, it is as if it slips through humoristically in their challenges to the governing bodies for which the past is frequently overvalorized. Although I do not believe there exits a direct line of influence from Darío and Rodó to Arenas and Eltit, their writing does elicit similar questions concerning the worldliness of their affiliations and the relation between mediocrity and marketability. Within *Ariel*, the migration of discrepant bodies, rather than ideas, that are darker and poorer than the previous ones, threatens to distort the future of the Southern Cone and turn it into a monstrosity that resembles the United States. While these concerns are present in Rodó's essay, it also attempts to divide the material and the theoretical. As we shall see in the present discussion of cosmopolitanism with respect to Arenas and Eltit, the movement of ideas and bodies is connected, and we critics function as disciplinary shopkeepers in the process of keeping abreast of this inventory.

My use of *cosmopolitanism* premises itself on a range of positive and negative nuances in the context of Spanish American literature and culture. In an article (1979) entitled "Cosmopolitanism and Internationalism in the History of Ideas in Latin America," Noël Salomon explores the vast semantic field in depth by juxtaposing it to *internationalism*. As in the Anglo-American context where *cosmopolitanism* has historically more inclusive and exclusive faces, *cosmopolitismo*, as we have begun to see, is invoked to both combat and celebrate imperialism. Salomon begins with a discussion of its Greek etymology and then speaks of sixteenth-century Renaissance humanists, with the intention to demonstrate that " 'cosmopolite' was apparently not taken to be the opposite of 'patriot' or 'indigenous' " (Salomon 1978, 83). Salomon's principally diachronic study of cosmopolitanism within the Romance languages, like McKillop's, describes both exclusive and inclusive versions of cosmopolitanism. Salomon describes how late-eighteenth-century anticolonialist sentiment saw itself as having emerged from *cosmopolitismo*. For instance, in the 1793 epistolary novel, *Cartas marruecas* (*Moroccan Letters*), written by José Cadalso (Spain, 1741), the protagonist Nuño is said to love all the foreigners of Madrid "as they were his fellow countrymen . . . being a true cosmopolitan unto them" (84). A cosmopolitan is thus someone who recognizes the humanity of the inhabitants of all parts of the globe. In nineteenth-century France, when *cosmopolitan* began to be used as an adjective, it not only meant someone open to the world, but also someone uprooted. Overall, Salomon looks favorably on the other term announced in the title, cultural *internationalism*, and refuses to see them as opposites.

Jean Franco similarly conflates *internationalism* with *cosmopolitanism*, cosmopolitanism with eclecticism in a chapter entitled "Cosmopolitan or Universal?" of her now classic *The Modern Culture of Latin America*. What is distinct about Franco's approach is that she intuits the importance of economic class on cosmopolitan experimentation, while she emphasizes that modern Latin American artists signal their "right to participate in Western culture" (Franco 1970, 196), a cosmopolitan realm that is a modern brotherhood whose members are joined by diverse characteristics that include artistic experimentation, interest in "root" experience, the model of poetry as spirituality, the Americanization of universal myths, and the desire to participate in modernity as city dwellers. While critiquing Franco's explanations of the cosmopolitan for being vague and aesthetic, Esther Cimet (1973) asserts the need to connect even more concretely the issues of cultural and economic nationalism. Similarly, in numerous studies of *modernista* and *vanguardista* artists, *cosmopolitan* continues to circulate as a signifier of their aesthetics. Especially in the works of avant-garde writers, such as the Chilean Vicente Huidobro and the Argentine Oliverio Girondo, it is the simultaneity of time and place conceived of as the distinguishing factor of a cosmopolitan modern life and of the convergence of world cities.

What Franco does in her 2002 book *The Decline and Fall of the Lettered City: Latin America in the Cold War* is link the apparent spontaneous imperative toward cosmopolitan values among diverse Latin American writers to an institutionalized anticommunist agenda that made its mark on several journals supported by Congress for Cultural Freedom and the Rockefeller Foundation. Following the evolution of Franco's own thoughts on the subject is fascinating in and of itself. In her recent book, Franco traces the motivation behind what she referred to as the "right to participate in Western culture" in 1967, in particular, to *Mundo Nuevo*'s response to the overwhelming influence and distribution of the revolutionary journal *Casa de las Américas* (Franco 1967, 196; 2002, 45).

Foregrounding the power involved in the selection processes of forging truths and speaking for others must not mean shying away from the occasions to form distinct solidarities. In addition to self-critique, a "post-cultural" space, as imagined by Clifford, in which neither the interpreter nor the interpreted imagines a unified culture, is the basis for a positive strategy of coming to terms with the link between a professional worker, who is frequently an academic bound to his or her discipline, and his or her object of analysis. While Nelly Richard has critiqued the disciplines of social sciences or cultural studies for appropriating the subaltern in processes of self-legitimatization, feminist critics engaged in microinstitutions and microexperiences of knowledge take part in this process as well. Reckoning with these discrepancies forms part of my analysis of the intellectual investment in others who we frequently perceive as more local and authentic than us, in a process of forgetting to consider the movement of ideas and bodies to which they too are attached. At the same time that this book pays attention to intellectual self-fashioning, its interpretations of cultural production also take into account the need to look at what people do rather than profess, a process that Sheldon Pollock explains elegantly as the need "to think about cosmopolitanism and vernacularism as action rather than idea, as something people do rather than something they declare, as practice rather than proposition . . . This enables us to see that some people in the past have been able to be cosmopolitan or vernacular without directly professing either, perhaps even while finding it impossible rationally to justify either" (Pollock 2000, 593). My approach is mainly episodic, and my discussions of authors writing in distinct periods highlight the continuities and limits of a discussion on *cosmopolitanism.*

The sociopolitical consequences of cosmopolitanism's commensurability with the process of Europeanization are examined at length as they relate to the Cuban Revolution, itself a process that balances nationalisms and cosmopolitanisms through its historically internationalist dimensions. Precisely because of how significant the destiny of place, and even more specifically, the destiny of Cuba's place, has been to defining world politics, most frequently in negative terms, cultural critics must insist upon other ways of viewing the identifications and misidentifications among individuals and groups. Nevertheless, out of this actual place of Cuba has emerged Cuba, an idea that executes a vitality and passage toward a defiant cosmopolitanism among intellectuals from diverse parts of the world.

Among the principal institutions in the island's negotiation of the national and international sphere are the Casa de las Américas and the Cuban Institute of Cinematographic Art and Industry (ICAIC), which, along with a number of journals and prize-awarding bodies, have formed a complicated cultural landscape. The negative dimensions of this institutionalization have never surfaced more dramatically as in the Padilla affair in 1971 and in the more long-lived Arenas affair; however, these are not the only cases wherein culture was affected seriously by governmental mandates. The closure of the Pablo Milanés Foundation, a cultural organization, in 1995, the incarceration of the writer Raúl Rivero, along with many other officially denoted dissidents, along with other factions, such as the punk rocker Gorki Águila Carrasco in 2003, as well as the closure of the Spanish Cultural Center that same year are some of the more recent and notorious examples of this predicament. As Havana is undoubtedly the focus of this web, writers' relation to Cuba's capital reflects the weighty climate. In addition to symbolizing escape from the oppressive provinces, the capital of Havana comes to be identified as a prison in Reinaldo Arenas's novels.

While it would be easy to think that Arenas's self-obsession leaves no space for community, chapter 2: A *Guajiro*'s Cosmos delineates Arenas as a migrant writer with a vested interest in construing an alternate version of affiliations. Out of a life in Castro's Cuba that consisted of constant imprisonment and escape and culminated in his exodus in the 1980 Mariel boatlift, unique definitions of American identity are forged at the same time that they are cast as constricting. By embracing the imposed animalization of homosexuals, utilizing the local epithet *pájaro* (in Cuba meaning both queer and bird), Arenas arrives at a "discrepant" cosmopolitanism in which "migratory birds" are central. At the same time that Arenas's narrative focuses on several landscapes (Holguín, Havana, Paris, Miami, and New York), underlining his complex vision of a possible union of global and local symbols, his work challenges the urban connotations of cosmopolitanism through the shifting nature of his rural childhood.

Many of the details of Arenas's life have been brought to the large screen in Julian Schnabel's *Before Night Falls* (2000), through a commodification process that becomes the focus of chapter 4—Arenas was a prolific writer; the greater part of his oeuvre is composed of novels. At the time of his suicide in 1990, he had written 11 novels, many short stories, essays, poems, and an autobiography. What escapes the film, however, are the complexities that determined how Arenas constituted himself as ultimately Cuban in his inability to fit within the limits of the nation:

Tengo una idea muy especial de lo que puede llamarse la literatura cubana: creo que es una cuestión muy aérea y desasida y hasta cierto punto un verdadero caso de "apariciones." Es que los escritores cubanos, más que escritores propiamente dichos, son como "aparecidos." En un momento determinado hacen su entrada, comparecen, y después, a poco andar, ya no sabemos qué es de ellos ni lo que se hacen . . . Eso les da a los escritores un aura como de duendes, de seres mágicos, de criaturas—insisto—que aparecen y muy pronto ya no se sabe cuál es su destino. Quizás, y dentro de ese esquema, pueda yo considerarme dentro de una tradición de literatura cubana. . . . Porque lo mejor de la literatura cubana . . . se ha escrito afuera y quienes han vivido en la isla lo han hecho como fantasmas. Piensa en Lezama Lima, un verdadero "aparecido" al que nadie veía, piensa en Virgilio Piñera, que era un duende que de pronto surgía de la nada y al que durante un tiempo considerable ya nadie volvía a ver. . . . Esa literatura es entonces fantas-mática, errante, y a la vez fugaz. En esa fugacidad quizás pueda situarme. (Arenas 1993b, 51)

[I have a very special idea of what can be called Cuban literature: I believe that it is a very aerial and loose question and, up to a certain point, a true case of "apparitions." It is that Cuban writers, more than properly called writers, are like "show-er uppers." In a determined moment they make an entrance, they appear, and after, just a bit later, we already don't know anything about them or what they are doing . . . This gives writers an aura of elves, of magic beings, of creatures—I insist—that they appear and very soon their destiny is unknown. Perhaps, and within this scheme, I can consider myself within a tradition of Cuban literature . . . Because the best of Cuban litera-ture . . . has been written outside and those who have lived on the island have done so like ghosts. Think of Lezama Lima, a true "show-er upper" that no one saw, think of Virgilio Piñera, an elf who suddenly emerged from nothing and, for a considerable time, no one saw again. This literature is then phantasmic, wandering, and at the same time, fleeting. In this fleetingness perhaps I can situate myself.]

With this statement, Arenas makes explicit what his fiction does implicitly, thus securing a place in a paradoxically anchored tradition.[26] He shapes himself by distinguishing the particular literary and historical figures with whom he feels an affinity, many of whom are "aparecidos" from those he despises.

Chapter 3: Just a *Vieja de Barrio?* On Self-Fashioning and Diamela Eltit examines another writer who, like Arenas, has been viewed as ex-centric and conflictive in her national context. The works of Diamela Eltit, a writer and performance artist who promoted the Avanzada scene in Chile in the late 1970s, challenge the notion of propriety set forth in both public and private spheres. They reveal the mechanisms of power that function at all levels of society. Rather than operating in a moralistic sphere that the military dictatorship (1973–1990) led by General Augusto Pinochet manipulates to its advantage, Eltit's works examine the complexities involved in the construction of self and the execution of power. In recent years, the criticism of Eltit's fiction within Chile, especially by Nelly Richard and Eugenia Brito, and in North America by Jean Franco, Mary Louise Pratt, Mary Beth Tierney-Tello, and Gisela Norat, the translations of her works into English by Dick Gerdes and Ronald Christ, and her associations with, among many other universities, Berkeley, Columbia, Brown, Georgetown, and Johns Hopkins universities, have helped to shape her reputation, making her known primarily within academic circles as one of the most important writers from Latin America today.

That Eltit has positioned herself as a local intellectual is fascinating in light of how central her works have become to the discipline of Latin Americanism and the degree to which she is engaged with international theory, avant-garde literature, and the margins of urban space. While cosmopolitanism in relation to the works of Eltit, a Chilean who lived and wrote in Chile during Pinochet's regime, refers to a field that is distinct from Arenas's insular cosmopolitanism, both continually antagonize fixing identities rather than seek a totalizing definition of America's difference. The general questions throughout my analyses relate to aesthetics and the formation of solidarities, be they the alternative fraternities of exiles in the case of Reinaldo Arenas or vagabonds of Diamela Eltit.

A narrative of elitism, expertise, and complicity continues to evolve in chapter 4: Face to Screen, which relates the implications of the filmic translation of Reinaldo Arenas's identity in Schnabel's film *Before Night Falls* on audiences in North America to the legacy of Arenas's life and writing on intellectuals and writers within Cuba. Insider and outsider positions transform into the other. New management of discipline, order, and liberation result when official online journals, for instance, originating in Cuba are primarily accessed from abroad. The lack of filters in the Internet has the potential to undo concepts of national literature. Bearing in mind the connections that this book lays forth among critical encounters with the margins, authenticity, and posing, this chapter investigates the "fables of intimacy" utilized by Schnabel to position himself as an artist, in the Modernist vein and as an authority on this writer from a nation fascinating to many "outsiders" for its offerings of sociopolitical, climatic, and erotic differences. Schnabel's self-promotion as a rugged world citizen effaces the specifics of Arenas's defiant cosmopolitanism. It is in this symbolic Cuba/New York (Hollywood) that Arenas is transformed into a universalist.

As we come to see the multifaceted potential of cosmopolitanism without dismissing it for being comprised of ambiguities and afflictions, we arrive at another set of challenges. Whereas Schnabel's and his audience's encounter with Arenas transformed the political and symbolic weight of Arenas and his public, in chapter 5: Uncomfortable Homes, the anonymous voices of mental patients are disseminated and refracted through a distinct international lens. Focusing on the discourse of human rights, the form of the *testimonio*, and the Internet, chapter 5 emphasizes the intersections among cultural studies, critical cosmopolitanism, and consumerist discourse. How do art objects that center on images and words of interned patients with a limited circulation in a local context transform as these representations travel?

I read Diamela Eltit and Paz Errázuriz's photoessay on an insane asylum, *El infarto del alma* (1994), alongside both Eltit's *Mano de obra* (2002a), set primarily in a supermarket, and a 2002 issue of the Benetton fashion house magazine *Colors*, similarly focusing on insanity. All the while in the backdrop is José Donoso's 1970 masterpiece *El obsceno pájaro de la noche* that internationalizes the indigenous Chilean image of mystification and alienation of the *imbunche*, the child whose orifice has been sewn up. Echoing *El obsceno*'s old servants who "imbunchify" in order to possess the allusion of possession as they obsessively package the leftovers of the upper classes, *Mano de obra*'s twenty-first-century supermarket workers obsessively package and disappear within the products of their labors.

In this discussion, the question of approaching the other achieves a different momentum. A highly marketable version of multiculturalism emerged from Benetton in the 1990s alongside the most fervent debates on the politics of difference and pluralism taking place in a variety of spheres. The partial degree to which this fashionable packaging is sustainable as a challenge of the West's hegemony has been examined by several critics already. Given the fact that *Colors* is produced by this multinational fashion enterprise, how are we to read its testimonial-like photoessay of asylums around the world but especially in Cuba? Our own affiliations within a particular discipline are embedded in our responses to Benetton's multicultural campaigns, in general, and to the "Madness" issue, in particular. Our reactions are also involved in questions of accessibility, authenticity, and truth. Blurring borders of neoliberalism and discrepant cosmopolitanism, these texts destabilize the boundaries among scientific discourse on madness, commodity, and culture as they refigure the world according to a particular photographic aesthetic. This chapter cautions against sharp assessments of literature alone as an intermediary between madness and philosophy or as a tool to give voice to the mad. Engagement with discourses on madness, as Shoshana Felman concluded, has the possibility of "mystifying effects of the marketplace of fashion," but even within an apparent display of the containment of the mad in Benetton's *Colors*, the contradictions of the solidified national sphere can be adduced (Felman 2003, 13). Discourses on madness have become definitive in literary and cultural critique because they epitomize discourses of exclusion. To house a discourse of madness within cultural critique or within fashion, as this analysis of cosmopolitanism demonstrates, begs us to toss aside disciplinary rigidities and look at distinct professional assessments of difference in the process of examining the limits of our investment in discrepant cosmopolitanism.

A *Guajiro's* Cosmos

To rural schools in the Cuban countryside, the revolution's youth is sent away from their familiar terrain for the purpose of acquiring local and experience-based knowledge. While in the 1960s the more practical reasons for such a systemized stint related to the nation's agricultural demands that necessitated a larger and more productive workforce, the theoretical justification for the combined manual and intellectual labor was found in Marx, Engels, Lenin, and, of course, the nineteenth-century thinker glorified by the revolution, José Martí. Such time away from home, despite, within the country, does not always guarantee the solicited social outcomes, as Wendy Guerra reveals in her vignette "Olga ya no es nombre ruso" (Olga is no longer a Russian name).[1] Accompanied by a cousin who needs to retrieve her student records before departing from her homeland with her new foreign husband, the narrator observes two young girls kissing each other in front of the institutional building of the rural *Pre universitario* (grades 10, 11, and 12).

In the days of the "Special Period in Times of Peace," an official term conveying the enduring exceptionality of the socioeconomic circumstances in post–cold war Cuba, the institutions where students are sent away from the city before university do not turn out to be only breeding grounds for socialist formation, for Martian weaving of theory and practice, but also for exploratory sexual relations, resembling more directly ploys for economic advancement. Guerra suggests that young women who came of age in the 1990s, in a practically bankrupt nation, negotiate their sexuality with the goal of becoming more solvent as individuals. The vignette's title refers to the fact that the Soviet Union is no longer the singular exotic place to which Cubans have access, nor is it the screen through which Cubans may perceive the world. What Guerra insinuates is that when young women return from their countryside hiatus, they are eager to invent ways of combating their economic conditions, leading them away from the designated goal of the acquisition of local knowledge and almost accidentally outside of the nation. A perceptual slip exists wherein they must operate under anachronistic norms set forth by a nation with a strong autonomous ideology that survived through intense internationalist backing. As a consequence of this seemingly anachronistic national obligation, these young women align themselves with a world outside of Cuba. The symbolic value that Guerra ascribes to the girls' affection for one another cuts to the heart of the effects of a disintegrated economy on gender explorations. "Ya cualquiera aquí se llama Olga—dijo corriendo en el minúsculo tramo de inmigración a la aduana. Tan femenina como viril, tan ebria como lúcida, tan ilustrada como vacía, tan cubana como del mundo" (Now anyone here is named Olga—she said running down the miniscule stretch from immigration to customs. As feminine as virile, as inebriated as lucid, as enlightened as vacuous, as Cuban as from the world) (Guerra 2003, 275). In the case of these Cuban youths, this category of worldliness depends on different temporary alliances that are united at an official national institution.

Guerra's description of a more individualistic imperative toward worldliness is really an interpretation of sexual politics inflected by global capitalism within an environment of gasping socialism. The market's supply and demand informs their conceptualizations of worldliness. In the everyday context, the actions of these homoerotic *Pre universitario* girls, desiring to leave Cuba, are not so different from those of the *jineteras*, the overused term to describe those who "hustle" with foreigners. As subjects abroad, they end up translating the world to their compatriots in the modern electronic epistolary, telephone, and even in person upon their no longer unimaginable return to the island. They also represent their faraway home in the metropolis. We may say that they are another breed of "actual cosmopolitans" who potentially contaminate the pure national sphere through exploratory tactics fine tuned in the countryside.

I introduce Reinaldo Arenas's rural cosmopolitanism using this vignette to emphasize the different economic and social factors that combine in a term whose nuances, as we have seen, have been frequently viewed to be part of an ideal framework and not significantly grounded in everyday local realities. The *pre*-girls, alongside that of Arenas, contradict this premise. The process of socialization in the rural schools, accordingly, leads to exits, in which material gain is desired, while Arenas's vision of himself within Cuba's rural landscape largely depends on viewing worldliness as an ideological category. This chapter focuses on the tensions between distinct modalities of cosmopolitanisms within Arenas's writing, while chapter 4 takes these modalities to a different realm as it examines how his aesthetic and ideological mutability complicates critical appropriations of his writing. Having come of age at the height of revolutionary exaltation of the countryside's value to the nation, Arenas fashions himself as a *guajiro* (country-bumpkin or hick). He repeats this characterization upon numerous occasions in his writing and even pronounces it in French in the international film *Mauvaise Conduite* (directed by Spanish/Cuban exile Néstor Almendros and Cuban exile Orlando Jiménez Leal with contributions by a varied group of intellectuals and artists including Susan Sontag, Juan Goytisolo, and Arenas).[2] In fact, unlike the other testimonies to the oppression of the 1970s in the documentary rendered mainly in English and Spanish, Arenas introduces himself by saying "je sui un paysan," as if it were a promise—whether of translatability or intranslatabilty is questionable. Born in the prerevolutionary rural Oriente province, outside of Holguín, in a town called Perronales, Arenas expresses great reluctance to urban landscapes. To a large degree, they are portrayed as stale and inherited. Still, in contrast to other artistic stances in this book, Arenas resorts to the category of "cosmopolita" in the process of plotting his own symbolic map of the world. Although he conveys reluctance toward elitist "cosmopolitas," whom he perceives as thinking themselves above the actual knowledge of place, another more nuanced version of cosmopolitanism characterizes his own writing. It is not the opposing term to *country* as in the binary country/city or to the *national* as in the binary *cosmopolitan/national*. Emerging out of a sense that individuals are continually suffocated, it is rather an expansive, yet sharply contradictory, worldview that is linked to the author's conceptualization of flux in nature.

Life in the countryside, unleashed of the city's institutional restrictions, can be the most liberating. Yet, Arenas explicitly rejects *costumbrismo* and *regionalismo*, currents that he suggests are favored by dictatorships, and instead reclaims rural nature and the sea for their mutability (Arenas 1986, 92). More humane and worldly affiliations may arise from them.

> Creo que el campo es más universal, más "civilizado" que la ciudad. De hecho un hombre de campo tiene que ser más cosmopolita que el habitante de esos modernos pozos de concreto, donde todo perece en

aras de la identidad (impersonalidad) monolítica, tanto en arquitectura como en costumbres

[I believe that the countryside is more universal, more "civilized" than the city. In fact a man from the countryside has to be more cosmopolitan than the inhabitant of these modern pools of concrete, where all vanishes in altars of monolithic identity (impersonality), as much in architecture as in habits.] (Arenas 1986, 84–85)

Against the revolution's insistence that educational programs uphold telluric visions and moral integrity as ultimately nationalistic, Arenas's writing gestures toward the geographical expanse of the countryside as a principal impulse for imaginative innovation. Cities progress limitedly and deteriorate; nature evolves expansively and rejuvenates.

As Arenas's characters form unique affiliations with marginal figures and the most marginal aspects of canonical ones, a cohesive social structure begins to come apart and in its place is construed an imagined cosmopolitan community that does not exclude the most local figures. Crucial to this invigorated space are libidinal energies for which political boundaries are insignificant. Arenas stakes this claim by sexualizing historical figures from distinct historical and geographic frameworks; before I elaborate on these processes of identification, let me recount briefly the symbolic weight of Arenas's vision in the 1960s and 1970s, during the first two decades of the revolution. At almost any point in this abbreviated review, it would be possible to tell the story differently by signaling additional economic and political events beyond Cuba that influence its internal politics. Such a complex simultaneity would not excuse intense degrees of oppression within, but would require thinking about them alongside imperialistic and mercenary fears.

Culture and Production

As is always the case with Cuba, external factors such as the U.S. embargo impede easily evaluating the nation's own cycles of expelling and incorporating "difference," as a category that departs from the revolutionary goals. There may be greater tolerance toward gays apparent in the public sphere, yet the large-scale crackdown on the rights of "dissidents," internationally criticized in 2003, extends to other spheres and makes it difficult to isolate any one aspect of identity.[3] In grandeur, Arenas's texts display something else; that is, male characters that allegedly couple with women frequently doing so with men. This unsaid representation, exposing the limits of visibility and tolerance, is a foremost way that Arenas's texts push beyond those prescribed limits of authoritarianism in religion and political ideology. In Arenas's "real" life, a life that is difficult to view apart from his largely autobiographically imbedded fiction, besides presenting a lost copy of *Otra vez el mar* (1982; *Farewell to the Sea*, 1986) and the fact that he published abroad as evidence of his illicit and illegal behavior, the Cuban Security Police also cited him for sodomy.[4] While the possession of rights is not the only ingredient of joy, restrictions on them, as the earliest of Arenas's publications allude to, can also impede individuals from experiencing pleasure. *Celestino antes del alba*, Arenas's first novel, represented the violence bred by patriarchy. As such, although it was awarded an honorable mention by the Concurso Nacional de Novela Cirilio Villaverde in 1965, only after another two years in a single print run of between 2,000 and 3,000 copies, rather than in a run between 10,000 and 25,000 typical of the more institutionally supported texts, was it published.[5] In *Antes que anochezca*,[6] Arenas explains that two judges in particular were responsible for this outcome: Cuban critic José Antonio Portuondo and internationally acclaimed Alejo Carpentier, both aligned with official revolutionary politics. The resistance on the part of the Cuban union of writers and artists called La Unión Nacional de Escritores y Artistas Cubanos (UNEAC) to seeing it in print was not entirely unpredictable since the norms of revolutionary art were already delivered in 1961 by Fidel Castro himself in "Palabras a los intelectuales" (Words to the intellectuals), the most memorable part of which is frequently quoted: "Dentro de la Revolución, todo; contra la Revolución, nada" (Within the Revolution, everything; against the Revolution, nothing).[7] Preceded by the Playa de Girón/Bay of Pigs, just about two months before, Castro's words confirmed the extent to which the revolution's restrictions would prescribe the role of artists. Already, Sabá Cabrera Infante's short film *P.M.*(1961), featuring the nightlife of Havana, had been censored and his brother Guillermo's cultural supplement *Lunes de revolución* was shut down.[8]

In his not so modest prologue to *El color del verano (The Color of Summer)*, Arenas comments that little good literature emerged from his own generation:

> Mi generación . . . con excepción de mí mismo no ha podido producir un autor notable. Y no es que no los hubiera, es que de una u otra forma han sido aniquilados. (Arenas 1991, 247)

[My generation . . . has not produced a single noteworthy writer, with the possible exception of myself. And it's not that there never were any; it's that one way or another they have been annihilated, destroyed, done away with.] (Arenas 2000, 254, trans. Hurley)

His writing has informed many about the measures taken in the 1960s and the 1970s to silence "antisocials," in general, and homosexuals, in particular. Although the 1984 documentary, *Mauvaise Conduite*, may have left spectators with the false impression that the forced labor camps called Unidades Militares de Ayuda a la Producción (UMAPs) carried into the 1980s, the personal testimonies of oppression exposed less than two decades after their occurrence have impacted an international discussion of gender and human rights within Cuba.

To the extent that it appears to be a rationalizing cliché to think of those times as difficult for Cuba, as a premier leftist nation, and for its citizens, they were. The Padilla affair invoked much more than a national quandary. The same day that Padilla was released from a month's incarceration, he delivered a haunting self-confession in which he inculpated his wife and many of his friends. Strict governmental policies on culture resembling the thematic and formal uniformity of Stalinistic programs characterized the gray period that began in 1971.[9] One outcome of the Padilla affair was the First National Congress on Education and Culture specifying the limits on religion, sexuality, and cultural activity in the revolutionary state.[10] Viewing homosexuality as a problem in need of a solution and homosexuals as a threat to the society's health required homosexuals to not "intervene directly in the formation of our youth by means of artistic or cultural activities" and not "represent our country artistically abroad" (Johnson 1977, 102). In 1979, homosexual acts were decriminalized, but oppressive political and judicial acts against "antisocials," though difficult to document, have not disappeared.

During the revolution's first two decades, the notion that homosexuals ought to be cured focused on levels of visibility. Official discourse positioned them as degenerative, egomaniacal, and sex-obsessed, which turned an already-existing preoccupation with the morality of homosexuality endemic in, among other societies, Catholic ones, into a sort of hysteria, also comparable to 1950s' United States. Beyond these general similarities, a very particular discourse on masculinity that focused on the *hombre nuevo* (new man) was cultivated throughout Cuban society.[11] Homosexuals were seen as the products of corrupting influences from abroad and leftovers from bourgeois regimes that needed to be eliminated for the "new man" to produce. Work camps were instrumented as mechanisms to strip homosexuals of useless symbols and replace them with those of the new society.[12] Somewhat of a challenge to the vision of Cuba as a nonevolving repressive state for homosexuals is the 1993 internationally successful Cuban film *Fresa y chocolate* (Strawberry and Chocolate) directed by Tomás Gutiérrez Alea and Juan Carlos Tabío. Yet, as Emilio Bejel suggests, even in *Fresa y chocolate*, the revolutionary and the *pájaro* (fairy) never enter into a sexual relationship and the heterosexual paradigm is sustained through the departure of the *pájaro* and the romance of the revolutionary and an aging prostitute (2001, 160–61).

While there have since been artistic and sociological campaigns aimed at greater societal sensitivity toward homosexual difference, "cycles" of oppression and tolerance continue to define Cuba's sociopolitical climate.[13] As Arenas points out in *Necesidad de libertad* (1986), more reactionary periods within the United States provide Castro with justification for implementing severe oppressive tactics. Critical cosmopolitanism would mean embracing the privileged position of looking at this period from a temporal or geographic distance and finding an ethical means to convey this complicated dynamic.

Costuming Cuban History

In Arenas's writing, the revolution's transformation of the cultural sphere is so complete that the author can hardly imagine a space that is not affected by it. What I mean by this is that his almost incessant probing and critique of institutions reveal a desire to be supported and embraced by such institutions, rather than be entirely separated from them. A complex dialectic emerges out of his depiction of himself as victim of the guardians of convention—the home, the national writers' and artists' union, and the national father Fidel Castro—and his fierce desire to surpass the seemingly all-inclusive battles. Through comical distortions, exaggerations, and overall resistance to unity of form and content, Arenas constitutes an alternative common base in which neither category—the Cuban or the foreign—is presumed to be unified or stagnant. Exile—an obvious infraction on the revolution—becomes as much a theme as it is a narrative and semantic device that works on the level of grammar wherein predicates of sentences are split and made distant from their supposed originating subjects.[14] Self-obsession, fear, and anger, the common symptoms of an exile's suffering, penetrate Arenas's work, as much before as after he left Cuba. Exile as a worldview is of utmost importance in Arenas's five-part series termed *pentagonía* (a combination of *pentalogía* [pentalogy] and *agonía* [agony]). It follows the metamorphosis of a character through Cuban history: he is Celestino in *Celestino antes del alba* (1967; first published in English with the title *Singing from the Well* in 1987); Fortunato in *El palacio de las blanquísimas mofetas* (1982; *The Palace of the White Skunks*, 1990); Héctor in *Otra vez el mar* (1982; *Farewell to the Sea*, 1986); the tripartite character Gabriel/La Tétrica Mofeta (The Skunk-in-a-Funk)/Reinaldo Arenas in *El color del verano* (1991; *The Color of Summer*, 2000); and the unnamed character in *El asalto* (1991; *The Assault*, 1994). The dates of publication aside, especially because they hardly coincide with the order of writing, it is important to recognize, as has Carmelo Esterrich, that geography does not dictate Arenas's exilic perspective. "Así, la Pentagonía se convierte en una especie de diálogo entre postura distanciada dentro de la isla y la lejanía del exilio" (In this way, the Pentagonía becomes a kind of dialogue between the distanced posture from the island and the distance of exile) (Esterrich 1994, 25). Arenas's characters are conveyed as exiles from themselves, in part, because of the weight exerted by perceptions of others of them. Geography does not complete the operative conceptualization of either exile or cosmopolitanism.

"Deliberate and nuanced cosmopolitanism," for Gustavo Pérez Firmat, refers to the double focus of *criollist* writing that negotiates peninsular and insular codes in the process of founding a national literature. Arenas shares this propensity for intralingual translation that, involving "intense national reflection," linguistically resists the stability of the dominant culture, by adjusting accepted vernacular codes and insisting that this sort of subversion be placed within a Cuban tradition (Pérez Firmat 1989, 5). It never sets aside linguistic, geographical, cultural, and political references to Cuba, but examines the construed uniformity of origins by highlighting their implication in extra-national spheres. From the first of Arenas's novels, formalistic strategies reinforce the dynamic relation between inside and outside. In *Celestino antes del alba*, a *kunstlerroman* about a young boy who defers his artistic talent and its consequential repression onto a cousin, italicized citations of more and less renowned writers outside and inside of Cuba—Sophocles, Jorge Luis Borges, Arthur Rimbaud, and Pan Yuan Tche, as well as the Eliseo Diego, the protagonist's own mother, a crazy uncle, and a grandmother—are set on whole pages apart from the rest of the text. In contrast to the principally grounding effect of epigraphs, these multiple and diverse citations visually display emblems of cultural movement. When the narrator's crazy uncle, a commoner, is put on the same plane as the canonical Jorge Luis Borges, not only are the barriers between private and public discourses dismissed, but so are the hierarchical notions of the nature of art. Along with the theater plays that continually interrupt the novel's linear progress, these citations function as paratextual signposts akin to José Lezama Lima's *curso délfico* (Delphic course) in their eclecticism. Arenas's personal grouping of citations confirms that those influences closest to home have at least as much footing as these disperse references in the international sphere.[15] We may also think of these citations as having entered the text as exiles from their original context, yet to be thoroughly integrated into their new one. Through a valorization of the persistence of this exilic condition, Arenas links himself to those historical others expelled from their home for ontological, existential, political, and material reasons. With an emphasis on the malleability and constructed character of truths, a far-from-sacred heirloom is formed out of typical Arenian exaggerations of personal statements and historians' accounts. Parodic responses to the difficulty of assessing one's own relation to national history become part of the nation's countermemory, by which history is split and made discontinuous.[16]

Figures and symbols are dislodged from their sacred contexts through Arenas's parodic tactics and become imitations of grand narratives. As they highlight individuals' "strangeness," Arenas's narratives question the possibility of forming affiliations with others on the basis of prescriptions for commonality that generally operate within dominant communities.[17] According to contemporary Cuban writer Abilio Estévez, Arenas once said in a French newspaper, "The world and I are at war." Estévez's interpretation is this statement's flipside. "Reinaldo Arenas damns us and we come to love him, as we love the demon who saves us by showing us the frightful sight of our own lives" (Estévez 1995, 313). This demon within the Arenian idiom displays itself in the spirit of carnival as an unabashedly incomplete body, replete with prohibited libidinal energies. It relates to the sort of disdain for the other that psychoanalyst Julia Kristeva, referencing social anthropologist Mary Douglas, attributes to the other's proximity to what is most despised in one's self. Alan West-Durán revels in this type of parody using the parodic form itself. His Cuban *Fidelio* brilliantly conveys Arenas's take on the double life of the Cuban society.

Arenas impersonates Fidel in order to rescue his jailed lover (called Rococo), who is a jaguar that during the day looks like Lezama and at night like Virgilio. The prison is built in the form of a pineapple. But, as chance would have it, the head of state visits the prison that day, bringing about the encounter of the two Fidels. Naturally, each accuses the other of being an imposter. Who is more faithful (or is it fi(s)tful)? A judge is needed to ascertain the highest degree of fidelity: Raúl Castro is brought forth, dressed as *vedette* Rita Montaner. (West-Durán 1997, 182)

Parody exceeds the original in West-Durán's series of staged impersonations and, as a result, the leader must question whether he is himself authentic. Even though the leader came into the prison, presumably convinced of his position, Arenas's mask, donned in the process of liberating his lover, arouses suspicion: "Naturally, each accuses the other of being an impostor. Who is more faithful (or is it fi(s)tful)?" The mutual regard of the two Fidels epitomizes the link between a leader and his national subjects.[18]

Behind the strategy for the pervasive images of the leader is the hope that through their repetition, he singularly may come to replace citizens' links to their own diverse and sometimes conflicting ethnic and racial heritages. *El color del verano* indulges the more intimate possibilities of this apparent hope through an almost psychoanalytical report on Fidel, who is referred to in the novel as Fifo, one of the Cuban people's more affectionate names for Castro. Fifo's origins are the point of focus, as the text ridicules the revolution's attempt to supplant genealogical and class differences. Accordingly, Fifo inherits "ansias bugarroniles" (Arenas 1991, 411) (the wish to be a surly bull macho and screw *other* machos) (Arenas 2000, 423, trans. Hurley) from his great-great grandfather. Fifo's homosexual tendencies and a passion to be a "real" man are explained by the fact that his mother was both a "whore" and a devout Catholic, and his father was a Galician macho as well as a rapist of almost anything. Out of this pact, the narrator claims, emerges Fifo's vision of a revolutionary Cuba as a place where neither homosexuals nor prostitutes exist. However, the immensity of Fifo's dedication to his vocations can be measured by the way the 1999 carnival is publicized as an event celebrating the fiftieth, as opposed to the fortieth, anniversary of the revolution.

Nations are literally inscribed by the geography of bodies. For instance, at the center of an international orgy is the gigantic phallus of "La llave del golfo" (The key to the gulf), whose name in the book is also Lázaro Carriles, a character based on Arenas's real-life friend Lázaro Gómez Carriles. The reference, however, is also to Cuba's trademarked position at the entrance to the Gulf of Mexico, presenting a duality that clearly challenges the nation's fundamental exceptionality. Cuba gets sucked off from all sides. "Reyes, obispos, obreros, militares, jóvenes comunistas, jóvenes terroristas, monjas de clausura, señoritas" (Arenas 1991, 417) (kings, bishops, working men, soldiers, Young Communists, young terrorists, cloistered nuns, virgin young ladies . . .) (Arenas 2000, 440, trans. Hurley) all perform oral sex on "La llave," while Fifo, from his hot-air balloon above, masturbates and monitors. His overarching capacity to dominate transcends the precarious transportation. As the nation is satisfied, an even more domineering form of voyeurism and exploitation comes into play. Foreigners seem unable to hold back from beckoning to the master of ceremonies, a token of his capacity for seduction. The internal sphere, meanwhile, experiences another form of chaos. The rumor is that the Bulgarian embassy is opening its doors to those Cuban nationals who seek asylum.[19] The discrepancy between projections of Cuba by foreigners and the reality of Cubans' lives is at the forefront of these passages.

The initial playlet of *El color del verano* captures the sort of histrionic polarization that the United States came to know through the "Elian affair" in the spring of 2000, but these characters are, for the most part, writers and intellectuals. The fact that, during this period, a monument of Martí holding a child that strongly resembled Elían González was erected in Havana heightens this connection between posthumous history and Arenas's fiction. "La Fuga de La Avellaneda: Obra ligera en un acto (de repudio)" (The Flight of Gertrudis Gómez de Avellaneda: A Light Comedy in One Act (of Repudiation) focuses on one of the most canonical nineteenth-century literary figures in both Cuba and Spain. In order to make the carnival even more grandiose, the leader has resuscitated the romantic poet who left Cuba for Spain in 1836, Gertrudis Gómez de Avellaneda, but in defiance of his orders to participate in the carnival's festivities, she embarks only to find herself in the Antilles among Fifo's sharks. This comedy is set in the Malecón, mobbed by Fifo's supporters who are ordered to repudiate her, and Key West, with Cuban Americans begging her to join their flock. José Martí joins the scenario, floating in between the straits, delivering lines that are interspersed with his own poetic verses critical of the United States. Insults are shouted from both sides until La Avellaneda sinks. The descent of a movie screen introduces yet another genre wherein the deteriorated statues of Martí and La Avellaneda take center stage. Death permits cultural figures to be immediately ideologically frozen and utilized for whatever circumstance. The degree to which national and exilic interests appropriate prerevolutionary Cuban artists for their particular objectives makes it seem as if those faraway temporal figures had lived for the revolution's rhetoric. In a contradictory fashion, this project of mastery and consolidation reveals just how "important" artists actually are for this nation. At one point in Arenas's narrative, the poet Andrés Reynaldo, an anagram of the author himself, appears behind the statues, begging the filmmaker Néstor Almendros to portray them. An inversion occurs with the artist's insistence on appropriating history in the form of a photographic moment with these two great historical figures. In a sense, he substitutes for Fifo as the master of the narrative and thus takes a jab at authoritarian nationalism. The episode is also reminiscent of Arenas's collaboration with Almendros on *Mauvaise Conduite*, a documentary that, as previously noted, was highly critical of the revolution's policies toward homosexuals.

Arenas carries intertextuality to its limits by fusing his identity with those of these other beings for the purpose of telling his own story and that of his nation. What Sylvia Molloy takes as "allobiography" refers to the technique by which writers integrate additional characters into their autobiographies in order to facilitate telling their own lives' stories.[20] It is particularly useful for examining Arenas's identifications, especially with Friar Servando Teresa de Mier Noriega y Guerra (1765–1827), the preacher of the groundbreaking Guadalupan Sermon and a precursor of Mexican independence, as well as with the Countess of Merlin Mercedes Santa Cruz y Montalvo (1789–1852), the exile, writer, and singer, who has been identified as Cuban, Spanish, and French.[21] In the process, the outing of sexual activities or of other bodily functions promotes a notion of communities that is deeply suspicious of achieving an authentic and common base. *El color del verano* may witness the most excessive carnivalesque inversions, but it is by no means the only text where familiar values are refigured through doubling and mergers. In "Viaje a la Habana," a story in which the taboo on incest serves as the backdrop for exploring the regenerative splendor of pleasure and the limits of provincialism, the encounter of the self in the other is reached at the peak of copulation. The laws of civilization may attempt to forbid incest, yet primordial desire resists the imposition. At the same time, on account of the immense esteem with which Cuba holds particular figures and the prohibitions that accompany it, the nation's own policies can seem both incestuous and provincial. To paraphrase briefly Benigno Sánchez-Eppler's brilliant reading of this story (1994), its principal protagonist Ismael is in the position of the most canonical writer

José Martí who, from his exiled home in New York City, writes to Ismaelillo, his son in Cuba. The sensuality with which Martí describes his longing for his son, a symbol of his homeland, is converted by Arenas into an overt sexual act between father Ismael and son Ismaelito. With regard to the cosmopolitan mergers being discussed here, it is fascinatingthat both texts are initiated with a letter, that of Martí to his son, dated 1882, just a year after his wife and son returned to Cuba, and that of the wife Elvia to her exiled husband Ismael in Arenas's story, dated 1994, 15 years after he left Cuba. Such textual refigurations further delineate Arenas's challenge to the literary canon and the more general norms of heterosexuality. Ismael locates himself in the sexual act, when he is most physically linked to the other, his sexual partner.

What is even more significant for my reading of the persistent costuming of Cuban history as a principal component of Arenas's cosmopolitanism is that the story takes both its title and epigraph from La Condesa de Merlin's record of her return to Havana. The purity and autonomy of the self as well as of the local sphere is challenged through the combination of literary, geographical, psychological, and social migrations that occur in "Viaje a la Habana." To think of the self only as it is viewed in relation to the many others who populate his or her imagination is manifest in the epistolary form. Like *Viaje a la Habana* (1844) by La Condesa, Arenas's story focuses on the events and observations of a Cuban exile upon return to the island. Passages of "Viaje a la Habana" read as if they were from an alternative and precise tour guide to the peripheries of Havana and to the geographical boundaries put into place by the government to ensure that particular groups have access to particular places. Ismael's exile was precipitated by his desire to break all the rules and feel alive. He had endured all the steps necessary to hide his homosexual tendencies. He wed and even impregnated a woman who conceived a son, but the consequences of his adventure were felt immediately. Sergio, the boy with whom he took that risk, turned him in immediately to the Comité para la Defensa de la Revolución (CDR), whose "incestuous" function is to monitor the neighborhood's behavior and activities. Ismael was imprisoned for his weakness.

"Viaje a la Habana" interweaves free indirect and direct speech, as well as a first-person account rendered in italics, allowing the narrative to go back and forth between the past, the present, and then Ismael's subjective past. The epigraph "*Sólo encuentro un montón de piedras sin vida y un recuerdo vivo!*" (All I find is a pile of lifeless rocks and a living memory!) poetically reveals how, through citing another's memories, here, those of La Condesa, one's own are recalled. Once back in Cuba, the tale's protagonist, Ismael, engages in yet another dangerous act that reverberates with the previous one. After making love to a stranger, Ismael discovers that this stranger is his son.

> Sensación de flotar, certeza de diluirse, de integrarse, de fundirse a alguien que siendo él mismo—él mismo—es el opuesto, la resistencia anhelada y amada, *que siendo uno mismo puede darnos el placer de ser otro, ese otro yo tan desgarradoramente dado ya por desaparecido y de pronto, en medio del infierno, en plena llama, encontrado.* (Arenas 1995a, 147–48)

> [Sensation of floating, certainty of dissolving, of becoming integrated, of merging with someone that being himself—himself—is the opposite, the longed for and loved resistance, *that being oneself it can give us the pleasure of being another, this other I, so uncontrollably believed to be disappeared, and all of a sudden, in the middle of hell, in flames, found.*]

Breaking away from his own fears and giving into another's as well as his own desire, Ismael is reminded of being alive. This episode of a sexual union between father and son is a mirror for others including that of Arenas and the dramatically sexualized nineteenth-century female literary figure La Condesa de Merlin and that of Arenas and José Martí, which we observed in the Andrés Reynaldo episode in *El color del verano*. These sorts of literary unions breathe life into the "pile of lifeless rocks" into which Arenas perceives the revolution to have converted art. While Arenas's protagonists continually place their desires on Cuba, it is a Cuba that is most itself when it envisions itself as other. The above words also caution against facile critical consumption, whereby difference and lack of understanding are retained on account of the other's resistance.

The frequency with which Arenas's texts register such a merger with La Condesa de Merlin makes it worthwhile to examine them more closely. The function of this transgendered identification involving desirous, almost compulsive, movements toward and away from her is reminiscent of José Fernández's relation to Russian diarist Marie Bashkirtseff; both female characters are ridiculed by the literary establishment and find their identities in French, a language that is not their native tongue. Both nineteenth- and twentieth-century writers are particulary unsettled by these kinships. For Adriana Méndez Rodenas, Arenas possesses a "psychic connection" with La Condesa, who lived primarily in France in the first part of the nineteenth century. She "served him rather as a gendered alter ego in the same sense that Fray Servando Teresa de Mier played the role of authorial double in *El mundo alucinante* (1969)" (1998, 131). Arenas really goes beyond, "on occasion pay[ing] . . . homage" to La Condesa de Merlin, as Sylvia Molloy refers to the author's influence on contemporary Cuban writers, such as Arenas, and functions as an "allobiography" in Arenas's autobiographical fictions. On several occasions within Arenas's own life, he signed his letters as La Condesa, Doña Mercedes Santa Cruz. While the more urgent explanation for this pseudonym is that if his letters were intercepted, their author may remain anonymous, we may think of this letter-signing policy as the subversive other side to officials' practical canonization of literary figures.[22] A gendered relation between "home" and "host" nation can be studied by looking at the manner in which Arenas parodies Sarduy speaking in the first person as La Condesa. He establishes a continuum between her and Sarduy, primarily through a parody of their sexual identities and relationships to their "home" and "host" nation. We could go so far as to say that considering Arenas's epistolary practice, Arenas also suggests a tentative link with Sarduy. Molloy's comments on La Condesa are helpful here to understand the ramifications of these identifications. La Condesa finds "her identity as a writer *in* exile and *because of* exile . . . Only from the otherness she has, quite literally, espoused— she takes on her French husband's name and writes her memoirs in French—can she gain access, obliquely, to the scene of writing" (Molloy 1991, 87). The passage from Doña Mercedes Santa Cruz to La Condesa de Merlin is crucial to keep in mind as we consider these comparable contexts of "victims of authority" and intra- and transnational identifications (Molloy 1991, 90).

Although Sarduy's exile in Paris took place more than a century after La Condesa's, the two coincide in Arenas's fiction.[23] In the binary natural-rooted/cosmopolitan-rootless, the narrator of *El color del verano* endeavors to figure himself as the arbiter of national culture in opposition to another Cuban writer whose luck in successfully maneuvering distinct international spheres is renowned.[24] Arenas even schemes a certain animosity between La Condesa and Sarduy through which Arenas can revisit his difficult feelings toward Sarduy, the roots of which are located in the hostile politics of publishing. Having spent two years on a government scholarship for the study of art criticism in France beginning in December 1959, Sarduy never returned to revolutionary Cuba. Almost immediately after arriving in the French capital,

Sarduy met and established an intimate friendship with François Wahl, one of the directors of Éditions du Seuil (Gónzalez Echevarría 1993a, 20). While, according to the translator Lilianne Hasson, in the early years of the diffusion of Sarduy's texts in France, Sarduy was somewhat opposed to the promotion of Arenas, it was he who commissioned the translation of *Otra vez el mar* with Le Seuil. Claudio Canaparo, in fact, quotes a letter that another of Arenas's French translators, Didier Coste, wrote to the author concerning the departure of the sympathetic Claude Durand at Seuil and his replacement with Wahl, a situation, he claimed, that would make it more difficult for Arenas since Sarduy desired to be the most prominent Cuban writer in France.[25] It is in the book of essays entitled *Necesidad de libertad* that Arenas's critique of Sarduy, referred to by his nickname La Chelo (because of his resemblance to the Cuban actress Chelo Alonso), is least restrained. Readers of *El color del verano* see the Sarduy-based character, also called Zebro Sardoya, as a war-profiteer, a fawning individual with a fierce desire to be known. In a letter from La Condesa to her daughter, written in the wake of the Cuban Revolution, Zebro is described as "uno de los maricones más temibles de la tierra . . . mi querida Leanor, el nombre de ese maricón de raza negra y cuna pordiosera es Zebro Sardoya, aunque todos lo conocen por la Chelo. Hija, ese ser satánico, que tanto daño me ha hecho, nació en las planicies camagüeyanas en medio de verdes cañaverales" (Arenas 1991, 257) (one of the most fearsome faggots on the face of the earth . . . The name, my dear Leanor, of this fairy sprung from the Negro race and of mendicant origins was Zebro Sardoya, though all the world knew him as Miss Chelo. This satanic being which has done me such great harm was born on the flatlands of Camagüey in the midst of green cane fields) (Arenas 2000, 264, trans. Hurley). Arenas not only ridicules La Chelo for particular provincial origins but also for being opportunistic and convictionless. La Chelo's and La Condesa's exaggerated and compensatory worldliness undermines its force as a critical category.

> Ni cubana, ni española, ni francesa (pero dominando todas esas culturas y espantos) tenía ese aire de mundanidad, de soltura y desdén que es sólo propiedad de alquien que no pertenece a este mundo y por lo tanto nada le importa demasiado. Con mi capital y un préstamo que me concedió personalmente El Emperador abrí un fastuoso salón en el número 40 de la rue de Bonday. Mi salón era visitado por Rossini, la Persiani, Alfredo de Musset, la condesa de Villani, la Malibrean, Goya,

George Sand, Balzac, El Vizconde de Chautebriand [*sic*], Madame Recamier, Fray Servando Teresa de Mier, Simón Bolívar, la Emperatriz Josefina, Martínez de la Rosa, Chopin, Liszt y otras personalidades para las que yo cantaba . . . Canté para los griegos luego del gran terremoto; canté para los polacos después de la insurreción; canté en beneficio de los habitantes de Lyon con motivo de los desastres causados por una inundación del río Rhone; en 1931 canté a favor de los martinquenses a causa de gran temblor de tierra que asoló a la Martinica . . . Partout ou il avait une grande infortune je travaillais a [*sic*] la soulager. (Arenas 1991, 256–57)

[Neither Cuban nor Spaniard nor Frenchwoman, though mastering all those cultures and their horrors, had that air of worldliness, of *savoir faire* and scornfulness that is the property only of one who belongs not to this world and therefore cares little about any of the things it holds. With some of my own capital and a loan given me personally by the Emperor, I opened an elegant salon at number 40, rue de Bondy. My salon was visited by Rossini, the Persianis, Alfred de Musset, the Countess de Villani, Mlle Malibran, Goya, George Sand, Balzac, the Viscount Chateaubriand, Mme Récamier, Fray Servando Teresa de Mier, Simón Bolívar, the Empress Joséphine, Martínez de la Rosa, Chopin, Liszt, and other personalities, for whom I sang . . . I sang for the Greeks after the earthquake; I sang for the Poles after the insurrection; I sang for the benefit of the inhabitants of Lyon at the flooding of the Rhône; in 1931 I sang for the people of Martinique when that terrible earthquake devastated their poor country . . . *Partout où il avait une grande infortune, je travaillais à la soulager*] (Arenas 2000, 263, trans. Hurley)

Here La Condesa is described, not for her excess of sexual desire, but for her excess of compassion, so global that it levels all difference. Beyond the specificities related to the vision of Sarduy and La Condesa, the above extract addresses the way critics legitimatize authors according to how they measure up to some national or global standard, as in the case of Darío, who was valorized by Valera for his proximity to a French standard. The relations among Sarduy, La Condesa, and Arenas are imbued with a dose of camaraderie, tension, and jealousy that manifests the limits of worldliness and reflects a more general suspicion toward the journey of an intellectual from the so-called periphery to the "cosmopolitan" capital, of the sort that gave rise to rastaquouères. A mockery is made of La Condesa's desire to console others with the prowess of her voice. When a disaster does not present itself to her, she invents one in order to perform this role.

This scenario marries *soulager* (consolation) to sexuality, emphasizing the greediness of the protagonist La Condesa and the superficiality of such bearers of cosmopolitan humanism. Similarly, La Chelo physically transforms himself to cater to the sexual orientation and nationality of his partners. Doing to La Chelo what the narrator has been doing to La Condesa already, the narrator admires La Chelo's ability to seduce, while mocking his ubiquity.

> Como si eso fuera poco, la camagüeyana se puso un bollo plástico y costosísimo y con él sedujo a las damas más refinadas de la cultura de la política francesa. Ese bollo tenía la particularidad de ser portátil y de fácil desconexión, por lo que cuando había que seducir a un hombre que ocupaba un cargo prominente, la loca se desprendía del bollo y con mil sacrificios hacía uso de su miembro natural que por ser negro no era pequeño. (Arenas 1991, 260)

> [And as though *that* . . .[26] were not enough, the Queen of Camagüey got herself a ruinously expensive plastic cunt with which she seduced the most refined ladies of French politics and culture. This cunt had the advantage of being portable and easy to disconnect, so when she wanted to seduce a prominent man, the faggot undid the cunt and with a good deal of grudging willfulness made use of her natural member, which, her being Negro and all, was not small.] (Arenas 2000, 266, trans. Hurley)

The expression in homosexual communities of being "international" (either a top or a bottom) is the point of departure for the narrator's tirade. These adjustable sexual organs imply a lack of integrity and potential for betrayal, as well as a predicament over a wide spectrum and necessity to categorize sexual identities. An extended use of "allobiography" converts La Condesa into a spokesperson who, like *El color del verano*'s narrator, may critique, mimic, admire, and envy La Chelo for her success and ubiquity. The novel's very techniques of narration and multigeneric form enact this challenge to singular articulations of space and identity, and the way that these two categories are made to come together.

Arenas's distrust of realism comes to the fore in his description of not just Sardoya's sexuality, but also literary creation as a potential act of betrayal.[27] *El color del verano* acts out Arenas's critique of *criollismo*. *Criollismo* of the first half of the nineteenth century consolidates the particularities of the Americas under a local rubric. If readers were to substitute the bourgeois content for one more applicable to a socialist world, even more immediate sources for the ridicule could be found in the efforts to validate local Cuban and Latin American characters and themes over other worldly references by revolutionary congresses, especially in the 1960s and early 1970s.

> María de las Mercedes Santa Cruz, Mopoz, Jaruco y Montalvo, Condesa de Merlin, reunía todas las cualidades que hacían de ella una de las criaturas más afortunadas de la isla de Cuba en el siglo XIX. Su acaudalada familia tenía un enorme central azucarero y una gran dotación de esclavos. (Arenas 1991, 252)

> [In the person and estate of María de las Mercedes de Santa Cruz Mopox Jaruco y Montalvo, Condesa de Merlin, were joined all the qualities needful for happiness, and indeed she was one of the most fortunate creatures on the island of Cuba in the nineteenth century. Her wealthy family possessed an enormous sugar-cane plantation and sugar processing establishment—and (very important) a large company of slaves.] (Arenas 2000, 258, trans. Hurley)

Soon, however, the narrative is overwhelmed by La Condesa's sexual precociousness that leads her to a life principally guided by sexual escapades. A sudden shift in narration from free indirect speech to the first person singular and plural forms practically melds the previous narrator into the object of the narration. However, at the end of the segment narrated in the first person, La Condesa reveals to the reader, who is an extension of her daughter, Leonor, the receiver of these letters, that her own life is being chronicled. "Y os dejo el relato de mi tragedia en las manos de mi rústico cronista" (Arenas 1991, 259) (And I leave you with the story of my tragedy in the hands of my rustic chronicler) (Arenas 2000, 265, trans. Hurley). With this guiding metatextual statement, the narrative suddenly shifts, forcing readers to contend once again with how truth is constituted. The frequent transformations of narrative voices allow characters to be perceived from multiple perspectives and transcend the imposed singularity of the self. This happens not by consoling or being everywhere, but rather by forcefully seeking out the other and the other's eccentricities. The move from third to first person narration signifies a merger that, far from consolidating the facts, continues emphasizing difference and multiplicity in a manner akin to cosmopolitanism.

While much of Arenas's writing celebrates La Condesa's exilic, marginal, and sexualized persona, it also conveys a suspicion toward the authenticity of her literary production that echoes dominant attitudes of her time. "Se le había entregado también el Premio Nobel de

Literatura precisamente por aquellas novelas que nunca había escrito"
(Arenas 1991, 257) (she had received the Nobel Prize for Literature,
specifically for those novels she'd never written) (Arenas 2000, 264,
trans. Hurley). Such queer mimicry references a nineteenth-century
misogynistic notion that La Condesa was not the true author of
her works, but, even Méndez Rodenas, a renowned scholar on La
Condesa, refuses to reproach Arenas entirely for this attack: "Arenas's
problematic translation of Merlin into his own novelistic idiom suggests, at one level, a psychological projection and, at another, a deep
identification springing from his own tortured sense of gender and cultured marginality" (1998, 239). In this fictional critique of Sarduy and
La Condesa, the narrator finally gets to arbitrate national culture, but
refuses to explain the background of his claims. The author's desires to
affiliate with the world and have one's voice heard beyond the place of
origin are at stake, but they sometimes become blurred by what may
seem on the outside to be petty battles.

While many of the characters with which Arenas identifies are
Cuban, the protagonist of his international prizewinning book, *El
mundo alucinante*, is not, but has in common with La Condesa, an
exaggerated identification with Arenas. After delivering a sermon in
support of Mexican independence and the syncretism of a baroque
culture, the novel's protagonist, a leader of Mexican independence,
Fray Servando Teresa de Mier, can barely ever stop fleeing. Arenas's
historical novel maps Servando's trajectory of escape from the
Inquisition in and out of prison and through Spain, France, Italy,
Portugal, England, the United States, and Cuba. Having consulted the
first volume of Servando's *Memorias*, Artemio del Valle Arispe's biography *Fray Servando*, and Lezama Lima's *La expresión americana* for
information on the friar, Arenas reproduces, more than the precise historical data, the spirit of Servando's rebellion and exile and enlarges its
corporal, sensual, and sexual dimensions. Arenas's characterization of
Fray Servando leads to the notion that Servando's Americanness was
derived from a sense of foreignness. It turns out to be parallel with
Arenas's own configuration of exile as historically characteristic of
Cuban identity and himself as most Cuban in this uncanny attachment
to the nation.

The novel begins with a most striking expression of Arenas's
identification with Fray Servando in a letter dated July 1966: "Lo más
útil fue descubrir que tú y yo somos la misma persona" (Arenas
1982d, 19) (What has helped me most to "apprehend" you has been
my discovery that you and I are the same person) (Arenas 1994, ixx,

trans. Hurley). However, the interweavings are even more extensive. "Y yo, que me vi en él como nunca me he visto ni en mí mismo" (Arenas 1982d, 172) (While I, who had seen myself in him as I had never seen myself even in myself) (Arenas 1994, 129, trans. Hurley) captures Fray Servando's intimate connection to Simón Rodríguez (1763–1827), Simón Bolívar's tutor in the writings of the Enlightenment thinkers, Baron de Charles-Louis de Secondat Montesquieu, Voltaire, and the romantic Jean-Jacques Rousseau, among others. Considering Lezama Lima's characterization of Fray Servando and Rodríguez as American romantic figures, joined by their continual flight, in contrast to Bolívar who "se detiene al nombrar una realidad" (stops upon naming a reality), it is not surprising that his disciple, Arenas, links the two (Lezama Lima 1993, 130).[28] Lezama Lima suggests that Rodríguez was a special kind of master whose pedagogy "no debe haber sido ejercida a través del ethos, de una circunstancia causalismo de la conducta, sino a través de lo que había en Bolívar y en él de más endemoniado y primigenio" (ought not to have been exerted through ethos, from a causal circumstance of conduct, but rather through what there was in Bolívar and the most devilish and base in him) (1993, 116–117). Rodríguez was impoverished in real life and forgotten by history. He "poseía un daimón muy irritado para ser un ciudadano del mundo" (possessed a very irritated logic for being a citizen of the world) (Lezama Lima 1993, 117).

Along these lines, Arenas's friar is devilish and fleeting with a compelling and irritating logic that negotiates a sense of strangeness with a sense of place, but he is not the only character to undergo fascinating transformations that signal a conflicted relation to place. Rodríguez's forsaking of his father's surname for his mother's is exploited in *El mundo alucinante*. The character's use of both Samuel Robinson and Simón Rodríguez highlights dimensions of duality, constant fleeing, and frustration over the conformity of signifiers. The meta-merger—Samuel Robinson/Simón Rodríguez—encapsulates the cosmopolitan process of self-representation in the representation of another.

The friar's outlook on sex parallels his views about the world at large that, informed by the precepts of Catholicism, seek to surpass all perceived limits and encounter greater transcendence. Echoing Lezama's belief that Fray Servando does not break with tradition but rather enlarges it, by finding himself within it, Arenas is impressed by the friar's combat with ideology using that same system (Lezama Lima 1993, 112). "Era el personaje tratando de combatir una ideología en un sistema inquisitorial partiendo de la ideología misma" (It was the character trying to combat an ideology in an inquisitorial system setting out from the same ideology) (Arenas 1983, 115). Not constrained by conventionality, the friar's bonds in *El mundo alucinante*, like Arenas's with its principal character, are not only transnational in their identification and scope, but also national in their consequences. Even though Arenas's adaptation of Fray Servando's story of oppression was written a few years prior to the author's own difficult travails in the 1970s, it is a commentary on oppression in Cuba, the consequences of which were becoming predictable. The UNEAC awarded *El mundo alucinante* an honorable mention, though not first prize. It was considered too erotic to be published (Santí 1984, 230). Arenas's allobiographical rendering of himself through Fray Servando rests on a shared experience of the exilic condition, as well as an understanding of persecution and power that transcend particular circumstances. In the case of Fray Servando, Arenas attributes universal quality to the sequence of constant fleeing, conversion to hero status postrevolution, and subsequent imprisonment, once the revolution becomes as stale and corrupt as the previous empire (Arenas 1983, 116). Rather than imagine exile and nation as opposites, the novel pushes toward the notion that at the base of American nations is this foreign spirit, as fleeting as it is erotic.

Having lived most of his life as an outcast, Servando is transformed into a hero of Mexican independence and, together with Cuban poet José María Heredia (1803–1839), is housed in the presidential palace and where he is overcome by a sense of suffocation. While the return home could signal a triumphant implementation of ideological dreams, *El mundo alucinante* demonstrates how all too often they become mirages. Not only is the new Mexican national palace full of repulsive relics, but the friar and Heredía are also turned into relics through the grotesque institutionalization of the revolution: "qué somos en este Palacio sino cosas inutíles, reliquias de museo, prostitutas rehabilitadas" (Arenas 1982d, 293) (who are we, huddled in this palace, but useless *things*, relics in some museum, rehabilitated prostitutes) (Arenas 1994, 235, trans. Hurley). The notion that once the revolution is institutionalized in the State the rebellious thought that initially characterized it is contained is most clear in the two exiles' competitive complaint-ridden parley over their new living conditions. The complaints of the friar upon his return home reflect the tenuous foundations of American nations.

Even more than the repetition of the same chapter titles with different versions of stories in *El mundo alucinante*, the transformation of Fray Servando into Doctor Maniau signals a provisionality of truths and identities. When Fray Servando escapes to France, he does so using not only the passport but also the entire costume of the dead French doctor Maniau: "no soy emigrado, sino mexicano, y no traigo sino este pasaporte (era el de Maniau) de México para España" (Arenas 1982d, 155) (I am not an emigrant, but a poor Méxican, and all I have is this passport that was Maniau's, from México to Spain) (Arenas 1994, 113, trans. Hurley). Disguised as a Frenchman, Servando affiliates with his designated nation, but as soon as his identity is affirmed in the phrase "No soy, sino [soy]" (I am not, but rather [I am]), it is quickly destabilized by the very guise and another syncretic juncture.

> con esa tristeza del desterrado que es desterrado de su destierro, eché a andar por toda la ciudad, para mí desconocida. Y así fue que en una calle del barrio de Sancti Spíritus, oí un cántico de salmos en castellano . . . Me dirigí hasta allá, y, sin pensarlo, entré rápidamente en el recinto de donde salían los cánticos.
>
> Estaba, pues, dentro de una sinagoga. Y era la pascua de los ázimos y el cordero. (Arenas 1982d, 156)

> [with this sadness that every exiled man must feel when he has been banished from his homeland, I set off walking again through the city, which I had no knowledge of. And so I came, in a street in the quarter called Spiritus Sancti, to a place where I heard a psalm being chanted in my own tongue . . . I hurried over and, without thinking, rushed in into the room from which the chant was issuing.
>
> I was, then, inside a synagogue. And it was Passover, the feast of the unleavened bread and the lamb.] (Arenas 1994, 114, trans. Hurley)

The Catholic friar's encounter with the origins of psalms he had heard in a synagogue ruptures any essentialist sense of identity and linear progression. Though value is placed on knowledge of place, in its circumstantial absence, signs of shelter are enough to sustain one's soul.

Guilt: Gallicization and Beauty

> Era un niño flaco, pero con una barriga muy grande debido a las lombrices que me habían crecido en el estómago de comer tanta tierra . . . Un día sentí un dolor de barriga terrible; no me dio tiempo a ir al excusado . . . Lo primero que solté fue una lombriz enorme; . . . sin duda, estaba enfurecido por haber sido expulsado de su elemento de una manera tan violenta . . . Yo le cogí mucho miedo a aquella lombriz, que se me aparecía ahora todas las noches y trataba de entrar en mi barriga, mientras yo me abrazaba a mi madre. (Arenas 1992a, 17)

[I was a skinny kid with a distended belly full of worms from eating so much dirt . . . One day I had a terrible bellyache. I did not have time to get to the outhouse, and I used the chamber pot . . . The first thing that came out was a huge worm . . . no doubt enraged at having been expelled from its home in such a violent way. I was deathly afraid of this worm, which now appeared in my dreams every night trying to get into my belly while I embraced my mother.] (Arenas 1993a, 1, trans. Koch)

This event is recalled in the first chapter of *Antes que anochezca*, after the autobiographer describes his current condition as a subject dying of AIDS. Once this strange foreign body—the worm—is expelled, Arenas is immediately confronted with the other's potential for affect. In this anecdote, the worm is much like the individual in the collective sphere that, viewed as a parasite, is excreted from the larger body. The parasite, once recognized by the host, adopts host-like qualities. The consumption of dirt in the shed is the first of a series of images conceived as natural, beautiful, and civilized. Urban life, for the auto-biographer, is largely construed as artificial, ugly, and barbarous. From the outset, Arenas presents himself as a country-bumpkin, who is, at his roots, not *culto* or cultured. So *avant la lettre* have readers heeded this characterization that the quarrels in which Arenas was entangled in exile (about which we discuss in detail in chapter 4) were frequently explained by his being essentially and authentically a country-bumpkin. However, using Arenas's own tracts, a country-bumpkin, because of a certain connection to nature in constant flux, is almost obliged to be more cosmopolitan than a city dweller. This distance from not only the fixed, erudite, but also decaying city pervades Arenas's oeuvre, but is personified in a character in *El color del verano* named Alejo Sholejov, a compound that references two writers. The writer Alejo Carpentier, for instance, was cradled by the revolution early on with an appointment as cultural functionary and by leniency toward publishing abroad. Then with the surname Sholejov, Arenas links Carpentier to the Russian writer Mikhail Sholokhov whose socialist realist portrayals earned him the Stalin Prize in 1941. While the style of socialist realism, prescribed by Stalin, by no means gives justice to Carpentier's writing, it refers to the combination of privileges Carpentier attained from the Cuban government and his writing's apparent distance from a Cuban reality. The narrator of *El color del verano*'s "Un paseo por la Vieja Habana en compañia de Alejo Sholejov" (A Walking Tour through Old Havana in the Company of Alejo Sholekhov) ridicules Carpentier's erudition and need to justify Cuba by way of "universal" symbols. He takes the *barbacoas*—the makeshift homes into which sometimes up to one hundred people were crammed—for the manifestations of a style that was present in France in the early part of the century.[29] Sholejov invents Havana employing French surrealists André Breton and Robert Desnos, among other European sources, but his theories do not coincide with what is being observed. He bores his audience, made up of the minister of culture, Fifo/Fidel, and members of what Arenas coins UNASCO ("desde luego, francesa" [Arenas 1991, 88] [made up entirely of Frenchmen] [Arenas 2000, 89, trans. Hurley]), with metaphors in which a part of each term either does not exist or may exist but with a contemporary function overlooked by the didact. Carpentier's position as Cuban representative to UNESCO in Paris is the historical backdrop for this particular humanitarian intervention. Even Fifo is so fed up with Sholejov's discourse that he demands he be executed but changes his mind when he discovers that UNESCO has promised to donate money toward the reconstruction of Old Havana. Cuba's dependence on external funding for sustaining its economy and ideology is a principal theme. The manner in which the Carpentieresque character hobnobs with the French, the Russian, and the Cuban, incarnate in Castro, suggests Carpentier's struggle between letters and action. Although Arenas has evaluated Carpentier's writing in a more nuanced light in other contexts, here the latter is not only consolidated almost tragicomically, but is also payed homage.[30]

At once highly influenced by French modernism and eager to cater to the revolution, Sholejov possesses conveniently coherent affiliations that do not translate successfully into cultural realities, but make them conform to interpretative models applicable to another geographic sphere. Sholejov may be civilized according to societal norms, but these norms are antithetical to Arenas's ideal of intimacy within nature and beauty. Arenas's doubt that Carpentier is an adequate translator of Cuban realities also permeates *Antes que anochezca* where he takes a typical jab at his accent: "le comenté a alguien del público cómo aquel hombre ya no hablaba español, sino que producía un sonido gutural con un acento francés tan marcado que parecía una rana" (Arenas 1992a, 267) (I stopped to comment to someone in the audience that the man could not even speak Spanish anymore, that all he could do was produce a guttural sound with such a heavy French accent that he sounded like a frog) (Arenas 1993a, 243, trans. Koch). As the examples of the *modernistas* demonstrate, the accusation of being Gallicized is a not so subtle questioning of virility. Reminiscent of his vituperative approach toward Sarduy, Arenas complies with an ample body of genealogical criticism on this canonical author that is in part explained by the personal injury to his literary career in which Arenas felt that Carpentier was complicit. This Carpentier does not resemble the quintessential transcultured subject, for whom the particularity of place is crucial, propagated by North American cultural critics like Mary Louise Pratt and Timothy Brennan. Professional criticism frequently entails selecting those elements that are most important for the proposed claims. Translation processes are not always successful in Arenas's version of cosmopolitanism, especially when insistent misinterpretations are afforded by a convenient internationalism, embodied in UNESCO. Resistance to this type of misinterpretation derives from subjects' willful rendering of only parts of themselves, but even such an act of resistance needs to be seen as part of a process of commodification.

For Arenas's Carpentier, actual urban wanderings end up being the concrete justification of his intellectual voyages. For Arenas's Arenas, newly adopted places allow the character to hold on to his past and project him into the future. To the extent that *Antes que anochezca* critiques the U.S. healthcare system's undemocratic approaches to managing care, *El color del verano* displays other approaches to disease, spirituality, and representation that are not so widely accessible. Mapping Havana and New York and their respective peripheries is a significant component of *El color del verano*. For the exiled subject living in Manhattan, New York's other boroughs, Queens and the Bronx, are links to his rural origins. In Queens, a famous *curandera* prescribes Gabriel with a remedy to potentially save him from AIDS, involving an intricate process that requires a *bilongo* (a little packet containing the wings of a chicken) and a *ceiba* tree. In a letter that Gabriel in New York directs to Reinaldo in Havana, he conveys that the difficulty in finding this natural denizen of the tropics has sent him on a journey North to the Bronx Zoo where he locates a single *ceiba* that is closely watched by a guard. The notion is that subjects are continually under vigilant surveillance, even when they are extracted from their natural roots. The CDR may be a thing of the narrator's past, but capitalism's efforts at categorization for the benefit of commercial packaging is equally catastrophic. Back in Queens, the *curandera* advises Arenas to throw the *bilongo* behind a Catholic altar, a syncretic realization connoting the historical disguising from the dominant classes. He goes to the most splendid cathedral on Fifth Avenue, St. Patrick's Cathedral, where his object to realize the obligations of his spirituality is thwarted by the material and psychological conditions of another. A black man exposes himself at St. Patrick's and causes a scandal. The narrator's discovery that the man on display was in fact a Cuban, who also had in common the experience of the *Mariel* boatlift is especially significant. In an utterly Arenian fashion, they convey the travails of displacement—the efforts at maintaining a spiritual life and the fraught nature of forged exilic communities. Arenas too arrived in 1980 as one of many undesirables who, on account of Fidel Castro's duping the United States, were perceived *en masse* as criminals. International history expels these personages from their homeland, but as Arenas's faith implies, this homeland itself is a hybrid reality complete with international sources that are the result of the slave trade. To take this a step further, such encounters of alienation recall James Clifford's "discrepant" cosmopolitanisms that are inextricable from "violent, histories of economic, political, and cultural interaction" (Clifford 1997, 36). This mirroring indicates a consciousness beyond the individual experience of an artist in New York, toward that of an emerging community of those struggling on account of a new passage to the Americas. Other instances of extirpation and subjugation on account of difference from the norm pervade Arenas's United States. Gabriel, in fact, gives testimony to his suffering to Reinaldo, the writer, back in Havana. This careful division of the narrator into three parts permits the writer to claim different subject positions. The tripartite narrator is othered, making it possible for the character, Arenas, for example, to closely observe Gabriel or *La tétrica mofeta*'s (Skunk-in-a-Funk's) experience of the world. He deconstructs before the reader the implications of his actions, creating a simultaneity of place that recalls the avant-garde.

Arenas's cities are ripe with these sorts of alienating and barbarous episodes that I have just described. In *Antes que anochezca*, it is only when the autobiographer moves to the Cuban city of Holguín that he is prompted to acculturate and conceal his natural and beautiful tendencies. However, cities also give him access to mentors like Lezama Lima and Virgilio Piñera who impress upon him the idea that beauty poses a threat to dictatorships.[31] In this conflict between beauty and culture, the complexities of Arenas's self-fashioning as a *guajiro* begin to come to light. It is people with AIDS then, who, for the autobiographer, are at least symbolically far from the centers of consolidated power that are the most capable of approximating beauty because they have not much to lose.[32] In the memoir, a somewhat more nostalgic account than his fiction, the explicit beauty and eroticism with which Arenas represents his earliest childhood function as the origin of the explicit truths he reveals upon his deathbed.

> Creo que el esplendor de mi infancia fue único, porque se desarrolló en la absoluta miseria, pero también en la absoluta libertad; en el monte, rodeado de árboles, de animales, de apariciones y de personas a las cuales yo les era indiferente . . . eso me ofrecía un enorme margen para escaparme. . . . Andaba por los árboles; las cosas parecían desde allí mucho más bellas y la realidad se abarcaba de una manera total. (Arenas 1992a, 22)

> [I think the splendor of my childhood was unique because it was absolute poverty but also absolute freedom; out in the open, surrounded by trees, animals, apparitions, and people who were indifferent toward me. This gave me an incredible opportunity to escape it all without anyone worrying about where I was or when I would return . . . I used to climb trees, and everything seemed much more beautiful from up there. I could embrace its completeness.] (Arenas 1993a, 5, trans. Koch)

Arenas describes his childhood as authentic due to his proximity to nature—distant from so-called civilization's most fracturing elements. In nature, individuals can feel completeness because society has yet to impose its constructions of singular identity. This rural cosmopolitanism, seen as an attachment to the whole world, was already brought to life in *Celestino antes del alba*, where the simple, ingenuous voice of a young boy invents an imaginary friend, a cousin he calls Celestino, to help him defend himself against barbarism.

> Yo no sé, pero la mujer de Tomásico sí sabe; y cuando la llevamos hasta los troncos, que Celestino había garabateado, pensando que el pobre muchacho lo que hacía era poner el nombre de su madre muerta . . . ¡El nombre de su madre muerta!: ni siquiera se acuerda quién era su madre . . . y, si mal no recuerdo, una de las cosas que leyó la mujer de Tomásico decía: "Quién será mi madre," "Quién será mi madre," "Que la busco en el excusado y no la veo" . . .
> No puede ser, debe estar escribiendo algo muy lindo, que la muy yegua de la mujer de Tomásico no entiende, ni yo tampoco, y por eso dice ella que es algo asqueroso. ¡Salvajes!, cuando no entienden algo dicen en seguida que es una cosa fea y sucia. ¡Bestias! ¡Bestias¡ ¡Bestias! . . . Si yo pudiera por lo menos, aprender a escribir la palabra esa: "Bestias" . . . Pero no importa que yo no entienda lo que Celestino está escribiendo. Yo sé que es una cosa muy linda, que si fuera algo feo mi familia no lo perseguiera. (Arenas 1967, 167–68)

[I may not know how, but Tomasico's wife does—and when we took her and showed her the tree trunks that Celestino had scribbled all over, thinking the poor little thing was writing his poor dead mother's name—why, the name of his dead mother, nothing! He doesn't even remember who his mother was. Yessir, I mean it—and if I remember correctly one of the things Tomasico's wife read went "Who will be my mother," "Who will be my mother," "for I look for her in the privy but I don't see her" . . .

It can't be—he's writing something so pretty, he must be, but that old she-ass wife of Tomasico's, she doesn't understand, nor me either, and that's why she says it's filth. They're a bunch of savages! If they don't understand something, they automatically hate it. They say it's ugly or it's dirty. Animals! . . . I wish I could at least learn to write that word— *Animals* . . . But it doesn't matter whether I understand what Celestino is writing or not. I know it's something beautiful, because if it was really ugly like they say it is, *that* wouldn't bother my family one bit, and they wouldn't keep pestering him so.] (Arenas 1988, 159–60, trans. Hurley)

The discrepancy between that familiarity and the vast space beyond does not terrorize the narrator into consolidating beauty. Unlike his grandfather and even his mother who, if she wishes to survive, must go along with the patriarchal system and despise beauty, the protagonist does not wish to convert either it or the vast space beyond the village into something more manageable. By opposing those barbarians to Celestino, his cousin casts himself as an interpreter of what is beautiful. Following this analysis, he becomes civilized, unlike his savage family members who only accept what is ugly in their lives. While he may not be *culto*, he has the capacity to imagine the beauty of Celestino's creations—to dream of the world beyond his home, which is actually in flames. The household head is an authoritarian grandfather who raises his hatchet and chops down trees at any instance of rebellion, one of which is writing on tree trunks. It is not so much what is written that runs counter to the grandfather's commands and results in the cutting down of trees, but rather the very creative urge.

Largely told in the present tense, characteristic of the immediacy of expression, *Celestino antes del alba* narrates a single event several times in a different manner, allowing readers to see reality being made, as if they were the child narrator who observes the changes that occur in nature up close. Only in relation to his creation does the narrator become, like the written word, eternal. Tristán Corbière's "Soy el que, sin cesar, me hago" (Arenas 1967, 165) (I am he who, incessantly, I make myself) (Arenas 1988, 165, trans. Hurley) is one of those eclectic and exiled citations within the text, which speaks to the Kristevean concept of the *subject in process* that continually experiences libidinal energies. The text's attention on its own fictionality is most apparent in the narrator's response to his mother's use of the word *recondenada* (miserable) upon discovering her son's stash of the family's wine bottles. He swears that he could not have created such a mother. In addition to elucidating the consequences of beauty and civilization, ugliness and barbarity, the following passage assesses origins in a profound manner:

> Le he dado todas las botellas de vino a mi madre. Tendré que dejar la borrachera para el año que viene . . . La veo alejarse, y me digo, ¡ojalá no esté equivocado de nuevo!¡ Ojalá! sea esa mujer mi madre. Que no sean solamente ideas mías y mi verdadera madre esté esperándome en la casa, con una estaca en la mano. Pero no: yo nunca he inventado a una persona que haya podido decir *"recondenada"* en aquella forma tan única como mi madre lo ha dicho. Sí, no debo dudar: aunque fuese por unos segundos: he visto por primera vez a mi madre. Ahora no importa que la otra me caiga a estacazos. (Arenas 1967, 207–08)

> [I've given all the bottles to my mother. I'll have to wait till next year to go on my binge . . . I watch her go off and I say to myself, I certainly hope I haven't made another mistake! I hope this woman is really my mother. I hope I'm not making all this up, and my real mother's not waiting for me up at the house with a piece of kindling. But no—I've never invented a person that could say *miserable* the way my mother just said it. Yes, I shouldn't have any doubt—even if it was for just a few seconds, I've just seen my mother for the first time. Now I don't care if the other one takes a kindling stick to my head.] (Arenas 1988, 199, trans. Hurley)

The identity of the mother in question depends on her utterance of a single word: *miserable*. She is real, and not a figment of the narrator's anything but impoverished imagination, which conceives of a list of virtues and grotesque images that never give in entirely to nostalgic impulses.

Celestino antes del alba challenges the "pseudo-psychological condition" of nostalgia that perpetuates the notion that it is natural to be at home (Kaplan 1996, 34). Nostalgia appears in the form of a premature eulogy to a decaying house. In addition to possessing feelings, the narrator's home, a shared space, is also a repository for memories and the most intimate of secrets: "No, no puede haber otra casa que sea como ésta, y que esconda todas las cosas secretas que yo he hecho

en ella. La otra será extraña para mi, y yo también le seré extraño"
(Arenas 1967, 146) (No, there couldn't ever be another house that
would be like this one and hide all the secret things I've done in it. The
other one would be strange for me, and I'd be strange for it, too)
(Arenas 1988, 138, trans. Hurley). If the house falls down, not only
might the narrator's secrets disappear, but so would his memories of
positive experiences with his family. Links among the home, propriety,
property, and the nation are most evident in the story the narrator tells
about a red dirt castle he and his cousin built.

> Todo el día nos lo hemos pasado trabajando en el castillo de diez pisos
> y cien cuartos. En él van a vivir todos los pomos. Todos los pomos que
> abuela guarda en la locera vieja y que nosotros pensamos robárselos y
> mudar para este lugar, donde van a estar mucho más cómodos que allá,
> dentro de la locera, donde viven ahora apretujados unos contra otros y
> teniendo que compartir el lugar con las cucarachas y las arañas bravas.
> Pero acá van a vivir como si fueran reyes . . . aunque no todos van a
> vivir de ese modo. Celestino y yo ya tenemos planeada la forma en que
> vamos a dirigir el castillo. (Arenas 1967, 94)

> [We've spent the whole day working on the big ten-story hundred-
> bedroom castle. All the jars and bottles are going to live in it. All the jars
> and bottles Grandma is saving in the sideboard, and that we intend to
> steal from her and bring here, because they'll be a whole lot more com-
> fortable here than there in the sideboard where they're all squeezed in
> together and have to share the space with cockroaches and spiders that
> bite. But here, they'll live like kings . . . Except not all of them will be
> able to live so high. Celestino and I already have the way we're going to
> run the castle all planned out.] (Arenas 1988, 81, trans. Hurley)

Inscribed within this daydream is its very interruption. The children's
plans to control the castle are thwarted by authorities who do not
admit the two young construction workers into the party.

The anguish at not being allowed into something that you participated
in creating is persistent. Given this logic, guilt is a preexisting condition
that bears no relation to having committed any wrongdoing.

> Esta noche hay una fiesta muy grande en el Castillo de Tierra
> Colorada . . .
>   Hasta la puerta llegamos Celestino y yo, con el fin de ver la fiesta y
> comernos algún que otro pedazo de dulce. Llegamos a la puerta y trata-
> mos de entrar, pero los centinelas nos detienen con sus grandes espadas
> y nos gritan: ¡Atrás!

—Qué tontos son—les digo yo—; ¿no ven que nosotros fuimos los que hicimos este castillo y los que los hicimos a ustedes? (Arenas 1967, 95)

[Tonight there's a big party in the Red Dirt Castle . . .
    Celestino and I come to the door of the castle, to see the party and maybe have a piece or two of something sweet. We come to the door and try to go in, but the sentinels stop us with their big swords. They tell us—"Back!"
    "What geese!" I tell them. "Don't you see we're the ones that made this castle and even made *you!*"] (Arenas 1988, 82, trans. Hurley)

While the "ustedes" or "you" may refer to almost any kind of fraternity that excludes some in order to sustain a sense of cohesion, the Red Dirt Castle is also the art in general created by the cousins but from whose inheritance they are excluded.

This exclusion has become internalized. For his grandfather, as well as for the rest under his dominion, merely expressing oneself is associated with feminization. Acculturation starts from the first day of class when the narrator's peers make sure he knows that he is not one of them by labeling both him and his cousin as queers.

—¡Es el primo de Celestino!
—¡El primo! ¡El primo!
—¡Pégale ahora! . . .
—¡El primo de Celestino el loco! ¡El primo de Celestino, él que escribe poesías en los troncos de las matas!
—¡Mariquitas! ¡Mariquitas! (Arenas 1967, 34)

["He's Celestino's cousin!"
"His cousin! His cousin!"
"Hit 'im now!" . . .
"Celestino the crazy kid's cousin! He's Celestino's cousin, the one that writes poetry on the trunks of the trees!"
"They're both queers!"
"Queers!"] (Arenas 1988, 25, trans. Hurley)

Although the child's fears emerge from artificial constructions, it is impossible not to internalize them. The sentiment of having been left out of something that others are allowed to participate in becomes a fundamental aspect of Arenas's relationship to Cuban national culture and is attached to an overall feeling of guilt.

Between ¡Mariquitas! and Migratory Birds

Literature of the island and of exile are, for Arenas, one and the same. Though Cuban critics including Ambrosio Fornet, Amir Valle, and Víctor Fowler Calzada have promoted this notion in the past decade, when Arenas uttered it, the disparity between the two was well inscribed into explanations of *cubanidad*. Arenas not only reclaims nature beyond territories of place, but he also inscribes gender into territory. The fact that it is Arenas's "heterosexual" classmate who first articulates Arenas's gayness by calling him the derogatory *pájaro* (translated as "fairy" and "faggot" in English) in *Antes que anochezca* is especially interesting in light of the affirming centrality of *pájaros* in *El color del verano*. We cannot understand the full extent of Arenas's cosmopolitanism without exploring the translations and migrations of the meanings of the word "pájaro." The vast majorities, who supposedly locate their reflection in the Cuban Revolution, like the deviant *pájaros* (homosexuals), for instance, prefer flux to institutionalization. *El color del verano*'s twofold image of the *pájaros*' (homosexuals') migration and the islanders' flotation on a piece of land in the middle of the sea, detached from Cuba's platform, expresses this coincidence. Not surprisingly, one of the most deferred voices in the novel, belonging to an anonymous *loca* that is overheard in the García Lorca salon in Havana, is the one that comes closest to conveying Arenian cosmopolitanism.

This overheard comment in the Teatro García Lorca forms part of the chapter entitled "La conferencia onírico teológica político filosófica satírica" (The Grand Oneirical Theological Political Satirical Conference) in which intellectuals from Cuba and all over the world navigate their way into the salon designated for international events. The conference room overflows with water—the same water that continues to gush out from the freshly discovered cistern between the walls of an antiquated convent neighboring an old whore's room and covers all of Old Havana. Also present in the salon are internationals and Cuban intellectuals. Fifo is on the podium. Not present is the character Oliente (we are told that she smells of English perfumes and also, of course, *churre* or filth) who, having planned on contributing to the theological/philosophic aspect of the conference, was, like Celestino and his cousin at the celebration at the Red Dirt Castle, turned away at the entrance to the great salon.

This particular narration, regarding Oliente, involves an ultimately cosmopolitan negotiation between presence and deferral. Oliente slips his text into the room to be delivered by another participant. Indicative of the identity formation developed in this novel is the name of the character Oliente, whose words are so fundamental yet whose name means merely "smelling of." On the margins of the paper, Oliente noted who ought to deliver the segment in his place—the bishop of Canterbury; yet, the path of deferral is longer than that. The bishop takes one look at the passage and turns from red to black (becoming the object of desire for all the surrounding queens). The text, written in Latin, is then passed on to the queen of Holland. Apparently she has not a problem dealing with the two languages and immediately translates from Latin to Spanish, although she does skip over some seemingly extraneous expressions. The discourse focuses on the condemnation of pleasure in the modern world and on the secret armies of intellectuals who still uphold pleasure: "Se había perdido el sentido de la vida porque se había perdido el paraíso y se había perdido el paraíso porque se había condenado el placer" (Arenas 1991, 388) (We have lost all meaning because we have lost paradise, and we have lost paradise because pleasure has been condemned) (Arenas 2000, 397, trans. Hurley). The circularity of this logic is similar to the strategies the nation uses to maintain its unity. The national *cofradía*, whose leader is Fidel, condones pleasure and enforces its cohesion by condemning homosexuals. Desire and libidinal energies are free and therefore cannot possibly be attached to a place. Attaching them to a place would cause them to lose their meaning. They are what they are just because they are forcefully removed from any topos and through desperate measures, they are liberated and free. Following the Arenian line of thinking, it is difficult to put limits on or to localize this desire.

"*Salí esta mañana y aún no he retornado*" (Arenas 1991, 390) (I left this morning and I haven't returned since) (Arenas 2000, 400, trans. Hurley), the commentary by an anonymous *loca* in the first person singular, incites Oliente to create a theory about the *pájaros'* collective experience. Although the following discourse by an anonymous *loca* in the García Lorca theater is filled with tensions and pain, it attempts to reckon with the incapacity to realize a place for desire.

> ¿Quiénes son los que retornan? Las aves migratorias, los pájaros, en su perenne afán de encontrar el clima adecuado, el nido, el árbol, el gajo donde quedaron los recuerdos. Un homosexual es un ser aéreo, desasido, sin sitio fijo o propio que anhela de alguna manera retornar a no se sabe exactamente qué lugar. Estamos siempre buscando un sitio que al parecer no existe. Estamos siempre como en el aire y atisbando.

Nuestra condición de pájaro es perfecta y está muy bien que así nos hayan calificado. Somos pájaros porque estamos siempre en el aire, en un aire que tampoco es nuestro, porque nuestro no es nada, pero que al menos no tiene fronteras. (Arenas 1991, 390)

[Who, what, is it that returns? Migratory birds—<u>birds</u>—in their eternal quest for the clime, nest, the tree, the branch to which their memories are forever turning. A homosexual is an aerial, untethered being, with no fixed place, no place to call his own, who yearns to return to . . . but, my friends, he knows not where. We are always seeking that apparently nonexistent place. We are always in the air, keeping our eyes peeled. Our aerial nature is perfect, and so it should not be strange that we have been called <u>fairies</u>. We are fairies because we are always in the air, in the air that is not ours because it is unpossessable, though at least it is not bounded by the walls and fences of <u>this</u> world.] (Arenas 2000, 400, trans. Hurley; underline in original)

In this quotation, the local epithet *pájaro* becomes a locus for an alternative community that, always searching, is in a perfect condition. This community reveals its most painful moments in the geographical exile (within the letters to and from the protagonist) in which the pain of the plague, AIDS, incites the first person plural—*nosotros*. In other words, rather than out of asserting cohesiveness by excluding all those who do not comply with its model of uniformity, community forms out of the shared experience of pain.

Arenas reveals that the image of gnawing masses at the island's platform is in dangerous proximity to the *pájaros'* perfect yet painful migratory condition. From so much gnawing at the island, the island's superficial layer separates from the base. It is not just the *pájaros* who enact this separation, but also a large part of its inhabitants who continue quarreling even as they float around. The rupture and movement characterized by this partition are characteristic of translational cultures, whose many representatives, according to Pérez Firmat, include Fernando Ortíz and Carpentier. Arenas translates denigration into liberation through linking the migratory *pájaros* to a national culture. It demonstrates the movement inherent in even the most situated of positions.

3
Just a Vieja de Barrio

The *pájaro* of Arenas's Cuban countryside who migrates to the city but never fully leaves behind the *campo* has its parallels in the *périca*, the "nobody" or streetwalker/flâneur of the Chilean neighborhoods. Like Arenas, a large part of Diamela Eltit's writings is invested in reclaiming the local space, of which many were deprived by a repressive regime, and in reassigning its value in the world. She too enacts a performance of herself in her writing. Especially in Eltit's firt novel *Lumpérica* (1983; English translation *E. Luminata* [1997a]), the female body, literally made open to the public through a photograph of the author's self-mutilation, becomes a starting point for complex negotiations with the self and the other. To consider a cosmopolitan realm within Eltit's works begins to challenge the assumed and reductive categories of the global and the local. Coming together in Santiago, Chile during General Augusto Pinochet's dictatorship, Eltit and other participants in the Escena Avanzada questioned social and geographic barriers by interrupting public space with nonfigurative artwork and more traditional linguistic structures with fragmented discourse. On the most general level, what we may say of Eltit resonates with what was said about Arenas: by reinserting the body into a national discourse that promoted itself through spirituality and other transcendental values, Eltit's performances attempted to disturb its forces of normalcy. Its effects on audiences have been documented. Much of this can be attributed to Nelly Richard, whose proximity to the Avanzada's production as a cultural critic makes her as much a spokesperson for as an inspiration to the group. To a large extent, Richard and Eltit go hand in hand. Richard facilitates reading the group's creations as both ethical and aesthetic. In response to a question of whether avant-gardism can affect societal change if it does not incorporate the masses—somewhat distinctly charged within the Chile of dictatorship and later, within Latin American cultural critique, Richard has insisted that incorporation of the masses merely reproduces the totalizing function of the authoritarian regime. In place of final interpretations is an aestheticization of the marginalized within art that blurs boundaries between the simulacra and the real. At times, the degree to which Eltit's writing is involved in experimentation makes it difficult for readers to acquire the distance that is necessary for critiquing without abandoning the tactics of transgression that her writing and its most intimate critic prescribes.

Resistant Invitations

To carve out what I call a "differentiated" space from which alternative cultural praxis during the recent experience of dictatorship can be evaluated, let us begin to examine the vaguely acerbic interpretation of sociologist José Joaquín Brunner.

> El propio "pathos" de la situación autoritaria, con sus secuelas represivas, reforzaba esas visiones alternativistas, haciendo virtud de la necesidad. Se llegó a elogiar los márgenes, a identificarse uno con los desterrados y excluidos, a imaginar que la "cultura oficial" podía ser atacada, desarticulada y contrarrestada "desde fuera," por obra y gracia de nuevos lenguajes, nuevos contenidos y nuevas instituciones situadas metafóricamente en los extramuros de la ciudad sitiada. Incluso, había una cierta pureza en el no-contaminarse, un excedente de valor simbólico y prestigio que venía de ser aceptado como marginal o excluido. (Brunner 1990, 22)

> [The very "pathos" of the authoritarian situation, with its repressive results, reinforced the alternativist visions, making virtue out of necessity. These consisted of praising the margins, identifying with the exiles and the excluded, imagining that the "official culture" could be attacked, disarticulated, and counteracted "from outside," by the work and grace of new languages, new contents and new institutions situated metaphorically on the outskirts of the besieged city. There was even a certain purity in not contaminating oneself, an excess of symbolic value and prestige that came to be accepted as marginal or excluded.]

This sociological approach touches on a key point about neo-avant-garde production that has been largely obscured in literary critique; that is, the role that purity has in legitimizing the neo-avant-garde's vision of its own provocative language. As is often the case in critical writings, these artists demanded a certain type of reader who could knowingly participate in the ceremony, but what is afforded by participation if readers are not as highly regarded as the producers because of their inherent distance from the particular experience of marginality?

To be a full-fledged "accomplice" in the manner codified by Richard resonates most with her own professional activity as an intermediary.

> Under censorship, the various mediations or substitutions used by the artists to transmit information has the effect of stratifying the meaning of the messages: each double or reversible sign contains a series of implicit meanings which are activated by the particular circumstances called for on the part of *accomplices*. (Richard 1986, 31)

These paradigms of reading become especially alluring because of the way in which they close off penetration from the outside. Such roadblocks, however, also inform approaches toward cosmopolitanism in literary studies. Bernardo Subercaseaux further prioritizes the experience of having lived through the Chilean dictatorship to the possibility of subverting cryptic language. Principal for him is "the internalisation of an environment, the presence of a reader who is an accomplice and co-author of a reading full of meanings pointing to the wider sociopolitical context, to the phenomenon of a (self)repression of language and to the historical rupture of 1973"(quoted in Richard 1986, 33). Complicity and appropriation are posited on opposite ends of a readership spectrum, wherein the latter implies violence. My contention with this spectrum is that, at the same time that travel to the margins and disinvestment with the center's apparent monolinguism are understood as legitimizing Richard's critique and Eltit's fiction, they themselves esteem the category of *insiders*. This value is complex since their own purity arises from their identification with the margins, necessarily involving mobility beyond their societal positions.

The warning to "international readers" against "compassion or solidarity" has ironically resulted in immense critical production (Richard 1986, 20).[1] Let us take, for example, an early critique of Eltit's writing, outside of Chile. Djelal Kadir places himself as an unapologetic outsider and insists on speaking about worlds that are not his: "Any reading tinged by the slightest ethical commitment will find an obligation to breach the gap between self and other, between one's own and the other's cultural boundary, not for self-confirmation or for appropriative ends, but out of the necessity to understand and for the genuine sake of solidarity" (Kadir 1993, 201). Although Kadir utilizes the same anti-appropriational language as Eltit and Richard, and goes a step further to assert an obligation implied by this step, he does not account entirely for Eltit's confrontational signal. The desirability of complicit readers suggests the impossibility of such a gap between self and other ever being breached fully. Coming in the form of critical essays, cautionary forewords, and autobiographical statements, resistant invitations set limits on how to approach texts and how far-reaching readers should believe these literary efforts to be. While it is certain that Eltit's writing is concerned "with the margins of culture, with literature, with a decidedly local sphere of public cultural practices," it is also immersed in an avant-gardism beyond Chile with decidedly cosmopolitan resonance (Tierney-Tello 1999, 93). To see *Lumpérica* as an embodiment of Eltit's "awareness of the post structuralist paradigm, in which the binary concept of 'critical distance' proves paradoxical," as does Robert Neustadt, is fascinating, but with respect to *Por la patria* (1986), he does not push this question of complicity and critical distance, far enough (Neustadt 1999, 54).[2] While Eltit's first and second novels share stylistic devices and even repeat certain motif-like phrases as "De vencida en vencedora" (From conquered to conqueror), *Por la patria* reconstitutes solidarities through framing and ironic self-fashioning. By representing the multiple facets involved in identity construction and solidarity, *Por la patria* engages its readers in a complicated call to solidarity. It acknowledges the advantages of maintaining distance from the center of power and also accepts the necessity of wielding power ethically.

   In Eltit's fictional narratives, her awareness of representation's limits is revealed through a conflicted necessity to preserve truth-value in order to form solidarities. Her foray into the testimonial genre with *El padre mío* (1989) and some of her explanatory essays on the nature of her work, written for distinct publics, tend to betray the framing of epistemological conflicts that occur in her complexly negotiated fiction. The proximity of Eltit's fiction to the genre of criticism validates paying attention to her own characterizations of her role as an intellectual. Taking her lead, we may arrive at a differentiated, rather than singularly complicit, understanding of this production. For North American theorist and cultural critic Bruce Robbins, "allegories of vocation" are "critical works which, while doing whatever other interpretive tasks they set themselves, also perform a second, most often implicit function, they invent and arrange their concepts and characters so as to narrativize and argue for the general value and significance of the intellectual vocation they exemplify" (Robbins 1993, 190). These are principal outcomes of Eltit's writings. Let us look at "On Literary Creation," in which Eltit makes apparent the relation between two frequently executed discourses: "literary practice requires me to establish another discourse, a cultural discourse that responds for my work. This second discourse, which is founded on the perceptions of the first—on uncertainty—is, of course, useless for comprehending the work itself, for illuminating it (unless we speak of the field of intentions and, perhaps, failures), but it can begin to generate a supplementary word: that of the author and her cultural determination" (Eltit 1992b, 144). The degree to which her fiction approximates theory and cultural critique makes me question the uselessness of her supplementary words. While Eltit constructs a unique narrative in which her fascination with vagabonds and the margins is the result of a special bond based on particular material, psychological, and social circumstances, it obscures another affiliation upon which her work is premised. It possesses commonalities with a long trajectory of modernist and avant-garde artists, frequently thought of as cosmopolitan. Though, as Gareth Williams has argued, unlike modernist approaches to similar themes, Eltit's approach does not promise redemption, it would be flawed not to associate Eltit's *pericas*, vagabonds, and insane with Baudelaire's *chiffonniers* (ragpickers), Borges's *orilleros* (dwellers of the outskirts) of Buenos Aires, and Cortázar's *clochard* (vagrant/tramp) under a Parisian bridge, among others.[3] *Lumpérica* and *Por la patria* involve a rigorous textual self-interrogation, a hybrid and transforming female body, complete with cuts, scabs, and decidedly un-cooptable masturbation.[4]

With these paradigms of artist and marginalized other in mind, revisioning cosmopolitanism as a tool for critiquing Eltit's work requires a closer examination of Robbins's and Clifford's analyses of the importance of cosmopolitanism in another discipline, anthropology. Clifford's claim that situatedness does not need to be the logical antithesis of cosmopolitanism and professionalism leads Robbins to praise him for having questioned the following assumption: "to open one's eyes finally and painfully to the 'situatedness' of a metropolitan or a cosmopolitan, is ipso facto to judge oneself intolerably contaminated and self-contradictory" (Robbins 1993, 191). In any speech act, the subject necessarily validates certain experiences at the expense of others and implicitly makes decisions about what and how to articulate according to the audience at hand. The issues around self-fashioning are intensified when it pertains to speaking for others.

In Clifford's allegorical reading of Conrad, *Heart of Darkness* becomes an alternative model of writing that is no less professional than Malinowski's professional ethnography. The decisive difference between them is that Conrad includes the experience of fashioning and self-fashioning, the activity of selecting and discarding, that is usually suppressed from ethnographic writing. His fiction includes the exclusions—the Lie to the Intended, the tearing off of Kurtz's "Exterminate the brutes!" from the official report—that are inevitable in all professional discourse. (Robbins 1993, 192)

The narrative's self-consciousness, characteristic of modernism, lays bare the contrasting elements that go into shaping truths. The notion that the ethnographer presents his cultural objects as "more 'local' than they are, in order to make himself a member of the 'local' culture of his fellow professionals" is especially fascinating in the context of Eltit's discussions of her own work (Robbins 1993, 193). By making the reader aware of the selection process, rather than concealing it, as would an ethnographer, Joseph Conrad tackles the problem of intellectual allegiances. "Professional discourse, the moral would seem to go, cannot be purified; it can only be saved by ironic self-consciousness of its impurity" (Robbins 1993, 192). In order to uphold "truths," such as those that appear in Malinowski's "classic ethnography that emerged from his fieldwork" (Clifford 1988, 97), *Argonauts of the Western Pacific* (1922), the professional ethnographer must dismiss the kind of polyphony that flourishes in his posthumously published intimate journal, *A Diary in the Strict Sense of the Term* (1967).[5] Robbins doubts that the Conradian ironic self-consciousness adequately toils with the problems associated with one's placement within a worldy profession and the desire for the "purity" and consolidation of the local. Rather, he argues for a combination of self-consciousness and the acceptance of a "post-cultural" space in which neither the interpreter nor the interpreted is obstructed by an imagined unified culture.

The "post-cultural" space to which Clifford refers, and toward which Robbins continually gestures, is not only a significant component in "allegories of vocation" within ethnography, but is of particular interest to Eltit's utilization of the margins and insertion within the discipline of Latin Americanism. Furthermore, Robbins's description is fundamental to postulating not only how studies of cosmopolitanisms contribute to our interpretations of Eltit's writing, but also vice versa.

Instead of a dichotomy of professional describers of culture, on the one hand, and their non-professional objects of description, on the other, Clifford now assumes a "post-cultural" space where the subjects and objects of description are at least potentially reversible, where the mobility required for observation and comparison is not monopolized by one side, where the word "local" has lost much of its contrastive force. His name for this space—a space that is not exclusively professional—is "cosmopolitanism." (Robbins 1993, 193)

Analyzing Eltit in the context of this version of cosmopolitanism, while keeping other versions in mind, offers a distinct framework for exploring several emergent issues.[6] Unlike Arenas who, by inverting the associations of cosmopolitanism and parochialism, develops a personalized version of cosmopolitanism that is linked to his memory of the fluxes in nature, Eltit casts cosmopolitanism in a more conservative light, as the homogenizing force of a deranged elite.[7] Considering the grotesque associations derived from cosmopolitan capital in the Chilean context, this stance is to be expected.

Illustrative of this position is the following ironic apology to an interviewer's suggestion that her representation of the uniqueness of Latin America in the novel *El cuarto mundo* (1988) using the term *sudaca* is outmoded for its proximity to essentialism.[8]

Lo siento mucho, pero no soy internacional, no pertenezco a todo el mundo. De partida, no escribo en todos los idiomas. Es decir, escribo en la lengua castellana y no veo que eso signifique ser internacional. Tengo una relación directa con ese idioma y con su historia. Tampoco es cualquier castellano: el código que utilizo y comprendo es el chileno. Mal me puedo sentir escritora del mundo, puesto que estoy trabajando con una sola lengua. Por otra parte tengo una relación de destino con Chile, y no te lo digo en el sentido romántico del término. Desde el alumbramiento a la muerte, mi vida está en Chile: ahí nací, fui formada y crecí. Tampoco tengo una biografía cosmopolita: soy una vieja de barrio, no más. Entonces, más allá de lo que piensen los cientistas sociales y los economistas, hay algo que es latinoamericano: una lengua y una forma comunes. A veces siento que los intelectuales que confunden Santiago con Manhattan, están al borde la chifladura. Definitivamente son dos lugares distintos. Los países latinoamericanos nos aspiramos a captar una miradita de los países ricos simplemente para no caernos del mapa. (Eltit 1991, 246–47)

[I am very sorry, but I am not international, I do not belong to the whole world. To start off, I do not write in all languages. That is to say, I write in the Spanish language and I do not see this as being international. I have a direct relation with this language and its history. It is not any Spanish either: the code that I use and understand is Chilean. I hardly feel myself as a writer of the world, since I am writing in only one language. Also I have a relationship of destiny with Chile, and I don't say it in the romantic sense of the term. From birth to death, my life is in Chile: there I was born, I was formed and grew up. I do not have a cosmopolitan biography either; I'm just a *vieja de barrio*,[9] nothing else. Then, beyond what the social scientists and the economists think, there is something that is Latin American; a common language and form. Sometimes, I feel that the intellectuals that confuse Santiago with Manhattan, are bordering on madness. Definitely, they are two distinct places. We Latin American countries aspire to capture a little glance of the rich countries simply so that we won't fall off the map.]

What is left out of Eltit's account is her own geographical positioning at the time of the interview—living in Mexico City as cultural attaché within Patricio Aylwin's government, is as fascinating as her insistence on differing from a tradition of intellectuals enabled by gender and socioeconomic privilege to form affiliations beyond Chile or to disavow their Chilean roots altogether. The situational nuances combined with her wish to not be perceived as a modern-day *rastaquouère*, as an overeager *international*, makes her impervious to other more liberating manners of perceiving the realities of these terms, as well as of the relation between Chilean vernacular and Spanish. Pride in having endured disparaging circumstances is an especially imaginable response, even more so, in light of the fact that the interview took place in the year after Pinochet was ousted. Beyond suggesting the tense relationship among disciplines in the social sciences and arts that during political strife became even more so, Eltit points to a contemporary debate over the discipline of Latin Americanism. Even as a government-employed cultural worker in a foreign country, she casts aside what she may share with cosmopolitans, whom she understands to principally possess class and intellectual formations outside of the nation. Nevertheless, her conscientious disassociation that entails envisioning herself as nothing but the product of her neighborhood is only part of the story. She projects an extra-textual self that has rejected a version of cosmopolitanism in favor of a situatedness in a particular urban experience within a country that lacks worldliness and confirms its existence by the gaze of the others.

There is another context of Eltit's fiction that we need to engage, beside her theoretical statements and authorial explanations. This trope of localness and humility is startling alongside her textual transgressions that entail hybrid figurations and linguistic structures that play with the proximity of argot and Chileanisms to "universal" languages, such as Latin and Esperanto. Readers may question the degree to which their difficulty in deciphering phrases in *Lumpérica* and *Por la patria* are because the author invented them or because they belong to other languages. *Por la patria*'s "l'invierno," (1986, 26) "mater" or "l'unta" (1986, 39) brings spoken colloquial Chilean Spanish to the written page, but visually, the initial apostrophe and unusual endings resemble some sort of invented, universal language that could possibly be rooted in Latin.[10] Rodrigo Cánovas explains it as an idiolect created especially for the occasion of merging public (national) and private (familiar) life into "la escritura de de un ser sufriente . . . efectuado (al modo barroco) en el cuerpo exangüe de nuestro idioma" (the writing of a suffering being . . . carried out (in baroque fashion) on the dead body of our language) (1990, 148). In response to the failure of language to transmit the experience of trauma, Eltit does not use an a priori Chilean Spanish, but rather creates another artificial Spanish for the fatherland in crisis. This also attempts to convey characters' dismay with Chile's contemporary situation wherein languages of the past are inadequate to describe the incomprehensible reality of the present. Eltit's denial of a neat correspondence between her postmodern Chilean texts and global trends brings out an interesting predicament concerning the conjunctions and disjunctions of the hybrid and the international wherein the former is privileged and the latter is cast aside as an interpretive category. The *bilongo*/negro/St. Patrick's cathedral episode in *El color del verano* elicits a similar tension. Emphasis on the distinctions between those categories—international and hybrid—is an important part of the symbolic currency of Eltit's works.

For that matter, Eltit's overall performance as a woman writer relies on a varied repertoire of humble origins, familiar scripts, jolting themes, and baroque stylistic devices. Critics are instrumental for directing the performance's realization, as the following newspaper interview in the Chilean *Hoy* entitled "Acoplamiento incestuoso" ((Incestuous Coupling) August 12–18, 1985) makes evident. It features a photograph of the author and her children, with a collage of haunting photographic images of male faces in the background. Here, the private and public realm is strategically blurred so as to suggest a natural link between the impoverished conditions of her biography and her relation to the patriarchal linguistic code.[11] Clearly, in this case as with many others analyzed in this chapter and in chapter 5, Eltit does not bear full responsibility for how her work is emplotted. However, guided by the journalistic medium, Eltit's words do convey a "cause and effect" logic, characteristic of a facile form of identity politics, in which neatly construed categories of class and gender figure principally. In this interview, the accompanying photograph encourages interpreting a firm link between women's struggle to obtain a voice under adverse material and social conditions in Latin America and her own difficulties to do so. Where such a "cause and effect" logic has definitive consequences on how to read Eltit is in the foreword to the English translation of *Lumpérica*.[12]

> Como yo no nací en cuna de oro y me enfrento diariamente a salvar la subsistencia de mi familia y la mía propia, estoy a perpetuidad en la vereda de las trabajadoras y porto la disciplina, pero también la rebeldía legítima y legal de la subordinada social. Por eso, tal vez, desde mi infancia de barriobajo, vulnerada por crisis familiares, como hija de mi padre y de sus penurias, estoy abierta a leer los síntom as del desamparo, sea social, sea mental. Mi solidaridad política mayor, irrestricta, y hasta épica, es con esos espacios de desamparo, y mi aspiración es a un mayor equilibrio social y a la flexibilidad en los aparatos de poder. (Eltit 2000a, 74)

> [Since I was not born with a silver spoon in my mouth and each day take on the salvaging of my family's subsistence as well as my own, I am continually made to toe the line of women who work, and I carry that discipline within me but also the legitimate and legal rebelliousness of the socially subordinated woman. Maybe that is why, after a childhood in a poor neighborhood, hurt by family circumstances, as daughter to my father and his hardships, I am open to reading the symptoms of neglect, whether social or mental. My greatest political solidarity— unrestricted, epic even—is with those spaces of neglect, and my aspiration is to a greater social stability and to flexibility in the power structure.] (Eltit 1997a, 9, trans. Christ)

What is qualified in her fiction comes across as unequivocally bold and unquestioned in this introductory statement to an international audience. This vein shifts slightly when she articulates that she is, in fact, a member of a professional group: "empleada que depende de su propio salario mensual, como responsable de mi espacio familiar y doméstico, como escritora . . . sólo soy una escritora entre muchas" (Eltit 2000a, 176) (an employee who depends on her monthly salary, as head of my household, as a writer . . . one writer, a woman writer, among many others) (Eltit 1997a, 11–12, trans. Christ). This last phrase detracts from the notion of writers as exceptional beings whose avant-garde sensibility may naturally unite them to the margins and places her, in a political way, as one among many. While the function of this subordination can be questioned, its broad acknowledgment of marginalities suggests a code for how to approach her first novel.

In contrast to Eltit's introduction where her own economic situation is definitive for how she views the particularities of her subject matter, the trope of mobility is inherent in another essay entitled "Nomadic Bodies."[13] It evokes a self-critical posture that helps to congeal the discrepant cosmopolitanism that I propose as a supplement to complicity. Eltit affirms her role as mediator as she contrasts the survival tactics employed by two sets of three women in an authoritarian society. In the process, she analyzes her own intellectual reaction to the intended emotionality of autobiographies published in Chile in the early 1990s when religious and national efforts to reveal the truth about the dictatorship with the goal of reconciliation were at their peak.[14] Eltit cautiously links the two trios on account of their temporal simultaneity: One trio was taken captive around the time the other hanged themselves. The first trio consisted of militant leftists, who were all active during Allende's government. Under Pinochet, Luz Arce, Marcia Alejandra Merino, and María Alicia Uribe worked clandestinely until they were captured and subjected to torture by the military intelligence agency (DINA). They all broke; not only did they inform, but they collaborated so completely that they later became officers in that same organization. Disarming to Eltit is the way in which power—no matter the source—traverses these women's bodies. Even though Arce and Merino express a desire to be perceived as traitors in their written texts, Eltit argues that *betrayal* is not the appropriate term to describe their adverse actions, since it "pierde su efecto por la repetición. Más bien sus cuerpos no son sino espacios por los que el poder transita locamente mutando a la manera de los camaleones" (Eltit 2000a, 73) (loses its effect in repetition. Instead, their bodies are nothing more than spaces through which power passes, madly transforming in chameleon fashion) (Eltit 1997b, 48). The second trio is the Quispe sisters—Justa, Lucía, and Luciana. They hanged themselves after doing the same to their two dogs and decapitating the rest of their animals. What is curious is Eltit's use of the term *nomadism* to refer to both groups' actions but with utterly distinct resonances. The testimonies of Arce, Merino, and Uribe are unethical because they express "una mala lectura de los códigos socials y muy particularmente a una profunda crisis experimentada con las condicionantes de género, que las autoras solo son capaces de resolver utilizando un procedimento de inversión: ser masculinas a cualquier costo" (Eltit 2000a, 74) (a bad reading of social codes, especially a profound crisis felt in the area of gender conditioning, which the authors are only able to resolve using a procedure of inversion: to be masculine at all costs) (Eltit 1997b, 48). Although it is an admittedly very vague argument, Eltit makes the point that the endurance and longevity characteristic of these indigenous Quispe sisters contrasts with the principles of possession, territorialization, and occupation that define autobiographers. "En medio de un paisaje impresionante, la diversidad de los sobrevivientes de las antiguas culturas indígenas mantiene aisladas sus tradiciones, sus ritos y sus fiestas. La vida en el altiplano transcurre, secretamente, con un alto grado de nomadismo, escindida entre pasado y presente, entre un mundo y los otros, diversos, extintos mundos" (Eltit 2000a, 76) (Set in a spectacular landscape, the survivors of the ancient indigenous cultures keep their traditions, rites, and festivals isolated. Life on the highlands takes place secretly, with a high degree of nomadism, divided between past and present, between one world and others, different, extinct worlds) (Eltit 1997b, 49). Eltit's theoretical fascination with the sisters' relation of place and mobility has much in common with the "situatedness-in-displacement" that, in other contexts, has been referred to as a virtue of cosmopolitanism (Robbins 1993, 185). Furthermore, her characterization of their practices as being faraway, in a distant geographical space, echo the importance of situatedness within the discipline of cultural critique, out of which arises a new form of mobile proximity or cosmopolitanism. The Quispes's exercise of power, thus, goes against not only the negative nomadism pertaining to the uncontrollable power that flows within individual bodies in the nation, but against the grander discourses of humanism against which Eltit defines herself. That is to say, I am most fascinated by the implications of Eltit's authorial turn and the manner in which Eltit inserts herself into a spectrum of spatial determinants.

> Lejos en el interior de un distante microespacio geográfico, las hermanas Quispe decidieron abandonar voluntariamente la vida, pero mediante el modo en que cursaron sus deseos, gestionaron un nuevo microespacio simbólico, cruzado por éticas y estéticas en las que insertaron cifradamente sus historias de vida y de muerte y garantizaron, mediante un elaborado rito, la huella social de un asentada pertenencia y dominio sobre sus espacios y sus bienes. Pero también se reservaron la libertad radical de dejarlo todo, de llevarse todo, de terminar con todo.

Y, me parece importante que ustedes sepan que los únicos bienes materiales que las hermanas Justa, lucía y Luciana Quispe poseían eran veinte cabras, dos perros y sus propios cuerpos. Nada más. (Eltit 2000a, 76–77)

[Far away, in the interior of a distant geographical microspace, the Quispe sisters voluntarily decided to abandon life. They employed a method that transmitted their desires that enabled them to create a new symbolic microspace, crisscrossed by ethics and aesthetics in which they inserted, in coded language, their life stories and their death stories. Thus they guaranteed, through an elaborate rite, the social track of an established belonging and control over their spaces, and their things. But they also reserved the radical freedom of leaving it all, of taking it all with them, of ending everything.

It's important to me that you know that the only material wealth the sisters—Justa, Lucia, and Luciana Quispe—possessed consisted of 20 goats, 2 dogs, and their own bodies. Nothing else.] (Eltit 1997b, 49–50)

This final "nothing else" echoes the one that Eltit uses to affirm her "vieja de barrio" status, and as such, is equally suggestive. Shifting from being a more traditional critic of texts and culture to being an embodied mediator between the reader and the dead bodies, Eltit lends momentum to the final passage that, while relating the material wealth of these sisters, accomplishes *something else*. That *else* speaks in favor of bringing a distinct control over bodies back into discourse on a micropolitical level, while it establishes a relationship between us and them that could be a first step in our assessing our own relationship to power. Through relating the sisters' relation to power to her own critical discourse, Eltit transforms the sisters' apparent silence into a powerful form of resistance that she favors over the customary and silencing confessional modes of Arce and Merino. Eltit's own endurance of the dictatorship imparts credibility to her role as mediator. How to read discourses provoked under such extreme conditions is but one of a series of questions regarding authority and readership that conceptualize "este gesto de lectura es un acto político otro" (Eltit 2000a, 69) (the act of reading as a different kind of political act) (Eltit 1997b, 46).

¿Desde qué lugar podía yo juzgar la situación de mujeres violadas, torturadas, encarceladas en un medio feroz que yo, desde otro lugar, también había habitado? ¿Acaso el leer intelectivamente el discurso emocional de dos mujeres no quebraba el necesario compromiso de género de la una con la otra? ¿Por qué no olvidar esos discursos impuros y hacer como si no existieran? ¿Acaso no era, en cierto modo, ventajista que una escritora que nunca habia militado en un partido político se conviertiera en lector de la feroz crisis de dos mujeres militantes? (Eltit 2000a, 69)

[From what position could I judge the situation of women who had been raped, tortured, imprisoned in a ferocious environment that I had also inhabited but from a different position? Does perhaps the intellectual reading of the emotional discourse of the two women not break the necessary contract of the genre? Why not forget those impure discourses and pretend they didn't exist? Was it not in a certain sense advantageous that a woman writer who had never been a militant in a political party become a reader of the savage crisis of the two militant women?] (Eltit 1997b, 46)

Eltit's reading of these narratives conveys an intense self-consciousness that points toward the difficult union of critical distance and proximity that is inevitable in studies of cosmopolitanism wherein distance from the source of pain is not entirely surmountable. The "vieja de barrio" rhetoric is not a mere aside to an ethical nomadism in her texts, but rather it authenticates her philosophy through creating a hierarchy of interpreters. In the act of esteeming her own native fluency of the contours, habits, and everyday fluctuations of a local place, Eltit suggests the tenor in which her equipped, yet displaced readers must humble themselves before the authenticity of her aesthetic approach—which coincides with the honest suffering, the "nothing else" of the hanged sisters.

Eltit's allegories of vocation tend to downplay what I perceive to be an easily identifiable commitment to theory in her work. An explanation of such hesitance can be located in Richard:

La palabra teórica del postfeminismo—y el tramado internacional de referencias culturales que la intertextualizan—aparece aquí despositaria de un saber—poder cuyo manejo, juzgado prohibitivo, provoca rechazo entre las mismas mujeres a las que iba originalmente destinado a beneficiar. Una palabra liberadora que afuera se profiere contra el sistema de dominancia (masculinidad hegemónica y cultura institucional), es aquí juzgada colonizadora. (Richard 1989, 71)

[The theoretical word of postfeminism—and the international plot of cultural referents that intertextualize it—appears here as a depository of a knowledge-power whose handling, prohibitive court, provokes rejection among the same women that it was originally destined to benefit. A liberating word that abroad is uttered against the system of dominance (hegemonic masculinity and institutional culture), is here judged colonizing.]

The "aqui" and "afuera" structure of this rejection is instructive. Read in light of the English foreword to *E. Luminata* wherein Eltit connects her aesthetic praxis to the sociopolitical divisions in her country, the novel's emphatic rupture with a linear notion of history would seem as if it were the spontaneous result of the author's down-home formation, of having emerged from the working class in the "third world." The national and international disciplines that inform her approach—the theory—seem inconsequential.

Lumpérica's deconstruction of language and highly baroque style, theorized by Eltit as a mode of deterritorialization related to the subjugation of particular social codes, responds to both theoretical trends and a definitive sociopolitical climate. That theory is inextricably linked to the novel transforms the notion that such reflection has its origins faraway and has particularly oppressive local consequences. Yet, in another essay entitled "On Literary Creation," Eltit further scripts the tensions between the national and international spheres, in a manner that critics of Fredric Jameson's "Third-World Literature in the Era of Multinational Capitalism" (1986) will recognize. By obliging Latin Americans to connect to a local place, international publishers restrict the dimensions of national literatures. This observation is particularly important to bear in mind, considering the manner in which Eltit strategically circumscribes herself and work. Let us examine the discomfort generated by Eltit's foreword to English readers that echoes the discomfort of a public square in Santiago during the curfew hours, the sole temporal period and principal setting of *Lumpérica*. Rather than invite readers in directly, the foreword continually implores them to be cautious in their approach toward the foreign text.[15]

> sigo pensando lo literario más bien como una disyuntiva que como una zona de respuestas que dejen felices y contentos a los lectores. El lector (ideal) al que aspiro es más problemático, con baches, dudas, un lector más bien cruzado por incertidumbres. (Eltit 2000a, 174)

> [I continue to think of literature as disjunction rather than as a zone of answers that leave readers happy and contented. The part of me that writes is neither comfortable nor resigned and does not want readers who are not partners in dialogue, accomplices in a certain disconformity.

The (ideal) reader to whom I aspire is more problematic, with gaps, doubts—a reader crossed by uncertainties.] (Eltit 1997a, 8, trans. Christ)

A superficial paraphrasing of this pre-sign or *ante-letrero* of the text would read "you will not feel at home here, and if you are not willing to enter an uncomfortable pact with me, I do not want you as a reader." Nonetheless, this explanation pleads for a different response from readers, the expectation that they will decide to accept Eltit's premise of not feeling at home. On one hand, Eltit's international readers question the value of feeling at home. On the other, the author's positioning herself as a homegrown writer suggests origins to be paradigmatic for determining how we read certain texts. Such a paradox works to her critical advantage, especially when it comes to subverting the traditional testimonial: readers more easily accept Eltit's experimental project, upon considering it as having originated from an authentic Chilean, nonprofessional insider, rather than from a professional outsider with a formation in both philosophy and literature.

Pericas: The City under Dictatorship

Defined by the *Dictionary of Chilenismos* as "persona cualquiera" meaning your everyday person, *perica* also suggests the vulgarty and trashiness akin to a streetwalker. The *perica* moves back and forth between approaching and resisting other subjects. While the figure defines *Lumpérica*, it also pervades *Por la patria* and *El padre mío*. To perceive its significance within the cosmopolitan context, again we must look toward Bruce Robbins's and Jean Franco's writing on postcolonial subjectivity and postmodern consciousness, respectively. Robbins's cosmopolitanism is "not one obsessed with embodying a preconceived totality, but one which does not judge in advance the macro-political scale of its units, which sees 'worlding' as process, to quote Gayatri Spivak, and a process in which more than one 'world' may be realized, where 'worlds' may be contested" (Robbins 1993, 188). Furthermore, Robbins privileges the *cosmos* or the actual process of making up of the self as in the adjective "cosmetic."[16] The "body-machine," central within Franco's discussion of *Lumpérica*, informs the present conceptualization of cosmopolitanism as a critical category in Eltit's work.

Lumpérica (1983) is an attempt to constitute a post-modern consciousness; if the novel has any fixed point it is a "person" in a central square of

Santiago whose body reflects a neon sign. It is as if in a world saturated by prefabrication and in the absence of a Cartesian subject, only the body machine establishes disjunction and conjunction with the world. (Franco 1994, 344)

The *perica* in the central square of Santiago signals a new approach toward knowing the world for which disjunctions are indispensable because they are the very basis of the subjectivity and sensibility of an un(identified) and un(individualized) subject that is often disregarded by literature.

Ronald Christ's more explanatory definition, as it relates to his translation of the novel, cannot be overlooked.

The fusion and dispersion in Eltit's language, the membering and dismembering, begins as early as her book's title, which, in the original (*Lumpérica*) fuses the German *lumpen*, a word perhaps more usual in Spanish, where Marxist terminology is commonplace, than in current American English, and *perica*, which denotes everything from babe and chick to an undetermined person, a sort of boulevard Jane Doe, a prostitute too: a walker of the streets who may also be a streetwalker. (Christ 1997, 213)

Christ's walker of the boulevard or the streetwalker presents clues that direct us to carve out a space where Eltit's first novel could conceivably fit beside modernist letters regarding the city. Within such writings about the city, tendentiously classified as cosmopolitan, *Lumpérica* signals an abrupt difference. Although it shares with them a fascination with two related motifs—gazes exchanged in the streets and the relationship of the individual to the masses, it refracts onto that modernist imaginary, fueled by possible transcendence, the impossibility of universal claims regarding both the subjectivity of the walker of the streets and the aesthetic experience as a whole. The experimental language and style is rooted in various traumas related to colonization and patriarchy and exacerbated by neoliberalist policies. Unlike the urban imaginary created by Baudelaire in the oft-cited sonnet "À une passante" (To a Female Passerby), published in 1861 in *Les fleurs du Mal* and in the essays of *Le Peintre de la vie moderne* (1863, *The Painter of Modern Life* [1964]) in which subjects, overwhelmed by the more-than-human crowd and energy of the streets, grasp to hang onto what makes them human, *Lumpérica* renders subjects via both the electric light, symbolic of both repression and truth, and the free-market economy.

Charles Baudelaire's poem begins "La rue assourdissante autour de moi hurlait" (The deafening street was screaming all around me), but out from this personified massive image emerges a singular woman who causes the poet's body to contort "comme un extravagant" (like a madman) at the moment of regarding her (quoted in Benjamin, "On Some Motifs in Baudelaire" 1969, 169). Eros and Thanatos converge in this urban encounter of the late nineteenth century. The velocity of the event, which bespeaks an even quicker negotiation between superficiality and penetration, distinguishes the poetic voices of both "cosmopolitan" pieces. The following passage from *Lumpérica* dramatizes that speed.

> El primer peatón cruzó la plaza, seguramente para acortar camino. Su mirada distraída la enfocó vagamente, luego de manera abierta. Sus ojos cruzaron. Ella sostuvo la mirada por un instante, pero después la dejó ir hacia la calle de enfrente. La gente era ahora heterogénea, mujeres, hombres, estudiantes. Todos ellos iban a alguna parte y los ruidos crecían en el momento en que el día ya estaba totalmente despejado. (Eltit 1983, 195)

> [The first pedestrian crossed the square, certainly for the sake of the short cut. Her absent-minded gaze focused on him vaguely, then openly. Their gazes crossed. She held the gaze for a moment, but then turned hers toward the street opposite. The crowd was mixed now, women, men, students. They were all going somewhere and now the noises grew louder just at the moment when the day became completely clear.] (Eltit 1997a, 203, trans. Christ)

The electric light that combines with the figure in the square to create the hybrid entity named L. Iluminada, along with the *lumpen*, form important cognitive markers.[17] Baudelaire's rendering of modernist urban subjectivity also suggests that in addition to the flâneur and the crowd, there is an important third element—the metaphor of electricity that invests the flâneur with an excessive amount of human energy.

> Thus the lover of universal life enters into the crowd as though it were an immense reservoir of electrical energy. Or we might liken him to a mirror as vast as the crowd itself; or to a kaleidoscope gifted with consciousness, responding to each one of its movements and reproducing the multiplicity of life and the flickering grace of all the elements of life. He is an "I" with an insatiable appetite for the "non-I," at every instant rendering and explaining it in pictures more living than life itself, which is always unstable and fugitive. (Baudelaire 1964, 9)

The crossing of gazes indicates the relation between the "I" and the "non-I"; the "I," in Eltit's novel, *L. Iluminada,* frequently stands in the center of the plaza and endows the crowd with a soul. These passages suggest that the nomadic intellectual is not removed entirely from the "lover of universal life" whose body contorts, as does a madman's. The flâneur who wanders through the arcades of the nineteenth-century's cosmopolitan capital is imperfectly exchanged for the *perica* who stumbles into the square in Santiago after endless wanderings, to be brought to life through fiction. Whereas we must insist that these are imprecise exchanges that always recall the disjunctions, this textual comparison provides the basis for envisioning a correspondence between *Lumpérica* and a cosmopolitan trajectory. Both artist figures revel in the capacity to see, while they maintain the prospects of remaining anonymous, a combination granted to them by their distinct urban surroundings—one, universally scripted as more local than the other.

Where the contrast between Baudelaire's lover of universal life named Monsieur G and the *perica* is stark is in respect to the scope of their gazes. Monsieur G rejoices in being "away from home and yet to feel himself everywhere at home" (Baudelaire 1964, 9). The spectator is a "*prince* who everywhere rejoices in his incognito" as well as in "ebbing and flowing" with the crowd's movements while being at the center of the world (Baudelaire 1964, 9). The crowd epitomizes the world, but the *perica* is involved in the square and its immediate surroundings. Although displaced, unsheltered, and on the streets, her situatedness is unquestionable. At the same time the novelistic *perica* connotes a group of unidentified singular beings—the many presences (Jane Does) in the plaza—the protagonist, L. Iluminada, is the ultimate *perica,* and she doubles as an artist. While her name hardly conveys the act of human creation, L. Iluminada embodies the *lumpen* of the square. From an illuminated message projected from a neon sign in the plaza onto her body, she becomes the illuminated or enlightened one.

The initial "making up" scene also introduces readers to another aspect of Eltit's participation in a discrepant cosmopolitan zone in which hybridity and artifice (recalling the cosmetic nuances of *cosmos*) serve as key elements. Rather than presenting an autonomous being in conjunction with the world, the narrative denaturalizes female subjectivity by signaling the way in which L. Iluminada constructs as well as dissects herself through dominant discourses.

Lo que resta de este anochecer será un festín para L. Iluminada, esa que se devuelve sobre su propio rostro, incesantemente recamada, aunque ya no relumbre como antaño cuando era contemplada con luz natural.

Por eso la luz eléctrica la maquilla fraccionando sus ángulos, esos bordes en que se topa hasta los cables que le llevan la luz, languideciéndola hasta la acabada de todo el cuerpo: pero el rostro a pedazos. Cualquiera puede constatar sus labios entreabiertos y sus piernas extendidas sobre el pasto—cruzándose o abriéndose—rítmicas en el contraluz. (Eltit 1983, 7)

[The remains of this evening will be a feast for E. Luminata, that woman who recrosses her own face, incessantly appliquéd, though no longer shining brightly as in time past when viewed under natural light.

That's why the electric light makes her up by splitting her angles, those outer edges at which she jostles toward the cables that carry the light to her, languishing her right up to the finishing touches to her whole body: but her face in bits and pieces. Anyone can testify to her half-open lips and her legs stretched out on the grass—crossing or opening—rhythmic against the backlight.] (Eltit 1997a, 14, trans. Christ)

The situation in which the grammatical subject "electric light" performs its action of "mak[ing] her up" is the first of many that disrupts the expectations of readers.[18] L. Iluminada implies a heightened awareness that defies the knowledge of an Enlightenment-style, compact, unitary subject. Readers instead catch her in the act of being made up by an electric light in a manner that does not resolve itself neatly in a totality, but rather writhes and dramatizes its disjunctions. The phrase "anyone can testify" speaks to the necessity of the other in confirming a subject's difference from the rest. Identity, however, does not presuppose this singular difference, but is rather depicted in a Foucauldian sense of plurality, in which "numerous systems intersect and compete" (Foucault 1977, 161). This protagonist is the space of multiple crossings—she is the nomadic protagonist situated for the night in a plaza in Santiago. The mutability and hybridity of the protagonist, like Arenas's multiple, fleeing, and transforming identities, counter the fixating forces, especially those of the dictatorship.

Within these contested perceptions of reality, it is impossible not to construe the electric light, as repressive as it is, as also talking back to the Enlightenment's faith in humanity, individuality, continuity, and liberty with artificiality and cutting.[19] The words in the above passage—"splitting," "crosses," "bits and pieces," and "half-open"— infer a process that disrupts what Foucault calls "pretended continuity"

(Eltit 1997a, 154).[20] *Lumpérica*'s initial sequence beneath which there is no essentialist body of knowledge, contrasts with the novel's next one, an interrogation scene carried out by an authority figure with an anonymous suspect or possible witness to a crime in the public square. The interrogator's characteristic search for answers is never satisfied, and instead, the questioning produces the sensation in both the interrogated and the reader that the content, apparently related to the plaza's activities, gets more and more trivial. In the process, it is revealed that the interrogator knows more about the so-called truth of the crime or the end result than was initially disclosed.

> —Yo también he estado allí y sólo por eso sabrás todo lo que estos podría alargarse para llegar de todas maneras a la inevitable conclusión. Así es que no dilatemos el asunto. (Eltit 1983, 45)

> [—I too have been there and that's exactly why you'll understand how all this could open up and lead one way or another to the inevitable conclusion. So that's why we're not building this thing up.] (Eltit 1997a, 57, trans. Christ)

The implication that the end is known eventually leads to the discourse changing into one that emphasizes the construction and simultaneity of events. Suddenly words are filtered, in the narrator's process to grapple with competing conceptions of reality. The frame of the investigation is apparent, highlighting the possibilities of multiple motivations and endings.

> Pero olvidemos lo superfluo, se constituye la cuarta escena:
> Pongámoslo de esta manera.
> La proyección de dos escenas simultáneas.
> 1. Interrogador e interrogado.
> 2. La caída de L. Iluminada

> Pero tal vez una podría fundirse en la otra y así es el hombre (cualquiera) el que estuviera a punto de caer en la plaza . . . Pero si tampoco fuese así y el hombre ése hubiese estado enfermo, realmente enfermo, . . . Si eso ocurriera, entonces se subvertiría la caída en la plaza y sería a ella tal vez a la que interrogaban y de su boca no habría salido palabra, porque interrogatorio aquí es vocablo sagrado y por cámara se habría valorado solamente su expresión . . . Alguien ya no estará allí, unos cuantos nombres serán borrados del kardex y el kardex destruido y la plaza dejará de ser importante. Vuelve a ser la decoración de la ciudad. (Eltit 1983, 46–48)

[But let's forget about the superfluous, the fourth scene is being set up:
Let's put it this way.
The projection of two simultaneous scenes.
1. Interrogator and interrogated.
2. The fall of E. Luminata.

But perhaps one might be fused with the other and that way it's the man
(any man) who was at the point of falling in the square . . . But if that's
not how it was either and that first man had been sick, really sick, . . . If
that had happened, then the fall in the square would be subverted and it
would be she perhaps whom they interrogated and not a single word
would have come from her mouth, because interrogation here is a
sacred word and only in the camera would her expression have been
appraised . . . Someone will no longer be there, a few names will be
rubbed out in the Kardex and the Kardex destroyed and the square will
cease being important. It will go back to being decoration for the city.]
(Eltit 1997a, 58–60, trans. Christ)

The Kardex, a filing system similar to a Rolodex, symbolizes the value
attributed to names and addresses in a dictatorship in which such data
could warrant bodily torture, disappearance, and also leniency. The
police created a register of suspected subversives out of the innumerable combinatory possibilities extracted from confiscated individual
address books of Chile's citizens with the goal of ensuring a "homeland security." They are used with one or more of the above objectives
in mind. In an equally persuasive way, the above sequence, taken
along with the "having been there" of the previous one, illustrates a
contrast between two approaches to knowing: one that predicates a
search for a particular end, carried out in the habitual present characteristic of history, and another that continually negotiates several possibilities of occurrences, taking place in a broad conditional realm.
While these two realms can be compared to Aristotle's categories of
history and fiction, the conjectures in the conditional realm are just as
likely histories. Readers, in turn, envision the police creating their own
history out of those combinatory possibilities.

The setting of the novel is suitable for approximating these simultaneous histories. The plaza in relation to literature needs to be understood, not as identifiers of a regional/cosmopolitan divide, but rather
as a limit space of nomadic resistance and statist constriction. María
Inés Lagos accurately points out *Lumpérica*'s temporal and spatial
constraints, stating that the novel not only takes place in a territory set
apart from the rest of a city, but in one under siege during the curfew

set forth by the government (Lagos 1993, 136). Undoubtedly situated, the scene of the entire novel is also a space of reaction where a disruptive version of cosmopolitanism is performed. The "desarrapados, pálidos y malolientes" (Eltit 1983, 7) (ragged people, pale, and stinking) (Eltit 1997a, 14, trans. Christ) roam into the plaza, against the prescribed territorial limits of the city's citizens, to observe L. Iluminada's defiant spectacle of bodily pleasure and displeasure. Complicated by the multiple interpretative circles inscribed within the narrative, the reading experience resembles the nomadic defiance of the city's *pericas*. Prevented from interpreting in a linear fashion, readers observe the vagabonds being filmed as they watch the spectacle of L. Iluminada deducing the illuminated message.

In this way, the plaza is central to the present interpretation of L. Iluminada's role as *perica*/intellectual/artist/nomad. Néstor García Canclini's description of the plaza's dual functions is especially useful to understand its hegemonic and subversive functions as a repository of official history and as a place where that history may be besmirched. L. Iluminada's presence there gives her the status of a public figure in a society that demanded women's obscurity from such life. The military government, reinforced by the overall patriarchy, monitored women's participation in public life and banked on their carrying out the function of patriotic mothers. L. Iluminada's intense association of her body with language acted out in the public space is a radical departure from that ordering. Familiar to both national unity and dissidence, the plaza in *Lumpérica* is the space from which emerges an "effective history" that, in contrast to traditional history, narrates what is closest to it, the body, but does not fear "descending" to "seize the various perspectives" (Foucault 1977, 156). Identity is a continual negotiation among body, word, context, and the other, in a manner that challenges the continuity and homogeneity sought by official history.

The avant-garde form is well suited for this intervention, since it brings readers up close and then dislodges them to reckon with the multiplicity of perspectives advanced by the text. The masturbatory and masochistic functions of L. Iluminada remind us of language's materiality, but, at the same time, this female avant-garde artist/intellectual is much more than the average, the *perica*. This image that combines the most anonymous and defined elements strikes an interesting comparison with Vicky Unruh's discussion of the "vagabond Eye/I." Using several examples from avant-garde prose and verse including Vicente Huidobro's *Altazor*, Unruh explains a "simultaneously self-expanding and self-erasing process" by which a "totalizing desire to absorb and express all linguistic possibilities" results in a disintegration of the poetic voice to a prelinguistic utterance (Unruh 1994, 78). In this way, it is not contradictory to suggest that L. Iluminada both embodies the *lumpen* and falls apart as a singular static body.

In a sense, even more than *Por la patria*, *Lumpérica* resembles an avant-garde aesthetic that makes readers aware of the text as artifice. Although *Lumpérica* may not have been a readily accessible tool for Chile's opposition, its emphasis on artifice critiques the discursive structures, that, valorized for their being natural, enable the continuation of physical oppression. The attention on the framing devices and the implementation of baroque linguistic experimentation are not solely aesthetically driven, but also are attached to the local conditions in which the consequences of a transparent and easily consumable defiance would have been severe. An analogy can be drawn between Arenas's downplaying of his texts' high literariness and his cosmopolitan *paysan* identity to Eltit's reluctance to theory and her neighborhoodly post-structuralist complicity. To the extent that *Lumpérica* is as much about the authoritarian dictatorship as it is about writing and theory, its protagonist has in common with other avant-garde artists the tendency to "conduct [her] activities . . . from within a contingent world"—so much so that her mind disintegrates in order to reload with the identities of the *lumpen* (Unruh 1994, 78).

> Se celebran en sus identidades. Son sus propios padrinos que se reciben y ella, ella es la que se rebautiza en cada uno.
> Es una fiesta.
> El luminoso sigue cayendo dándoles más posibilidades, ampliándoles la imaginería. Se ven proyectados hasta los bordes de Santiago, ornados de atavíos: por robos y excesos accediendo a todos sus lugares. Por puro deseo propietarios al venderse al luminoso como mercaderías. Esos son los que se esperan con ansias.
>   Por esto, están reducidos a goce cuando entre los haces de luz del luminoso se dejan entrever sus posibilidades. Ya se ha consumado la transacción y por eso la felicidad de esos cuerpos imprime gracilidad a sus movimientos.
> La armonía se ha asentado en la plaza.
> L. Iluminada tampoco permanece ausente del espectáculo. Ha vaciado su mente de toda memoria y ahora construye y planifica sólo con los pálidos como referente: plasmados en su futuro. (Eltit 1983, 11)

> [Their identities are being celebrated. They are their own godparents who are being received and she, she's the one who is rechristened in each one of them.

It's a feast.
The illuminated message continues falling, giving them more possibilities, extending their stock of imagery.
They are seen projected to the limits of Santiago, decked out in finery: by thefts and excesses gaining entrance everywhere. Proprietors out of sheer desire as they sell themselves to the sign like merchandise. These are the ones who wait eagerly.
That's why they melt with joy when they can glimpse their possibilities amid sheaves of light from the illuminated sign.
The deal's done already and that's why the happiness of those bodies impresses gracefulness on their movements.
Harmony has settled into the square.
Neither does E. Luminata stay out of the show. She has emptied her mind of all memory and now constructs and plans only with those pale people as a referent: molded into her future.] (Eltit 1997a, 19–20, trans. Christ)

The notion of being rechristened in the *lumpen* reflects the expansiveness of L. Iluminada; she possesses an unusual capacity for seeing and creation. However, with that expansiveness comes the necessity of emptying her own mind in order to encompass the pale people. As they begin to penetrate L. Iluminada, the subject–object relation between intellectual and *lumpen* is slightly altered into one of intersubjectivity. L. Iluminada's moaning and groaning in the third section of the novel relates to that initial expansiveness and subsequent emptying. Like the avant-garde writings Unruh explores, *Lumpérica* contains its own ethical system of engagement in which a supposedly singular linguistic system surrenders to precommunicative utterances. Emerging from the female body, they disrupt the model set forth by the avant-gardes.

This frictional relation to literature, the self, and the world comes across succinctly in Section 5: ¿Quo Vadis? The following combinations imply diverse metaphors of comprehending the world, the corporal, the vernacular or local, the literary, the universal, and the spiritual "y palabra caída será: cuerpo y letra modulada sobre el pasto, frotará lengua y pasto, pierna y pasto" (Eltit 1983, 91) (and a fallen word she will be: letter modulated on the grass, she'll rub body and lawn, tongue and lawn, leg and lawn and the liquid) (Eltit 1997a, 98, trans. Christ). The act of rubbing, from a fallen or modulated position, critiques aggressively stable and hierarchical codes of comportment. Playing on perspectives in a manner that reveals the structures of dominant history continues to be the focus of the fifth section wherein the female subject performs her disjunction from them.

Está bajo el farol de la plaza y aunque cunda el frío por estos lados se tiende sobre el pasto a dormir. Pero el sueño no llega y se da vueltas para cambiar de postura . . . Desde lejos es una sábana extendida sobre el pasto, más allá no es nada. Está tan oscuro en la plaza. Desde la acera del frente es un cuadrante iluminado.

Como un zoom es la escritura. Reaparece la mujer que duerme o quiere dormir, pero no es así: es el placer de extenderse jugando con el deleite de su propia imagen. Infantil tendida es ésta. De mentirosa lo hace. Porque jugar a la distorsión de la mirada por falta de luz, ha sido una actividad explotada hasta el cansancio. Vence así el equívoco, crece la confusión y el insomnio es un hecho fugaz . . . ese extremo momento en que sus vellos se erizan levantándose de la pierna y creando otro circuito de cercanía. (Eltit 1983, 91)

[She's under the streetlight in the square and although the cold spreads along here she stretches out on the grass to sleep. But sleep won't come and she tosses and turns to find a different position . . . From far away she is a sheet spread out on the grass, from farther still she is nothing. It's so dark in the square. From the sidewalk opposite it's an illuminated quadrangle.

Like a zoom, that's writing. The woman who sleeps or wants to sleep reappears, but that's not how it is: it's the pleasure of spreading out playing, with the delight in her own image. Infantile stretching is what it is. Like a trickster she does it. Because playing at distorting the gaze with lack of light, that trick's been worked to death. She conquers this way the ambiguous, confusion mounts, and insomnia is a fleeting fact . . . that extreme moment when her down bristles up, rising from the leg and creating another circuit of proximity.] (Eltit 1997a, 99, trans. Christ)

Her trickster pose destroys the solemnity of the prohibition, tradition, and art in the name of play. To say that "playing at distorting the gaze with lack of light" has "been worked to death" resonates with Alejo Carpentier's post–World War II recognition in the prologue to *El reino de este mundo* (1949) that the avant-garde's mechanical experimentation was bankrupt. However, instead of turning inward toward identities and origins, Eltit's creation innovates this surfeit by interrupting the equation of mechanical play with an emphasis on the jouissance of the text.[21]

Section 5: ¿Quo Vadis? cuts into the present reconceptualization of cosmopolitanism in a more direct manner. The Latin title yields to a vernacular, as L. Iluminada, the intellectual, mediates between a reactionary and progressive role, between the Latin/universal, also described as cosmopolitan by Antonio Gramsci in his writings on the roles of intellectuals, and a vernacular discourse. L. Iluminada masturbates and experiences displeasure over the fact that it is raining in the square. She has her back to literature and constructs a "una narración transitoria que assume como modelo a una desarrapada" (Eltit 1983, 96) "transitory narrative that takes as its model a ragged bag lady" on the sidewalk (Eltit 1997a, 105, trans. Christ). The *lumpen* who are covered in plastic, almost as if they were books with covers, are read. Nevertheless, the realm of literature never represents them in their entirety. They take the chalk in order to inscribe themselves on the cement, as L. Iluminada translates the Latin into the Spanish "dónde vas" (Eltit 1983, 104) (where you going) (Eltit 1997a, 113, trans. Christ). Their actions are sustained by each other. "Se quedan quietos observando y como profesionales empiezan a tender su propio rayado en el centro. Es perfecto. Están enajenados en la pendiente de la letra, alfabetizados, corruptos por la impresión" (Eltit 1983, 105). (They stay still watching and like professionals begin to lay out lines in the center. It's perfect. They get carried away on the slope of the letter, made literate, corrupted by printing) (Eltit 1997a, 117, trans. Christ.) The *lumpen* then desist, to become once again the object of L. Iluminada's reading. This intellectual figure may emerge from a universal terrain, but is ultimately connected with the vernacular. Indeed, the *lumpen* affects the intellectual's reading and transforms itself, at least figuratively, through the linguistic system.

While on one level, the dictatorship, through restrictive cultural politics, demonstrated its adhesion to nationalistic values and production, on another, Pinochet's regime had free-market policies on its agenda. The references to being sold on the market in *Lumpérica* refer to a socioeconomic system that diminishes the marginalized/*perica* in order to sustain itself. However, by making a *perica* the narrative's protagonist, Eltit redefines the marginalized's subjectivity. Pinochet's properly ordered nation exerts a centripetal and chauvinistic force on its citizens, while it also has a vested interest in a centrifugal one, characteristic of an international neoliberalism, that is beneficial to a few. The sort of internationalism rejected by Eltit likely takes this particular centrifugality as a point of reference. In this way, the nation's insistence upon global market policies and the resistant writer's upon hybrid identities are flip sides of one another. The following passage in *Lumpérica* in which both the périca and the masses transform, gestures toward this complexity.

Gimen por luz, orgiásticos en sus convulsiones se masifican. Nadie diría que en Santiago de Chile podría ser esta bautizada para que esos se distiendan como gemas. Así es, con las ramas de los árboles que les lamen el rostro y ella se frota en su madera por el puro placer del espectáculo. Sumida en el éxtasis de perder su costra personal para renacer lampiña acompañada por ellos que, como producos comerciales, se van a ofertar en esta desolada ciudadanía. (Eltit 1983, 8)

[They moan for light, orgiastic in their convulsions they clump together. Who would think that in Santiago de Chile there could be this baptized one, just so those people might swell like buds. But that's how it is, with branches of trees licking the faces and her rubbing up against their wood from sheer pleasure in the spectacle. Plunged into the ecstasy of shedding her personal scab so as to be reborn hairless in the company of people who, like commercial products, are going to be put on offer in this desolate citizenship.] (Eltit 1997a, 15, trans. Christ)

The narrator indulges in the experience of pained ecstasy. "Nadie diría que" conveys surprise over the possibility of normalcy being disturbed through the communion of the artist protagonist and the masses. The place of the surprise—Santiago de Chile—is crucial to the significance of the affirmation; that "nadie" is clearly reminiscent of Juan Valera and reflects a double subject position wherein there is an internalized sense of self; that is, the one who occupies the position of validation. Nothing but this excruciating, ecstatic, hybrid existence is promised. This artist/intellectual figure does not freely choose her relation to the nation. She is already contaminated by the economic discourse of a nation for which purchasing power accompanied by patriotic spiritual discourse accounts for a large portion of meaning for its citizenry. She reaches toward what appears to be more natural and situated than the nation, her own body. However, like the streets through which she has wandered and the square, dark with the exception of an electric sign, on which she sits, her body bears the effects of this history. By shaving her head and rubbing endlessly her private parts, she obstructs the neat passage of oppression and exclusion of the peripheric people. In reaction to its condition of always already being contaminated, this redefined subject does not search for origins, but instead emphasizes how contaminated she is, by rubbing herself, but not only for herself. Out of this omission and the clippings of meanings, Eltit shapes *Lumpérica*. It embraces incommensurability—the incoherence and instability of the marginalized. Like the aesthetics of consumption, which put no limits on the market, those that define *perica* avoid closure and continually approach the world from different incomplete perspectives.

Making Up the World through Testimony

In contrast to the rejection of cosmopolitanism and professionalism apparent in much of Eltit's cultural critique, *Por la patria* (1986) frames the negotiation involved in speaking for others. Published three years after *Lumpérica*, Eltit's second novel takes as its focus the coalition politics that were beginning to be active as "una verdadera oposición" (a true opposition) after 1983 in a Chile still ruled by the military (Tafra 1998, 95). Sylvia Tafra explains that important differences between *Lumpérica* and *Por la patria* reflect Eltit's interpretation of that changing sociopolitical arena.

> Si en *Lumpérica* las pulsiones de vida y muerte se neutralizan, mante-niendo a la protagonista en un *impasse*, en *Por la patria* triunfan las pulsiones de la vida . . . El polo de la enunciación lo representa un sujeto que fluye de una visión objetiva a la focalización interna y variable en diversos personajes, aunque generalmente se focaliza en la protago-nista. Esta mirada polivalente o pluriperspectivista apunta a la disolu-ción del sujeto en el proyecto comunitario de liberación que Coya, como "madre general," lidera junto al grupo de las otras "madres." (Tafra 1998, 95)
>
> [If in *Lumpérica* the drives toward life and death neutralize, keeping the protagonist in an *impasse*, in *Por la patria* the life drives triumph . . . A subject that alternates between an objective vision and an internal and shifting focalization in diverse characters, although generally focalized in the protagonist, represents the pole of enunciation. This polyvalent or multiperspectivist gaze points to the dissolution of the subject in the communitarian project of liberation that Coya, as the "general mother," leads, together with the group of other "mothers."]

This project of liberation continually references the subject that flows, but also succeeds in forming group solidarities in order to achieve a more habitable realm. While *Lumpérica* is more limited with regard to a communitarian project, the intellectual and the *lumpen* do penetrate one another in a manner that gestures toward an intersubjectivity involving nonfixed subjects.

In part one of *Por la patria*, "La luz, la luz, la luz, la luz del día" (The light, the light, the light, the light of the day) the characters are primarily in Coya/Coa's family's bar, in a marginal neighborhood of Santiago. Coya/Coa's father is disappeared, and her mother departs with a traitor named Juan. The naming of particular dates and places of actual roundups in Chile, such as August 24 and Pisagua, make this a particularly historical text. In the second part "Se funde, se opaca, se yergue la épica" (The epic is founded, is covered, is erected), the four women are incarcerated, but Coya/Coa gathers their testimonies and writes their stories. Although liberated by the novel's end, the characters are also back in the bar where the novel began. An exceptionally literary work, consisting of speeches, documents, short plays, and testimonies, *Por la patria* lays bare the constructed character of truths at all levels.[22] Unable to encompass her entire self into either gender— "No me atrevo a tomar la tercera silla" (Eltit 1986, 15) (I do not dare take the third seat), the narrator/principal character Coya/Coa, incestuous with both parents as her inheritance from Coya may suggest, remains dual and bisexual. "Mi hombro fue paterno totalmente masculino cuando porteé la entrada con mi pie femenino, la planta de mi madre me guiaba" (My shoulder was totally masculine when I carried the entrance with my feminine foot, the sole of my mother's foot guided me) (Eltit 1986, 15). Coya/Coa, continually masturbatory as Luce Irigaray characterizes the female sex, is a starting point for a multiplicity of voices that intercept a stable, stagnant conception of identity and truth with her duality, the result of inheritance and context. "Esa noche de la tragedia, alguien acabó en mi nombre y desde entonces respondo dual y bilingüe si me nombran Coa y Coya también" (This night of the tragedy, someone came on my name and since then I respond dual and bilingual if they call me Coa and Coya also) (Eltit 1986, 22). Against the plot's circularity, *Por la patria* also establishes a provisional linearity out of which the female characters may dispute repressive measures. A principal instance occurs after Juan— lover, torturer, and squealer—declares that he will be the counter-memory of Coya/Coa. She is disembodied "mojada, traspasada de agua" (moist and soaking in water) (Eltit 1986, 273) she has lost her pubis and her flesh, and in these conditions, she delivers a speech regarding memory and forgetting that culminates in "Seré de vencida en vencedora especie" (I will turn from the species of the conquered into the conqueror) (Eltit 1986, 275). With those words, the women are liberated, but again the fact that they all end up back in the bar attenuates how much hope readers are to find in these seemingly revolutionary words.

Many of *Lumpérica*'s themes and structural devices are revisited. The *perica* reappears and although her links to modernist predecessors are even more pronounced, so are the ones to various indigenous American belief systems, most notably those of the Mapuche Indians. Coya refers to the wife and older sister of the founding Inca emperor, and Coa to street argot. Particular spaces in the city register the psychic reality of characters. The neighborhood of Pisagua, the center of the dictatorship's roundups and raids, becomes the focus of encounter among four female characters that challenge the patriarchal order. Like *Lumpérica*, *Por la patria* is a text about writing. More than interrogating other works in which the city is practically a protagonist, *Por la patria* inserts itself into the genre of testimonial fiction and uses metatextuality to subvert the genre. As Rodrigo Cánovas makes clear, the stories in *Por la patria* do not "pretenden ser reales (no son testimonios de personas) sino verosímiles (se simula el género del testimonio, se lo actúa, se transita por él)" (pretend to be real [they are not testimonials of people] but rather likely [the genre of the testimonial is simulated, it performs it, it passes through it]) (Cánovas 1990, 149). However, unlike in *El padre mío*, where Eltit creates another nonsensical world as hermetically sealed as the one in which the citizens of Chile were forced to live, enclosing a "real" protagonist within, here the artificiality of the text foregrounds the difficulties of bearing witness. With the authorial persona Coya/Coa who seeks to "darles voz" (give them voice) (Eltit 1986, 194–95), *Por la patria* clarifies the difficult task of the female intellectual who is compelled to translate the traumatic experience of dictatorship, but is also aware that, in so doing, she may usurp the voices of some of the dictatorship's victims. Cosmopolitanism critical practices can adopt from this fictional gesture that relies on the persistence to translate, alongside an acknowledgement of the violence and negotiations that are involved in the act of "speaking for" the marginalized.

These complexities are made apparent throughout the novel. Taking into account the importance of the collective voice for testimonials, *Por la patria* brings to the surface the conflicting voices involved in the construction of that collectivity.[23]

He inventado un espectáculo de aceptación con la mirada capada.
Distante, atacada de una absoluta falta de contacto, temerosa de la oscuridad, escribo:
Parlamentos, documentos, manifiestos.
Hablo siempre de las cosas nuevas de la infancia, del estilo asombrosamente decadente de la patria.
Berta, trabaja infatigable, dejando sobre las hojas la caparazón adyacente de su experiencia frustrada, de su ambición por el indeleble primer plano.
Hubo entre nosotras una discusión explícita.

Cuando se habló de aquello, mi posición categórica la inhibió, le torció
su hegemónico proceder.
—O te ciñes al plan general o te retiras. Así le dije.
—Las mujeres se van a resistir.
—Las mujeres van a estar felices. Las mujeres éstas van a delirar de gusto,
le rebatí. Va a ser todo una toma colectiva del habla. (Eltit 1986, 199)

[I have invented a spectacle of acceptance with a castrated glance.
Distant, irresoluted because of an absolute lack of contact, frightful
because of the darkness, I write:
Speeches, documents, manifestos.
I speak always about new things from infancy, about the shockingly
decadent style of the fatherland.
Berta, works tirelessly, leaving on her sheets the adjacent shell of her
frustrated experience, of her ambition for the indelible limelight.
Among us, there was an explicit discussion.
When that was spoken of, my categorical position inhibited her, dis-
torted her hegemonic being.
—Or you yield to the general plan or you withdraw. That's how I said it.
—The women are going to resist.
—The women are going to be happy. These women are going to be
delirious from pleasure, I rebutted. It's going to be a whole collective
taking of speech.]

The ironic tone conveyed in the "collective taking of speech" ridicules
intellectuals' efforts to project onto others their own desire for collectivity. Affiliation with the masses, regardless of the empathy that it
purports to offer, is tenuous, at the least. Such an ethical cosmopolitanism highlights not only the selections and omissions endured in
creating a collective discourse, but also the need to continue exerting
power through negotiation.

Where the issue of collectivity is perhaps most questioned is in the
passage in which Coya/Coa, desirous and searching for her parents,
inscribes on the wall: "Paz y plenitud sobre el antro chileno" (Peace
and plenitude over the Chilean den) (Eltit 1986, 261). However, following this figment of liberation is a disagreement regarding meaning.

—Te libraste, supiste hacerlo a tu medida, impresionaste hasta la Rucia
que es muy dura.
—Fue algo sincero. Era la única alternativa para nosotras.
—Para ti querrás decir.
—Yo soy todas ustedes.
—Mentira, yo soy yo, no más.
—Sin mí, hace rato estarían perdidas.

—Es por ti que nos pasa esto.
—Mujer, estábamos todas en lo mismo. (Eltit 1986, 262)

[—You freed yourself, you found out how to do it your way, you even impressed Rucia who is very difficult.
—It was something sincere. It was the only alternative for us.
—For you, you mean to say.
—I am all of you.
—Lie, I am I, not more.
—Without me, you would be lost a long time ago.
—It is because of you that this is happening to us.
—Woman, we were all in the same situation.]

From this passage emerge the multiple voices forged into the collective voice, and on an extratextual level, it foregrounds the complicit role of the intellectual, who, in giving voice, will also need to lie or tailor her argument as in "Era la única alternativa para nosotras" to suit particular purposes, in this case, the provisional "breaking-free." The process by which truths and allegiances are established, on a more general level, emphasizes an implicit dialogue between intellectual and *lumpen*, as well as intellectual and community of other intellectuals or professionals.

This interaction opens up *Por la patria* to readers as a viable text with which to dialogue, though readers are still required to earn this position. In a conversation with Fernando Burgos and M.J. Fenwick, Eltit comments on her lack of desire to make *Por la patria* appealing to a larger public. Even though Eltit describes this novel as being sealed off from reception, its use of the familiar second-person singular of address, *tú*, ensures that the audience is never an abstract entity (Eltit 1995, 348).[24] Through the combination of this characteristic tactic of testimonials and an avant-garde metatextuality, *Por la patria* mediates between insiders and outsiders to a far greater extent than does the testimonial *El padre mío*. These extents of mediation cannot be ignored. *El padre mío* creates a world so hermetically sealed that it deprives what sustains it, this real-world schizophrenic vagrant Eltit calls el Padre Mío, of a biography. The text is a transcription of three of his speeches that Eltit taped during her encounters with him in the slummy outskirts of Santiago called Conchalí, in 1983, 1984, and 1985. Pursuing "una inestable investigación en torno a la ciudad y los márgenes" (unstable research around the city and the margins), she and the visual artist Lotty Rosenfeld encountered this personage who could provide them with "una estética generadora de significaciones culturales" (an aesthetic capable of generating cultural meanings) (Eltit 1989, 11). Eltit links her own urban wanderings to a mode of critically escaping the seclusion of the institutional vocation, but her own limited self-interrogation directs readers toward a potentially monolithic way of reading.

In contrast to the *lumpen* who transform and/or talk back in *Lumpérica* and *Por la patria*, the transformation of the witness, called el Padre Mío, however, is much more implicit. Her appropriation of his schizophrenic discourse defines both of their literary and political aims.

> Cuando escuché al Padre Mío, pensé, evoqué a Beckett, viajando iracundo por las palabras detrás de una madre recluida y sepultada en la página. Después de Beckett, me surgió otra imagen.
>   Es Chile pensé, Chile a pedazos. (Eltit 1989, 17)
>
> [When I listened to the Father of Mine, I thought, I evoked Beckett, traveling through the words behind a mother secluded and buried on the page. After Beckett, another image came to me.
>   It is Chile, I thought, Chile in pieces.]

El Padre Mío's fragmented speeches illustrate a breakdown of heroic and linear narrative that corresponds to Eltit's critical need for marginalization. Through a peculiar experience of el Padre Mío's disoriented language, which, asserts Eltit, is evocative of Beckett, the reader is to recall the experience of the dictatorship, not by a unifying act of interpretation or re-membering but by the narrative's own fragmentation. Complicitous readers are essential for understanding this act of resistance, but they need not be so for the reasons proposed by Ariel Dorfman in his discussion of the *testimonio* in Chile. "Aunque supuestamente el testigo apela al mundo entero (con explicaciones y notas a pie de página para lectores extranjeros) para que el oprobio caiga sobre los 'esbirros,' lo cierto es que el verdadero grupo se circunscribe y demarca más: se trata de aquellos que están convencidos de antemano" (Dorfman 1986, 195). (Although supposedly the witness is appealing to the entire world (with explanations and footnotes for foreign readers) so that their opprobrium will fall upon the "minions," the fact is that their real public is more circumscribed and precise: it consists of those who are already convinced beforehand) (Dorfman 1991, 159). Dorfman explains that within the nation, the masses would not read *testimonios* as urgent calls to action, and on the international level, their effectiveness as texts capable of enacting change is scarce. Although many testimonials originally published outside of Chile made their way back in through underground channels, suggesting their defiant nature, their viability is also determined by their readership's prior commitment. Eltit's ideal readers are equally complicitous, armed with a set of contextual and theoretical tools that include the knowledge of a pre-national, national, and international context, needed to apprehend the fragmented discourse. They must be able to traverse several linguistic registers and be familiar with the clues, as well as the model of testimonial that is being reexamined. The speeches of el Padre Mío, lacking any teleological aim in themselves, function as mimicry. With the aid of complicitous readers who accept this function of otherwise nonsensical language, his speeches succeed in debilitating those of the national father and acquire their function as testimony of the dictatorship. Eltit's use of citation is crucial. For instance, in the introduction, Eltit suggests that Padre Mío's speeches demand "habitar como testimonio, aunque en rigor su testimonio está desprovisto de toda información biográfica explícita. El mismo lo dice en una de sus partes: 'Pero debería de servir de testimonio yo. Hospitalario no puedo servir, porque ahí tienen empleada la táctica de la complicidad' " (Eltit 1989, 17–18) (to inhabit as testimony, although in fact his testimony is stripped of all explicit biographical information. He, himself, says it in one part: 'But I ought to serve as testimony. I cannot serve as the host, because there they have employed the tactic of complicity'). Eltit's decontextualization of his statement to serve the purposes of the interlocutor's problematic opening words is justified since all of el Padre Mío's speeches are out of context. In a sense, he suggests that she host his testimony. However, the distance between the artist's position advocating nomadism as an existential and political consciousness and el Padre Mío's experience of it "a la intemperie" (in the outdoors), is never discussed. In relation to Eltit's self-consciousness concerning own self-fashioning, *El padre mío* is more singular and domineering in its vision of cultural travel to the margins.

This realization leads to the following largely rhetorical question, of the sort that such a theoretical text elicits. Could there be a way to mediate el Padre Mío's loss of all explicit biographical information and his standing in for a powerful poetics of change through language? Unlike the mediation between the Quispe sisters' bodies and readers in "Nomadic Bodies," *El padre mío* fails to leave the gap between self and other open. Furthermore, like Domitila Barrios de Chungara and Moema Viezzar's *Si me permiten hablar: Testimonio de*

Domitila una mujer de las minas de Bolivia (1978) and Rigoberta Menchú and Elizabeth Burgos-Debray's *Me llamo Rigoberta Menchú y así me nació la conciencia* (1983), *El padre mío* begins with the voice of the *intermediaria* or interlocutor, the person who has taped the account. And like them, at least in Spanish-language versions, the witness does not share her authorial status, but becomes the agent that engenders a distinct interpretation of history. In an astute analysis of the relationship between author and object of narration, Ivette Malverde Disselkoen explains the significance of the title.

> desde su título el relato tiene múltiples sentidos. "Padre mío" alude, por una parte, al nombre que en el discurso de la "presentación" Diamela Eltit le otorga al esquizofrénico, por otra parte, mediante un desplazamiento, ese nombre designa en el discurso del esquizofrénico a la figura autoritaria en la que convergen los poderes sociales. Mediante la primera denominación puede plantearse que Diamela Eltit se constituye en la figura de una hija que posibilita la emergencia del discurso del padre que, víctima de la sociedad, ha sido marginado e impedido de decir "su verdad"por parte de la figura autoritaria que ha usurpado el poder y ha asumido el control social. (Malverde Disselkoen 1991, 70)
>
> [from its title the story has multiple meanings. "Father of mine" alludes, on the one hand, to the name that in the discourse of the "introduction" Diamela Eltit grants to the schizophrenic. "On the other hand, through a displacement, this name designates in the schizophrenic's discourse the authoritarian figure in which the social powers converge. Through the first denomination it is possible to establish that Diamela Eltit is constituted in the figure of the daughter that enables the emergence of the father's discourse that, victim of society, has been marginalized and impeded from saying "his truth" because of the authoritarian figure that has usurped the power and has assumed social control.]

The tape recordings of the schizophrenic reveal a way of putting meaning together that defies the patriarchal logic of the regime. By naming the book *El padre mío*, Eltit is able to double her existence. As Malverde Disselkoen explains, she is the author and the fictional daughter of the schizophrenic. Father engenders daughter, and in the process of the daughter enabling her father's narrative, the daughter achieves her own subjectivity as a marginalized author. In an interview with Sandra Garabano and Guillermo García-Corales, Eltit implemented the word "rescue" in relation to the discourse of the other: "me importó rescatar ese discurso del 'padre mío" (Rescuing this discourse from the father of mine was important to me) (Eltit 1992a, 71).

As he is stripped of a specific biography, *El padre mío* becomes literature. He exists only in connection to his daughter, a daughter who enables his mad discourse in order to encounter her own transgressive voice. Her version of the *testimonio* does not privilege his authenticity, but rather her specifically pure capacity to render his discourse.

While Eltit briefly comments on his unnamed status with respect to the material conditions of his daily life, this reference is strategic in the creation of an appropriate metaphor for the nation in which both a modernist aesthetic and Eltit, as its practitioner, are central. Unlike in her more obviously fictitious texts in which the intellectual's own making-up process is also emphasized, here all we see is her critique rendering el Padre Mío unspecific. "Aterrado en medio de un complot, el poder lo acechaba mortífero, convirtiéndolo en un sujeto que ya se había desprendido de todo, incluso de su nombre propio" (Terrified in the middle of a plot, deadly power watched him, converting him into a subject that had already given up everything, even his own name) (Eltit 1989, 15). In this passage, the interlocutor is likely so aware of her role in the organization of representation and factoring of truth that she does not need to delineate it. While Eltit's disavowal of "identitarian construction" has legitimate goals, it is impossible to ignore the complexity of the object's anonymity. That the text's principal concern is disciplinary—"Desde dónde recoger esta habla era la pregunta que principalmente me problematizaba" (From where to gather this speech was the question that principally was problematic to me) (Eltit 1989, 16)—creates a situation in which "the father of mine" is positioned as other to Eltit's disciplinary self-critique. Her introduction challenges what Richard calls "technical–ethical" discourse through the creation of a decentered literary one, while it also brilliantly retains the centrality of an empowered intellectual. In this gesture, what is contained rather than transgressed needs to be measured against the processes through which readers are legitimized, according to prescriptive definitions of complicity.

The claim made by Richard that *El padre mío* overturns the concept of the testimony as a vector of social conscience and of identity formation rooted in the act of a shared ethos is not entirely accurate, if we consider that complicity also perpetuates a version of uniformity (1994, 243). Eltit's framing and employment of irony in *Lumpérica* and *Por la patria* present allegories of vocation in which neither the intellectual figure nor the represented objects are whole and static, but *El padre mío*'s introduction is so tightly woven that the notion of there being no outside to representation backfires. In this equation in which the subject appropriates the object for her own purposes, contestation is made difficult. The introduction is yet another interpretative code that orders readership in such a way as to complicate questioning her critical approach. In that regard, we may cautiously draw a parallel between the sense of entitlement that pervades Eltit's relationship to her object of study and the empowerment that "faraway" publishers or critics acquire through their established notions of a cultural "here" or local space. This is to say that Eltit's representations of her own local and neighborhoodly dimensions confer authority upon her professional activity.

Eltit's self-fashioning as a Chilean writer during the Pinochet dictatorship entails resisting a set of assumptions about both nationalism and internationalism. It obliges her to retreat into spheres that may be cast as the most local—for instance, a photograph of her own body is placed within *Lumpérica* as a reminder of the necessity to consider materiality, over the transcendence of Pinochet's morality and the abstraction of cultural theory. Given this set of conditions, we engage the capacity for discrepant cosmopolitanism to negotiate the author's own theoretical stances and those of her national and international critics, suggesting that the outside not only informs Eltit's articulation of the local, but also broadens our interpretation of our own and her differentiatedness and complicity.

4

Face to Screen

"Authentic" is how Reinaldo Arenas's desire for liberation has been frequently described, in part, because of the depiction of individual experiences and expressions of beauty in his writings, which are often discordant with a model of collective experience that is upheld by the familiar and national spheres. Nevertheless, examining the manner that Arenas's writing renders a Cuban legacy as it also legitimizes links with other parts of the world complicates the characterization of its author as authentic. It is also possible to see this same "authenticity" as obliging Arenas into a cosmopolitanism particularly nuanced by his continued entanglement with Cuba. On a certain level, engaging cosmopolitanism with respect to Arenas emerges from a card dealt to him by the revolution whose influence on his formation was extensive. As a *becado*, an agricultural accounting student on scholarship at the University of Havana, Arenas was able to move from Holguín to Havana. His first residence in the city was nearby the university at the Hotel Habana Libre that, before the revolution, was called the Habana Hilton. Undoubtedly, his foray into the capital at the height of revolutionary enthusiasm had an immense impact upon his version of cosmopolitanism.

But the revolution, as we have seen, also impeded him from possessing his own reading constituency within the nation. Growing international recognition exacerbated Arenas's sense of himself as being fractured. Practically the only sphere left to him then was a form of cosmopolitanism that entailed publishing primarily abroad and acquiring a readership that was far from home. To the extent that Arenas's autobiography, along with several of his essays privilege an audience of non-Cubans, for instance, by explaining the meaning of particular vernacular words through their "standard" equivalent—for example, *guagua* to *colectivo* (meaning "bus," of which the equivalent does not occur in Eltit's work)—there are also other occasions when he refrains entirely from doing so. It is also possible to think of Arenas as if he were translating certain words to himself, as an exilic subject who is divided on two lands. The construction of himself as an "aparecido," a "shower-upper" or even as a phantom, relates to the split caused by his international repute and near national anonymity. The history of his novels' publication also attests to a "discrepant" or "nuanced" cosmopolitanism. Publishing abroad converted him into what he called in a 1985 interview with Lilianne Hasson "una bestia negra del sistema" "a black beast of the system" (1992b, 45). However, we cannot isolate this aspect of cosmopolitanism from less pleasing entanglements endured in exile.

The real-life identities of characters in *El color del verano* perplex many of its readers, especially those who are sufficiently informed in Cuban cultural politics to recognize several characters, but still trip over the vast majority. That older or more historical texts do not provoke anxiety in readers in the ways that contemporary ones, such as *El color del verano*, seem to, does not mean automatically that *El color del verano* is less difficult or less literary than its less inflammatory counterparts. Figuring out the role that the audience plays with regard to production of meaning in Arenas's texts requires interpreting specific passages that implicate diverse readers, in the large sense, of the revolution. In contrast to *El color del verano*, for instance, Arenas's essays do not account for a diversity of readers in that sense that they tend to project a singular, overdetermined, and more fixed voice upon them. They point toward an ideological complicity. *El color del verano*'s narrator continually pleads with readers, but recognizing oneself within its second-person singular "querida" (my dear) may not be that simple. The novel sets out characters in a manner more typical of post-Stonewall Act-up politics in the United States than Cuban cultural politics. To top it off, the narrator negotiates outing readers, by addressing them with a term of homosexual camaraderie, "querida." Even if readers resist being provisionally "outed" by Arenas for the duration of this novel and instead prefer to take it as a code map for those "in the know," they may direct their attention to distinct levels of Arenas's rebellion carried out exclusively through those merging of identities as we saw in chapter 2. Nevertheless, the novel is incessantly involved in the question of reception, continually representing Cuba as being read from the outside. The nation's leader is obsessed with the international interpreters and cameramen who will record and transmit the revolution abroad. In the end, the key to Fifo's attraction to those more supposedly ideological players are the economic fruits they may bear on Cuba. There are also the more capitalist hackers. The nuances of the invitees to Fifo's grand party are especially perplexing to the narrator since, among heads of state, are the Spanish publishers Alfaguara, but not Siglo XXI (Arenas 1991, 134). In this way, the novel comments on the high marketability of the revolution and about the nature of its diverse benefactors. Beyond Arenas's dubious vision of Sarduy's cosmopolitanism, Arenas's figuration of his contemporary relies heavily on his knowledge of the politics of publishing and the courtships that they entailed. These negotiations are not too distant from the more general discussion of how the novel regards the process of making oneself and selling literature. The aesthetic technique utilized in *El color del verano* of partitioning the principal protagonist into three illustrates the extent to which the writer is involved in the material aspects of the world. One of the narrators is named Reinaldo. A continually decentered position is executed through his narrations of another part of the character—the more contained Gabriel and yet another—the even more sexual and in-your-face "Skunk-in-a-Funk." In addition to the multiple interpreters of the revolution, Arenas brings into this novel a protagonist who is able to comment on distinct aspects of his own character. This liberating multiplicity, I must say, is virtually absent from most of his essays, where a centralized authorial position is the model for a unified audience that refuses to perceive the nuances of political struggles.

Studying Arenas today from the United States entails questioning the critical tactics of cosmopolitanism that we also embrace, and also entails being attuned to the consequences of our critical acts elsewhere in the world. Construed out of multiplicity as opposed to polarized unification, this perspective considers the implications of returning to one of the gloomiest periods in Cuba before another particularly complicated one. In the name of increasing terrorism, in the twenty-first century there has been an increased repression of dissent, in both the United States (post-Stonewall and post–9/11) and in Cuba (post-Soviet bloc). A discrepant cosmopolitanism addressing Latin American literature insists on bracketing political and historical contexts in order to assess the value of art objects, their inheritance, and their contribution to the literary canon. The publicized incursions on human rights in Cuba in the spring of 2003, including the murder of three Cubans after they hijacked the Regla ferry and the harsh sentencing of eighty "dissident" journalists, lead to a most general questioning of intent: "What is Castro doing?" and the rationalization, "Why is he doing it?" On the part of intellectuals, there is demand to condemn publicly, but in the aftermath of such diverse events as the U.S. invasion of Iraq, the United States' own negligence toward human rights in the name of protecting its citizenry from terrorism in Guantánamo, among other places, its Homeland Securities Act, and the approach that the U.S. Interest Section in Cuba took with its 2002 appointment of James Cason, as the Chief of Mission at the U.S. Interests Section in Cuba, this condemnation gets muddled. Such muddling is not particularly new, as the last four decades have illustrated. It is indubitable that, through these exceptional yet nearly habitual circumstances, the enemies have and continue to pop up everywhere.[1] In the act of interpreting events as either forms of crisis or endemic to the system, there are significant political consequences demanding that we keep our eyes on multiple parties at once: the supposed instigators, the victims, and those who just refrain from formulating opinions.

As even literary history points out, the resemblance between enemies is acute. For example, reflecting on the experience of exile in the United States from a former Communist country in an essay entitled "Alchemy," Croatian writer Dubravka Ugresic suggests that what breeds socialist realism and how-to-books in innumerable quantities in diverse market economies is the same desire for progress and instruction. Arenas's appeal lies somewhere else, residing in aesthetic and political practices that contrast sharply with socialist realism and how-to-books; yet, we must not overlook the most controversial aspects of this divisive figure: his outspoken and not always pleasing affiliations on national and international levels, conveyed through his fiction, essays, and interviews. Arenas's writing begs readers to consider multiple spheres at once—few are bereft of his critical gaze and in this way, even this writer who positions himself in opposition to innumerable categories—anti-Castro, antisocialist realist, anticapitalist—"instructs" us in the messiness, joy, and disagreeability of cosmopolitan perspectives.

For an exile, Arenas is not exceptional in terms of the exuberant centrality that his homeland plays in determining his worldview. Stated simply in nonliterary terms of one of the exilic and domino-playing characters in New York City of Orlando Jiménez Leal's film *El Super*—"El problema de Cuba es un problema del mundo" (The problem of Cuba is a world problem). While such a statement could logically be applied to any number of nations without it being subject to the accusation of being overly chauvinistic, in the case of Cuba, the crucial part that the island has played in global politics over the past century, but especially since 1959, is clear. But, it is not necessary to move so far away from the literary sphere to engage a similar mentality. In a somewhat cynical and argumentative tone that sounds like the less typically scholarly dimensions of the topic at hand, Wilfrido Corral wrestles with Arenas's self-positioning vis-à-vis that of Uruguayan exile and critic Ángel Rama. Corral speaks as an insider. He states that having worked at the Center for Inter-American Relations (later called the Americas Society), the institute that published *Review*, when Arenas was a writer-in-residence there, he knew the author. Corral suggests that what became bothersome to Arenas about Rama was really more a facet of Arenas's involvement with a New Jersey Cuban contingency who was connected to "la parte de la comunidad exiliada cubana más intransigente y organizada desde focos de la Florida y Nueva Jersey" (the most intransigent and organized part of the Cuban exile community in Florida and New Jersey) for whom the author became a pawn for some time (Corral 1999, 175). In *Antes que anochezca*, Arenas's angered perception of Rama emerges as a result of his article "Arenas al ostracismo" that describes the Cuban's exit as a governmental mix-up whereby one day, Arenas was asked to leave the country by one office and the next, was asked to stay by another. Rather than focus on Rama's positive comments, the autobiographic passage reveals a skewed interpretation of Rama's use of the word "ostracism" to affirm the Uruguayan as a blind supporter of the revolution. In fact, one of the only critics who escapes Arenas's accusation of hypocrisy is the great promoter of the boom of Latin American letters, Emir Rodríguez Monegal, who has been himself associated with the CIA through the journal *Mundo Nuevo*.[2] After interpreting Rama as a new breed of dangerous communist and his article as a personal insult, Arenas is outraged by Luis Harss's suggestion that Fidel Castro "podría ser un símbolo de 'identidad hemisférica' de la talla de Bolívar o Martí" (may be a symbol of hemispheric identity with the magnitude of Bolívar or Martí) in a special issue on exilic Latin American literature of *Review* overseen by Rama (Corral 1999, 177). Corral suggests that Arenas's bumpkin-like nature made him easy terrain upon which to play out such politics. The impact of Arenas's critique of *Review* on the publication was fierce, and is said to have resulted in the fact that, between 1981 and 1983, *Review* ceased publication.[3]

As revealed by his numerous affiliations with universities and institutions primarily in the United States cited on his curriculum vitae, Arenas may not have been as distant from the centers of U.S. cultural institutions as his textual selves portray him to be.[4] As we have seen in chapter 2, Arenas's simultaneous scrutiny of the local sociopolitical and cultural dynamics and his search for potentially liberating figures and ideas whether they be inside or outside of the nation reveals the degree to which his writing travails multiple and conflicting affiliations. To exclusive and traditional conceptions of the term *cosmopolitan* previously elaborated upon, this figure adds "contradictory." Roberto González Echevarría, for instance, differentiates between Arenas and those Latin American writers of the boom who are "highly educated, cosmopolitan and multilingual" on the basis of Arenas's fascination "by the infinite: by the sea, the stars, the expanses of the mind. He was always testing himself against such unreachable horizons. In his private life, erotic passion drove him to probe the limits of the social and the political" (González Echevarría 1993b, 33).[5] As this statement suggests, cosmopolitanism and pedigree are often thought of as indistinguishable, and, as such, even when his writing reveals a vast literary knowledge and even knowledge of French, Arenas remains that *guajiro* who was educated by the revolution.

In the 1993 review of the English translation of *Antes que anochezca*, González Echevarría also focuses on what has turned out to be one of the more controversial claims in the autobiography about homosexuals in the United States, whose habits of pairing were boring on account of prevailing equality. For Arenas, the overall queerness of the Anglo-American gay community led to the rather dull interchangeability of "masculine" and "feminine" roles: "todo se ha regularizado de tal modo que han creado grupos y sociedades donde es muy difícil para un homosexual encontrar un hombre; es decir, el verdadero objeto de su deseo" (Arenas 1992a, 132) (everything here is so regulated that groups and societies have been created in which it is very difficult for a homosexual to find a man, that is, the real object of his desire) (Arenas 1993a, 107, trans. Koch). And later he continues: "Al no existir estas divisiones, lo interesante del homosexualismo en Cuba consistía en que no había que ser un homosexual para tener relaciones con un hombre" (Arenas 1992a, 133) (the interesting aspect of homosexuality was that you did not have to be a homosexual to have a relationship with a man) (Arenas 1993a, 108, trans. Koch). Placing the concepts of risk and community on opposite poles of a spectrum of identity is frequently how critics contend with the conflict triggered by Arenas's perception of identity politics. However, this tendency reflected in González Echevarría's "Arenas saw in sexuality, as in writing, a way to freedom, but a freedom conceived in risk rather than community" fails to grasp that, like the concepts of cosmopolitanism and ruralism, risk and community can complicatedly coexist (González Echevarría 1993b, 33).[6] While, for readers in the post-Stonewall United States, it may seem obvious that Arenas is blind to the way dominant models regulate his own understanding of homosexuality—a blindness that is not apparently shared by the young kissing girls outside of the military academy in the wake of the millennium, that does not mean that no model of community can be harbored from his writing.

Arenas contrasts the tedium of sexual relations in exile with the excitement and gratification of them in Cuba. While Arenas speculates that this boredom is related to the United States' being an advanced society that encourages a separate community of homosexuals, he does not negate entirely some of the positive aspects of homosexuals' forming separate communities. "La militancia homosexual ha dado otros derechos que son formidables para los homosexuales del mundo libre, pero también ha atrofiado el encanto maravilloso de encontrarse con una persona heterosexual o bisexual" (Arenas 1992a, 133). (Homosexual militancy has gained considerable rights for free-world gays. But what has been lost is the wonderful feeling of meeting heterosexual or bisexual men) (Arenas 1993a, 108, trans. Koch). The cosmopolitan sense of belonging toward which Arenas's writing gestures entails the ability of appealing to the rights of an already recognized community in a manner that does not limit individuals' pleasures. What is certain is that neither individual rights nor collective well-being is sufficient for a person to experience a sense of liberating pleasure. With regard to this problematic, Brad Epps suggests that both Arenas and the Spanish exile Juan Goytisolo "indicate the risky freedom of gay identity," but that the Cuban's personal experiences as a detainee impeded him from "vindicating the signs of gay identity at the level of community" (Epps 1996, 416). Fraught with fear toward the centralizing power of community and anger at having been excluded from it, Arenas "risks" imagining a community especially in *El color del verano*. Collapsing Arenas's difficulty with community into authenticity, rootlessness, or ruthless individualism ignores the connections forged by Arenas, often in an extremely eccentric and exaggerated fashion, with a cast of characters, some more recognized within Cuban cultural history than others. These often negatively construed social bonds are coated with such cynicism, satire, and spite toward authoritarianism and provincialism that they are more difficult to detect.

Lest we foresee the coincidence of risk and community, we subject Arenas to further reductive mechanisms. On the one hand, enough of an actual community is exacted by Arenas's writing that, for some time now, exilic acquaintances and friends have dedicated collections of essays to the study of the author and his work, but, on the other, there has been a lag in the inclusion of such a discussion in collections of distinct thematics pertaining to the Caribbean, exiles, gays, queers, and even to the Russian linguist and critic Mikhail Bakhtin.[7] Continually seeking to unite that which is excluded from social, political, and cultural spheres, Arenas aggressively clamors on about how particular writers betray a concept of self by forging affiliations within dominant communities in order to enhance their status in the world. Specific geographic locales do not fare any better than the vast array of characters symbolizing this facile union for the sake of a linear conceptualization of "betterment." Three cities, in particular, besides Havana, figure prominently in his imagination because they house and consolidate particular dubious characteristics: Paris—the old "cosmopolitan capital" that helped to save Arenas's second novel *El mundo alucinante* from oblivion by publishing it in French and awarding it the prize for best foreign novel—is also where Cuban writer Severo Sarduy is transformed into an international success, and as such, is a kowtowing superstar in Arenas's eyes. Le Seuil, in a metonymic relation to Paris, is frowned upon. Miami—the new Latino mecca, that other face of Havana, falls under special attack and, as if in a mad brushstroke, is a provincial battleground uniting the most barbarous elements from the island. Then there is New York City, a place that he viewed as "much more cosmopolitan than [. . .] American" and much less asphyxiating than Miami, but it was also boring, inequitable, and hypocritical—characteristics that were exaggerated by Arenas's suffering from AIDS (Arenas 1982b, 60). We must question the lack of this sort of conflictive historical information in Julian Schnabel's biopic of the author, *Before Night Falls* (2000), at the same time that we may recognize its valuable function within the national Cuban sphere.

Salvage Ethnography

The link between salvage ethnography and the *testimonio* genre, as described by Amy Fass Emery, rests on a shared "necrological" intent to represent the "other" in the moment prior to its disappearance (Emery 1996, 15). Like the interlocutor of *testimonios* that focuses on disappearing populations, the ethnographer approaches an object of representation with the knowledge that what is alive today will tomorrow be an artifact of a distant past. While the object of representation of Schnabel's film, *Before Night Falls*, died ten years prior to the release of the biopic loosely based on his autobiography, this association of salvage ethnography and *testimonio* still has important echoes in my analysis of the film and in the "fables of intimacy" that circumscribe the author (Emery 1996, 20). Emery explains "fables of intimacy" in the context of discussing José María Arguedas, Darcy Ribeiro, and Miguel Barnet: "All three of these writers, trained as anthropologists, have written fables of intimacy that authorize them to speak of the Other, not as detached social scientists, but as Selves intimately involved with the Others they represent" (Emery 1996, 20). We may see these "fables" as a subset of "allegories of vocations," and as such they are of particular interest for elaborating an ethical cosmopolitanism. Bringing *Before Night Falls* into the context of salvage ethnography and *testimonio*, the genre for which the Cuban cultural institution Casa de las Américas established a prize in 1970, is complicated further by outsiders' fascination with the inside of a Cuban world that is supposedly set off from time's corrosive effects.

As U.S. citizens grow weary of the increasing restrictions that their government places on travel, their craving intensifies to experience firsthand what the rest of the world has been enjoying but they have only glimpsed, most recently in a paradigmatic film of salvage ethnography, in Wim Wenders's *The Buena Vista Social Club* (1999). A significant component of the analysis of a cosmopolitan appropriation (postmortem) of Arenas obliges us not only to look at the limits within geographical space, but how the Internet is capable of reforming visions of blocked-off territories. In this case, the Internet's effect on Arenas resoundingly transforms our notion of how he inhabits local and global spaces.

How do the filmic Arenas and the literary Arenas relate to the scholarly academy, the film industry, and post-Soviet Cuba, one of the last vestiges of an ideological dream? To answer this question I consider diverse narratives of affiliation with and representations of Arenas. This discussion will allow us to ask, more specifically, how a Hollywoodian rendition of hope disguises itself within the framework of independent film. By examining the coordinates of authenticity, male sexuality, and language in Schnabel's film, we can illuminate the ways in which less formal strategies of pedagogy, which include DVD commentary tracks and the Internet, transform the patrimony of Arenas in distinct international spheres.

Risking with Arenas

Schnabel might appreciate narratives of loss, but he did not "rescue Arenas for the world," as Philip Weiss (Weiss 2001, 68) described it in his *New York Times Magazine* article "Julian Schnabel's Lust for Life." What stands out in this passage is not a cosmopolitanism, in the sense of the cosmetic "making up" the world, but rather his feeling implies an imposition of his own will. The heroic dimensions of the Weiss/Schnabel narrative are captured in the heading on the article's first page: "Big." The director's words on the commentary track of *Before Night Falls* uphold a "fable of intimacy" that, in turn, supports Weiss's assessment. In decorating his project with undertones of war-like heroism, Schnabel gives in to a globalizing narrative that he conceives his individual craft to be stubborn enough to resist. The principal terms in tension that impact our understanding of cosmopolitanism in this context are not, as they were with our previous examination of Arenas, "country" and "city," or with Eltit, "international" and "hybrid," but rather "globalizing" and "independent." Who comprises the world for which Schnabel believes he has rescued the Cuban writer, who died little more than a decade ago? Is it the film critics who, having admittedly never heard of Arenas before the film, dismiss him as less talented than the painter Jean-Michel Basquiat, the subject of Schnabel's 1996 film? Is it the New York artists whose creative tourism had somehow sidestepped Arenas? Or is it perhaps the multiplex cinemas that favor Hollywood, leaving screens for a handful of independent productions? Schnabel's world diminishes the contributions of those who for many years have read Arenas in Spanish as well as in French, German, Portuguese, and in English translations. Rendered by Andrew Hurley, Dolores M. Koch, Alfred MacAdam, and Gordon Brotherston, and published by Viking/Penguin, Grove, and Harper and Row, these translations have served to acquaint Anglophone readers with Arenas's writing.

This is to say that while the culture industry promoting Arenas has benefited immensely from Schnabel's "big" contributions, it already existed when the New York artist/director stumbled on the subject matter. *Before Night Falls*, a digital dance film choreographed by Johannes Birringer (with the AlienNation Company), inspired by Arenas's autobiography, explores memories of sexual encounters as well as the roles that "displacement/exile, family, and sexuality play in the constructions and rememberings of national and individual identity" (Birringer, "Information Pack" 1998). Parts of the digital performance installation, *Before Night Falls*, showed in festivals in 1997 in Dresden, Atlanta, and Cleveland, and in 1998 in Houston at the Diverse Works Performance Space. Prior to that production, Birringer directed *Lovers Fragments/Fragmentos de enamorados* (1996), a multimedia performance that explores the homoerotic writings of Arenas and Roland Barthes. *Lovers Fragments* premiered as a film at the Casa de las Américas in Havana on December 22, 1995, a fact that may come as a surprise to those who claim that the Cuban Revolution does not permit open infractions (and who thus betray a lack of understanding of the nuances of exposure and concealment with which the revolution is sustained). The performance is a "meditation on sexual ecstasy, loss and reintegration in a time of great uncertainty and convulsion over questions of sexual and national identity" (Birringer, "Information Pack" 1996). Due to the difficulty of pieces, they appeal to a specialized audience. Yet their presence within an expanding archive of creative works referencing Arenas must not be ignored. In Jaime Manrique's 1999 book *Eminent Maricones: Arenas, Lorca, Puig, and Me (Living Out, Gay and Lesbian Autobiographies)*, an encounter between Manrique and Arenas serves as a point of departure for the author to speak about himself. Similarly, in *A la sombra del mar: Jornadas cubanas con Reinaldo Arenas*, Juan Abreu draws on a complicity with Arenas to talk of an epoch of repression, despair, and creativity. As literary critics have been fascinated with Arenas's texts over the past three decades, so have artists recently desired to make their affiliations with Arenas known to distinct worlds.

Before the film's release, Arenas's name could be found on many different Internet sites. Search engines, these contemporary tools of discovery still utilized more widely in economically privileged societies, sometimes accentuate the differences between margin and center, but they also have the effect of "deperipheralizing" certain phenomena. While the latter was perhaps not the case with Arenas, the many virtual sitings of him, from "Books about Entheogens and the Psychedelic Experience" to a list of names of "Famous or Distinguished Gays, Lesbians, Bisexuals" suggest that his patrimony was not in imminent danger of vanishing before the film, though it may have been at risk of being misunderstood.[8] For instance, seemingly based on its title alone, the first English translation of Arenas's *El mundo alucinante (Hallucinations: Being an Account of the Life and Adventures of Friar Servando Teresa de Mier*, (1971), is placed on a list of books about psychedelic experiences. The unusual "Google" discoveries are not unique to Arenas. As David Hochman (2004) suggests in "In

Searching We Trust," the margin of error in "Google" is high. To the librarian of Congress's remark that "it is a gateway to . . . unintelligible material," Hochman adds that its "own role in the zeitgeist is still indeterminable." These dimensions are important to keep in mind as we analyze the Internet's role in the passage through distinct niches of cultural objects from "far-away" places. Culture on the Internet is not so much fenced in, but continually remade, making it sometimes difficult to determine the distance between "us" and "them." Of course, the presence of Arenas in the world was not limited to the several hundred URLs, but rather extended to diverse cultural spheres. Although Arenas may not have been as internationally illustrious as fellow exile Guillermo Cabrera Infante (and the Cubans Cabrera Infante, Severo Sarduy, and Alejo Carpentier were never as known as the Colombian Gabriel García Márquez, icon of the boom of Latin American letters, or even the Argentine Jorge Luis Borges), he was not about to perish either.[9]

However, by ignoring those somewhat conceptually distant predecessors, using a rhetoric that shrinks the world, Schnabel is able to secure his status in it as an outsider. Schnabel's statement "I watch a movie like 'Castaway' and I want to commit hara-kiri," which appeared on the cover of the *New York Times Magazine*, creates a frenzy based on a gut desire, which, in turn, speaks to readers' fears of homogenization. If they are not yet aware of their anxiety, the narrative awakens in them this dormant sensation. Schnabel steps in to resist a globalized world of fast cultural demise wielding a somewhat passé bold masculinity combined with artistic integrity. Although the end is legitimate, the heroic narrative with which it is realized still participates in a definition of risk in terms of potential financial loss that does not converge with the definition of risk of the subject matter. The *New York Times* article states:

> Schnabel takes his self-belief to the next level, by staking his money on the project. He told me he had been financially responsible for "the whole nut" on both his movies, without going into detail, though it is said that he sold one of his early plate paintings to help finance *Before Night Falls*.
> He risked personal money, and to me that means a lot, says the independent producer John Pierson. (Weiss 2001, 48)

Schnabel "risks" his own money and, with the staged resistance of an outsider who is almost an underdog, succeeds in making the story of this Cuban writer known to many worlds.

The film has resulted in the proliferation of the figure of Arenas and, in the process, the opening of well-deserved spaces for Arenas's narrative within distinct canons of literature. Whether or not the film challenges perceptions and sensibility, the main effect of Arenas's subversive sense of carnival, is less clear. Rather than elicit a mathematically accurate response, this question delves into the complex process by which the figure grows in stature in a more elaborate culture industry that depends on the manufacturing of authenticity to sustain commodification and standardization.[10] The more general role that sex and violence play within mainstream cultural circuits in the United States is well known; but the relationship of images of male sexuality to capitalism and globalization is a more specific topic that requires investigation. It is interesting to relate the treatment of sexuality and nudity in this U.S. independent film to Paul Julian Smith's critique of the Cuban film *Fresa y chocolate*, directed by Tomás Gutiérrez Alea and Juan Carlos Tabío. Smith argues: "Reinaldo Arenas' *Before Night Falls* (recently published in English) . . . also manifests a shameless delight in gay sex with the most diverse partners and in the most unlikely circumstances . . . It is a pity that Alea's dour Diego is not allowed even a glimmer of Arenas' defiantly proud eroticism. And to argue that we should not expect too much from the first film with a gay theme from Castro's Cuba is to be ignorant of the history of Spanish-speaking cinema" (Smith 1994, 32). For Smith, *Fresa y chocolate* is "irredeemably bourgeois" due to the absence of pleasure (1994, 33). While ideologues' inability to restrict entirely the grandeur of creativity is evident in Schnabel's *Before Night Falls*, the proud eroticism that strikes at the fundamentals of social systems, for which productivity is everything, is less visible. Keenly aware of independent film viewers' threshold for representations of the erotic, *Before Night Falls* simultaneously plays into a dominant model of globalizing society, carves out a negligible space from which it resists that model, and reenacts the same process that it purports to critique.

In conveying the cultural and political dimensions of Schnabel's consolidation and diminution of a writer, it is difficult to avoid thoroughly a sort of "fidelity criticism" that demands that film be faithful to the literary text and ignores the contingencies of a different artistic medium (Naremore 2000, 9).[11] Such a practice of seeking unmediated truths—in autobiography, of all places—would run seriously counter to the Arenian questioning of the construction of authenticity. The selection of "raw material" for filmic rendering is particularly precarious in light of the fact that Arenas's oeuvre has been either cast aside or promoted by critics for its autobiographical nature and "almost symbiotic relation to his life" (Negrín 1997, 48). The multiple textual Arenases problematize the hierarchies of singularity, originality, and authenticity set forth in Schnabel's film.

Hope and High Art

Unlike most other scenes in the film, which only hint briefly at the function of hyperbole in Arenas's life, the failed attempt to escape in a hot air balloon gives the spectator several minutes to zoom in on one character's singular desire for liberation and to hear his continual laughter as he rises though the roof and over the buildings of Havana, full of hope, only to crash pathetically into the seawall at the Malecón. While the attempted flight of Arenas's combative friend Pepe Malas has no referent in Arenas's narration of the ransacking and discovery that took place at the Santa Clara convent, the film's union of massive colors—the green of the trees, the blue of the sky and the sea, and the grays of the convent seen from above—alludes to Arenas's carnivalesque aesthetic. Mirroring Pepe's limited upward mobility in chapter 22 are Lázaro's and Reinaldo's mobile gazes up at the skyscrapers in the New York City snow of chapter 24, which is titled "Stateless," and is the first sequence after their departure from Cuba in the Mariel boatlift.[12] The provincial anomalies of the sort that Miami is infamous for provoking have the potential to disrupt these emotional scenes of "universal" hope. Absent from Schnabel's film, then, are Arenas's Miami-focused ad hominem complaints that could ingratiate or alienate a wider audience, tired of Elián González, and arouse a more involved Cuban community within the United States. That the Havana/New York mirroring offers a great contrast, on an aesthetic level, cannot be doubted, but at the same time, the juxtaposition at least tentatively conforms to a more comfortable and familiar age-old "American" (Hollywood/New York) narrative of personal liberation, implicitly connected to upward advancement.

Schnabel's "independent" film also breaks up the homogeneity of Hollywood as it participates in the commodification and standardization of the sort I've just described. In light of this tension, we may consider the efficacy of "high art" in slowing down the leveling effects of globalization. With an aesthetic code that is difficult to penetrate, the performance of Birringer's AlienNation dance company might be said to undermine global homogeneity, with its discrepant cosmopolitanism, but, in reality, it does little to present Arenas to Schnabel's "world." The albeit limited circulation of an art object such as AlienNation's *Before Night Falls* is facilitated by the Worldwide Web. The director posts an e-mail address, and those interested in obtaining the products must negotiate with their creator. One must struggle to know AlienNation, rather than simply be handed the art object. The "bigness" or relative commercialization of Schnabel's independent film stands in stark contrast to the limited audience of the cryptic performance piece. By Hollywood standards, however, the relatively slow-paced, picturesque *Before Night Falls*, written by Cunningham O'Keefe, Lázaro Gómez Carriles, and Schnabel, might share an inkling of this status.

After the 1993 release of the autobiography *Before Night Falls* in English, sales of Arenas's novels picked up somewhat in North America.[13] According to Penguin editor Stephen M. Morrison (2001), before the film, Penguin Putnam sold somewhere in the range of twenty-five thousand copies of *Before Night Falls* in paperback. As a direct tie to the film, the cover has been redesigned and thirty-five thousand more copies are in print. *Before Night Falls* was on several regional and independent bookstore bestseller lists in the winter and spring of 2001. The other books in the *pentagonía* have also seen their stock rise. For example, between 1995 and 2000, Penguin Putnam sold a little over four thousand copies of *The Assault*. Between January and August of 2001, however, it sold around fifteen hundred copies of that same title. Schnabel seems to have taken on a sort of larger-than-life godfather role.[14] Thanks to him, the sustained confidence of people like the current president of Penguin, and then vice-president of the Viking division, Kathryn Court, in the ability of Arenas's oeuvre to overcome "obscurity" appears to have been vindicated.

According to the worldwide box office statistics *Before Night Falls* grossed $4.2 million in North America and $4.5 million worldwide; most critics have given the film positive reviews. It showed at festivals in Italy and Canada and was released in cinemas in the United States, Spain, Argentina, Brazil, Colombia, France, the United Kingdom, German-speaking Switzerland, the Czech Republic, and Israel. It won the Grand Jury prize at the Venice International Film Festival and was nominated for best feature at the sixteenth annual IFP/West Independent Spirit Awards Ceremony. The lead actor, Javier Bardem, was nominated for an Oscar.

Increasingly in the past decade, different media, with diverse target audiences, cultivate desire for Cuba all too easily. The cover of Michi

Strausfeld's anthology, *Cubanismo! Junge Erzähler aus Kuba*, pays homage to one common thread, with a pinup girl lounging on top of an antique automobile. While the cover of the Spanish version is seemingly less sensationalist, its shadowy image of a child pulling on a fence still appeals in a different manner to a market yearning to feel the allusive and somehow innocent and entrapped Cuba. The fact that we can't distinguish the child's features suggests that there are many more such images on an island whose appeal is shaped by its status as the last bastion of communism, by its globally enticing leader, its citizens' distance from the rest of the world, and its tropical climate whose fruits, embargoed U.S. citizens, especially, can only enjoy while being there.

Iván de la Nuez's discussion of the symbolic landscape of Cuba explores the ways the island has been conceptualized and marketed for distinct publics:

> Hoy Calibán—el mito poético de hace unas décadas—se ha convertido en el actor de un parque temático llamado Cuba, el habitante oportuno de ese abrevadero de nostalgias—de izquierdas y derechas, del *son* primigenio y del Ché Guevara, del Cabaret y la Sierra Maestra, del *Paradiso* de Lezama Lima y de la masa de puerco en los paladares—en que se ha convertido la isla. (Nuez 1999, 167)

> [Today Caliban—the poetic myth of several decades ago—has turned into an actor in a theme park called Cuba, into the witty inhabitant of this watering trough of nostalgias—of the left and the right, of the original *son* and of Ché Guevara, of the Cabaret and the Sierra Maestra, of Lezama Lima's *Paradiso* and of the slabs of pork in the *paladares*—that the island has become.]

What pleases the "highbrow" consumer need not excite the "middlebrow" one, as Cuba offers a spectrum of attractions. This version of the island nation is appropriately packaged for what Stuart Hall has referred to as the "global postmodern," a trend that, entailing "homogenization and absorption, and then plurality and diversity," cultivates a taste for multiplicity and difference that is controlled and limited by transnational corporations (Hall 1997, 34).[15] However, Hall also describes similar processes on the margins where increasingly "new subjects, new genders, new ethnicities, new regions, new communities, hitherto excluded from the major forms of cultural representation" threaten "discourses of power" (Hall 1997, 34).

In deciding where the film falls in this spectrum of multiplicity and limits, it is interesting to consider the resonance of Schnabel's sophisticated and painterly rendering of this Cuban "poet"—a portrayal that at times seems outside this dominant media culture and at others participates in its tropes. I say "poet" here because, in the more than seven thousand related Web sites I scanned through, that is how Arenas is frequently described. And, while his writing is certainly poetic, the word choice is surprising, since he has published far more prose than verse.[16] *Poet*, in the *Webster's Dictionary* sense of "maker," of "creative artist of great imaginative and expressive gifts and special sensitivity to his medium" is entirely conceivable, but still, using this term harks back to a time or space where poetry was of more importance. To begin to "prove" the impact of this categorization of *poet*, I add that in my exchanges with U.S. university students, the first statement regarding Arenas that they most frequently utter is: "Oh, I thought he was a poet" or "That poet?" The defamiliarization that accompanies *poet* links Arenas to an ideal plane of artistic plenitude in the form of individual liberation. Because of this, since on a romantic level, I like poets, it is somewhat difficult for me to consider the poet with respect to culture industries, but it is also because of this that I think it essential to do so. AOL/FineLine/Time Warner distributed the $8 million "independent" film. Many independent filmmakers hope for such a coexistence wherein their own "independent" creative expression pleases media conglomerates enough to ensure their products' adequate distribution.[17] In the case of *Before Night Falls*, for instance, the president of Fine Line Features, Mark Ordesky, mounted a "no-holds-barred campaign to score an upset at the Academy for Javier Bardem" (Weiss 2001, 84). While Bardem's performance was superb, how *Before Night Falls* expands the possibilities of cultural expression, ruptures different audiences' horizons of expectations, and falls into or sets aside dominant models of appropriating the margins remains to be seen.

Accommodating Sex and Language

In the oft-quoted and critiqued "The Work of Art in the Age of Mechanical Reproduction," Walter Benjamin (1969b, published in German in 1936) writes on the liberating potential of film to release art from its auratic function. The *testimonio* genre, according to Alberto Moreiras, shares with film this potential. Like other forms of reproduction, film enables people to access a history that, to paraphrase John Berger, the clerks of culture had kept previously behind glass. It is in this context that Miguel Riera's indictment of Arenas's representation of his sexuality in *Antes que anochezca* is fascinating: "Reinaldo . . . nos restriega la cara con su homosexualidad" (Reinaldo . . . rubs his homosexuality in our face) (Riera 1992, 59). For this critic, the autobiography is a sort of "desfile sexual" (sexual parade). If we take this reaction to be symbolic of Arenas's provocation, we have to ask ourselves whether the Arenas figure of the film retains this "in-your-face" quality, to a point of deterring readers of *Antes que anochezca* from feeling solidarity with him. It is difficult to speak of "in-your-faceness" in this context without bringing up prosopopeia, what Paul de Man refers to as the "trope of autobiography, by which one's name . . . is made as intelligible and memorable as a face" (1984, 76). Directly linked to studies of ethics and *testimonio*, prosopopeia, as defined by Moreiras, foregrounds the pain and loss that are involved in speaking for the other: "Prosopopeia refers to a mask through which one's own voice is projected onto another, where that other is always suffering from a certain inability to speak. The relational mediation is then always unequal and hierarchical, even at its most redemptive" (Moreiras 1996, 210).

Granting the other a face is key to textual and filmic autobiography. The urgency within *Antes que anochezca* results from the subject's energy to live, knowing that soon he will be overtaken by death. The unusual juxtaposition of "Introducción: El fin" rapidly informs the reader of that condition. Propelling this initial passage forward are prosopopoeia and apostrophe of the late writer Virgilio Piñera. By turning to Piñera ("le hablé de este modo" [Arenas 1992a, 16]; (I spoke to him in this way) [Arenas 1993a, xvii, trans. Koch]) and pleading for time to finish his story, the autobiographer suggests an internal audience whose complicity is grounded in common defense of Piñera, a homosexual who was officially silenced after his 1961 prognostication of a frightening Cuban future.[18] Although the initial passage's immediacy is paralleled in the film's first chapter, the film never grants Piñera such significance; rather, he is depicted as an almost anonymous remnant of a more artistically liberated time.[19] Arenas's own affiliations are demoted in favor of the perception of him as a natural artist.

The camera first focuses on the trees and sky above, a mother carrying a child, and then, finally, to an unclothed boy alone in a dirt hole but bathed in light. The camera moves away and then focuses on that hole, in which the child can no longer be seen. The hole, to which the camera returns before the film's final credits, foreshadows the obscurity and the tomb that looms over the autobiographer. The first spectacular and emotional scene contrasting the illuminated baby and the dark surroundings is one of discovery. The human face is present in both text and film. One of the film's challenges, however, is to sustain this visual "in-your-faceness" as the protagonist ages and becomes sexually active. How this "in-your-faceness" is to be interpreted is ambiguous and largely dependent on whose face the Arenian filmic image is projected toward. Some audiences might turn away, but those who would respond to these images in this way would probably not chose to see the film in the first place.

Antes que anochezca's subversive content is subdued, in part, due to the contingencies of film, and more specifically, because of those related to autobiography, as identified by Elizabeth Bruss. Film "disrupts the 'act value' necessary for autobiography [because, in part], where the rules of language designate a single source, film has instead a disparate group of distinct roles and separate stages of production" (Bruss 1980, 304). *Before Night Falls* is a negotiation among Schnabel, his crew, Lázaro Gómez Carriles, and the other multiple screens through which the director comes to know Arenas, a fact that is important to recall in considering the film's relation to an ideologically complex autobiography that, according to Emilio Bejel, significantly ruptures readers' horizons of expectation:

> Además de una infinidad de contactos sexuales de todo tipo: como el bestialismo y el incesto, en cuanto a la homosexualidad, narra tan numerosos y prodigiosos encuentros que el protagonista-narrador llega a decir que para principios de la década del setenta él estimaba haber tenido relaciones sexuales con unos cinco mil hombres. Lo que prefiero subrayar, . . . es, por un lado, el grado de ruptura que significa la declaración de tan espectacular actividad sexual marginada, y por otro, esa obsesión de contarlo detalladamente. Se trata no sólo de una confesión sino también de un desafío al lector, de un insulto al mundo establecido. (Bejel 1996, 37)

> [In addition to countless sexual contacts of all types (including bestiality and incest), he recounts, with respect to homosexuality, such numerous and fantastic encounters that the protagonist-narrator ends up saying that, by the beginning of the 1970s, he estimated having had sexual relations with about five thousand men. What I prefer to underline is, . . . on the one hand, the degree of rupture signified by the declaration of such a spectacular marginalized sexual activity, and, on the other, the obsession to tell it in such detail. We're not talking only about a confession but also about a challenge to the reader, an insult to the established world.]

The director, in contrast, moderates the on-screen Arenas, encouraging independent film viewers to empathize with him.[20]

In Cuba during the 1970s, the decree that homosexuals be "cured" focused on levels of visibility (Smith 1996, 69). The decision as to how much to show on screen hinges on various issues. Arenas's experiences with indoctrination and purges as a student mirror the outside space in which those men who looked most homosexual were punished accordingly:

> desde luego, no fui yo solo quien supo ocultar su homosexualidad y su rechazo al comunismo; muchos alumnos que eran homosexuales se las arreglaron para sobrevivir; otros, sencillamente, se negaron. (Arenas 1992a, 73)

> [I was, naturally, not the only one who managed to hide his homosexuality and his rejection of communism. Many of the students who were homosexual managed to survive; others simply denied their orientation.] (Arenas 1993a, 50, trans. Koch)

In 133 minutes, it is difficult to unravel the plenitude of Arenas's eroticism. Major studios are reluctant to distribute films in which the sexual content does not conform to stereotypical portraits of heterosexual or even homosexual relations. The transformation of Arenas's scriptural relation to his sexuality may have been a way of ensuring that his story would transcend those small and often underestimated markets of gay communities, academia, and artists dispersed in different parts of the globe. Furthermore, the possibility that Arenas's method of subverting categories of Western subjectivity through writing about these prohibited acts—sodomy and incest—has echoes beyond the Cuban context that could distract the "world" of film from approaching him.

Schnabel's film displays prison conditions in great detail, but what Arenas refers to as his "voracidad sexual" is limited to a few memorable images and Bardem's suggestive facial expressions (Arenas 1992a, 39). Because of his medium's constraints, the director is forced to transform a sustained buildup of Arenas's homosexual pleasure into a handful of brief, intense moments. The result is that his film falls into the workings of the globalizing social process, which depends on rapid forgetting so that it can promote anew. In the movie's first six chapters, the ones that take Arenas through his first meeting with Pepe Malas, the charismatic figure who sparks a change in Arenas's erotic behavior, two sequences stand out as encompassing the transformation of Arenas's homoeroticism. One of the surprising erotic scenes takes place in the school in Chapter 4, "1964." When class is dismissed, the camera zooms in on Arenas getting up and then on the bodies of two females walking. This zooming in suggests Arenas's own bisexual behavior at that time. Linking this ambiguous gaze to a dream sequence featuring Arenas's mother provides a possible anecdotal explanation of the writer's sexual practices. Might homosexuality result from a peculiar relationship with a mother, the film asks?[21] The continuous building up of desire in the text is, in the film, projected onto this singular, intense relationship with Pepe Malas. In fact, the most erotic episodes in the film take place in chapter 5, "Pepe." Here the spectator catches a glimpse of showering nude men, but the spectators' eyes are quickly averted from this scene of desire. In addition, the spectator previews the violently erotic encounter between Pepe and Reinaldo. For Arenas, the sense of conspiracy and complicity that comes with sexual pleasure between two men is key to the transgression of established order. Spectators, however, are left with only an inkling of this insult to their bourgeois values. We are far from the world of *Antes que anochezca*, where Arenas gleefully exaggerates the *guajiro*'s bond with his natural surroundings: "No solamente las yeguas, las puercas, las gallinas o las guanajas, sino casi todos los animales fueron objeto de mi pasión sexual, incluyendo los perros" (Arenas 1992a, 39) (Not only the mares, sows, hens, or turkeys but almost all animals were objects of my sexual passion, including dogs) (Arenas 1993a, 18, trans. Koch). In the film, naiveté, whereby the spectator can relish tenderness and pity toward the marginal figure, replaces these playful tales of bestiality and sodomy.

Schnabel's comments on the DVD regarding the use of English in Cuba and Spanish in the United States are curious, especially considering the above coordinates of in-your-faceness and prosopopoeia: "In this particular situation, here is a man who grew up in Cuba, but he came to the United States. He learned how to speak English, he does speak English, when he died he knew how to speak English, and he is really telling you the story from the grave, so he can tell you the story in any language he wants to" (Schnabel 2000, chapter 7). Schnabel's story begins with an unnamed immigrant who in the past learned how to speak English. Then it jumps forward, while still in the past, with "when he died he knew how to speak English," and finally, the spatial dimension of this third-person pronoun—he is in the grave—is realized. The prosopopoeiac quality of this insight is typical of autobiography; but in this instance, Schnabel temporarily erases himself in order to shift the choice from him to Arenas. This discursive slip suggests a desire, on the part of the director, for merger with the object of representation from which authority and authenticity are claimed.

By examining the film's use of English in Cuba and Spanish in New York, we begin to comprehend how authenticity relates to commodification. Arenas comes into his self, his "natural/biological," Spanish-speaking self, in Manhattan. His authorial subjectivity, his coming into his own through publication, coincides with this process.[22] While it was through Ruben Darío's apparent affinity with Pan's that Valera attempted to seduce 19th-century readers, it is through Arenas's veritable and strange linguistic world that Schnabel captures audiences in this part of the film. The cinéma vérité; that is, the clips based on Jana Bokova's *Havana*, also contribute to this coming into subjectivity. Schnabel justifies this duality using the rationale suggested above: "It's interesting that we've got a movie where the guy is speaking English when he's in Cuba, and people are speaking English in Cuba. When he comes to the United States, he is speaking Spanish, because I wanted everyone to feel like this is really the guy and this is a fiction we've just made and here when we're really interviewing him, he's going to talk his own language" (Schnabel 2000, chapter 7). The word "fiction" here conveys distance. Through the use of Spanish, viewers are urged to feel a burst of empathy toward a character now physically closer to us. The critical assumption is that the further away we are from certain experiences of pain, the less we may sentimentally account for them. That said, the Arenas who spoke English was a repressed self in a faraway, fictive place where maybe poets are raised. The greater the distance, the more difficult and the more fictive the struggles are. However, the cinéma vérité transports these struggles. The coming into subjectivity in Spanish entails the ability to "scream" without fear of condemnation (as the Arenas character puts it in describing the difference between U.S. capitalism and Cuban communism). Although this strategy effectively builds solidarity, the implications of what it means to be a now "real" subject in New York in relation to the globalizing world should be considered. As the logic of Valera went, Europeans had more potential to be cosmopolitan, because of their greater proximity to the city of lights. As a more "real" subject, one is more likely to be discovered, but as we have seen, effacement of "difference" is a sophisticated and varied process.[23]

Fredric Jameson never fully resolves the question of "what the linguistic or literary equivalents of 'imperfect cinema' might be" (Jameson 1996, 187); but he suggests that *testimonio* might share with cinéma vérité "a set of aesthetic positions against stars and against traditional narratives and fixed scenes" (Jameson 1996, 179). The staged reality, that "here we are feeling with the real Reinaldo Arenas," conjures up the sense that it is in New York City with Julian

Schnabel that Arenas is granted his proper voice. In this way, the shift to film also projects onto Arenas an even more marginalized status. "In prosopopoeiac representation solidarity turns into a production of abjection where the producing agency, *testimonio* criticism, retains an aura that has been literally sucked off the testimonial subject, now abjected" (Moreiras 1996, 203). We might keep in mind Moreiras's relation of criticism to the genre of *testimonio*, not for a precise analogic coincidence that takes Schnabel to be the producer and Arenas the object, but rather for its relevance in foregrounding hierarchies that reproduce themselves in unlikely places.

That Lázaro Gómez Carriles, whom, in *Before Night Falls*, Arenas calls the "most authentic person he ever met," was also a cowriter of the film undoubtedly helps to shape Schnabel's "fable of intimacy" and lends his production a stamp of authenticity. In choosing the best location to shoot the film, the makers strove for verisimilitude: Veracruz and Mérida, Mexico had to suffice, since Havana was presumably not an option for bringing to fruition a North American artist's adoption of one of the Cuban Revolution's *enfants terribles*. For the director, it is important to be definitive in tracing his steps through the Cuban capital. "I've been in all locations where Reinaldo lived, where Reinaldo passed through . . . I've been to clubs" (Schnabel 2000, chapter 6). This "I've been there" framework is reminiscent of many conventions exploited by the imperialist travel writers that Mary Louise Pratt (1992) has studied. However, such a thorough tour through the locations does not fully coincide with the liberties Schnabel takes with language (Cuco Sánchez, he admits on the DVD, has more of a Mexican than a Cuban accent). The documentary-like footage and the use of particular filters to make the film look like, according to Schnabel, "a 1959 *Life* magazine cover," further promote an authentic setting. To that extent, *Before Night Falls* resembles *The Buena Vista Social Club*, the popular movie that piqued the "world's" interest in Cuba.

The hype of *Before Night Falls* picks up where *The Buena Vista Social Club* left off in commodifying Cuba for the world. In framing the narrative, the director gauges time incorrectly, somewhat overestimating Arenas's obscurity and the world's homogeneity. However, the disappearing world's paradigm from which marginal beings need to be rescued has successfully raised out of oblivion Sabá Cabrera Infante's 1961 short film *P.M.*, which runs under the final credits of *Before Night Falls*. Although, at first, the *P.M.* clip of people dancing and chatting, mainly Cuban blacks, might seem to have more in common with *The Buena Vista Social Club* than Schnabel's film about this writer, the shared context of keeping an artifact away from the general public is grounds for bringing to screen this buried film. *P.M.* then, the final framing of Schnabel's movie, to a larger degree than the work of Arenas, has been forgotten, and so it is with that culmination of forgetfulness that *Before Night Falls* ends. Schnabel's film never has too far from mind the *Castaway* paradigm of movie viewers that depends upon accelerated forgetfulness. One might still ask: whose cultural memory is privileged if we accept the rescue paradigm, and what aspects of consumerism lead us to buy into the narrative of rescue and demise that coincides with the market's whims? If we posit this rapid forgetting as expected, we must also flatten the Cuban writer's personality to fit the dimensions of a modernist, heterosexist, capitalist order, and coincidentally a revolutionary one.[24]

The Other Pedagogues: DVD Commentary, Translation, Samizdat, *La Jiribilla*

To understand how the Web, which "knows no center or periphery but only nodes of (electronic) intensity and sites—not places—of accumulation and exchange" (Nethersole 2001, 640), opens possibilities of circulation for material whose diffusion had been previously severely limited due to its ideological content is crucial to our investigation into the worlds that converge with the representation of Arenas. Interrogating the way Arenas travels also tells us about how the relatively new technological media affect the way other parts of the world are envisioned. Similarly, the DVD commentary track of this film is a newly invented genre for which a somewhat different method of reception must be learned.

Because, through this genre, many spectators will come to know Arenas, it is crucial that critics use this new form cautiously to enhance their interpretation of cinema. The DVD commentary track, as Schnabel announces, serves important pedagogical purposes, so its ideology must also be worked through. As can be expected from even staged interviews, however, *Before Night Falls's* DVD commentary, made up of the voices of Schnabel, Gómez Carriles, Javier Bardem, Xavier Pérez Grobet, and Carter Burwell, is uneven, moving between astute and imprecise observations and confessions. Schnabel's rehearsal of some of the foundational tenets of Walter Benjamin, albeit in a jumbled fashion, brings up an unavoidable discussion on representation.

You need to go and look at a painting and stand in front of it to see its power . . . There is a huge difference between painting and filmmaking . . . It's more accessible to go to the movies. . . . People always thought my work was filmic because it was large . . . Americans don't have any idea in a sense about the Latin part of Latin America . . . I'm kind of Mexican in some way. I am really proudly Cuban. All the Cubans that see the movie feel like it is authentic, like it is real and it's not just a movie. It is education, real; something that could break down the walls of intolerance . . . At least somebody is trying to address that issue. (Schnabel 2000, chapter 27)

As these reflections suggest, the contingencies of DVD commentary oblige filmmakers to enter territories of interpretive discourse that they did not previously need to maneuver for large audiences. Attuned to the "intentional fallacy," the critic must find a delicate equilibrium between the makers' self-positioning and the art object taken on its own terms. The above explanation projects a humanism based on the desire to know others that, though present in Arenas's texts, is carried out on a smaller, more difficult, and nuanced scale. Schnabel's "authentic" Arenas feeds into the world's far-from-uniform desire for and expectations of Cuba. Cosmopolitanism navigates interpretive approaches toward the other: from Eltit's overriding complicity with the margins and demand for a complicit readership to Schnabel's homogeneous universe of democratic and free individuals. The accessibility and marketability of the film has led to an extremely rapid increase in the number of Web sites referencing the name "Reinaldo Arenas." From less than one thousand hits on the Google search engine before the film, to approximately seven times more in October 2001, to another one and a half times more a year and a half later, this quantifiable, yet still tenuous, interest in Arenas attests to the scale of Schnabel's world. In turn, it begs us to wonder about the comfortable synthesis that emerges from the film, and whether the film, like the Arenas most identifiable in the autobiography and in *El color del verano*, continues to guard against "overstep[ping] restricted positions" (Sommer 1993, 408) and interpreting in the vein of what Moreiras (1996, 206) calls, invoking Doris Sommer, "stereotypical male sexuality." For Sommer, the process by which *testimonios* enact this resistance also can have the effect of preventing a too simplistic and short-lived identification.

These questions bring out the distinct vantage points of insiders and outsiders vis-à-vis representations of a Cuban homosexual writing against the system. The uniqueness of collective Cuban experience is frequently emphasized in different registers of speech, from everyday familiar conversations to official declarations regarding the nation's special position in a world that is increasingly homogenized. This distinction grounds the frequent usage of *nosotros* (we) and *ustedes* (you plural)—a use of pronouns that guarantees there will be no confusion as to who is "in the know" about particular bodies of knowledge. The United States has been especially instrumental in maintaining this gap open between *nosotros* and *ustedes*, but the burden of Cuban national pride rests on ingredients other than opposition to the Yankee. Because a North American (who feels both Mexican and Cuban) has now spoken for this dead Cuban writer, cultural workers within Cuba partake in the translation and "marketing" of him. The fact that in the spring of 2001, cultural workers were invited to showings of the film in an auditorium at the writers' union seating approximately forty persons, a social space of great ideological importance, illustrates that the symbolic significance of Arenas is in the process of being transformed. The sometimes heard remark "No one from the United States can come give us ethics lessons" suggests that the specific paradigm of Schnabel's representation of Arenas is seen to ape faithfully a general model of U.S. imperialism. Other more lighthearted spectators envision the filmic Arenas as "shaking up" less than the literary one. For the most ardent adherents to these beliefs, Arenas has been misappropriated by the "cosmopolitan" center. However, as a consequence of Schnabel's "fencing in" of this faraway personage, a nuisance of the past is revived in the Cuban context, as a challenge to those who had hoped that it had disappeared. It as at this juncture between intentional and accidental consequences of cultural acts that Arenas's importance for discrepant cosmopolitanism lies.

The us/them and literary/filmic divides alluded to in criticism of the film within Cuba is interesting to consider in light of César Salgado's 1995 interview with the principal translator of Arenas's oeuvre into English, Andrew Hurley. It delves into issues of identity politics and interpretive communities that are also relevant to the biopic. Underscoring this us/them divide, Salgado encourages Hurley to speak about the complex reactions that a North American community might have to Arenas's works. While Salgado's identity politics do not coincide with those manifest in Arenas's fiction, especially in the speech on the pained liberation and migrations of the *pájaros* (birds/fairies) in *El color del verano* (Arenas 1991, 390), *Antes que anochezca* takes a stance that has more in common with the interviewer's, equating attachment to origins with a capacity for understanding:

> Lázaro ha sido en el exilio para mí el único asidero a mi pasado; el único testigo cómplice de mi vida en Cuba; . . . Y nosotros los cubanos, . . . el sufrimiento nos marcó para siempre y sólo con las personas que han padecido lo mismo, tal vez podemos encontrar cierta comunicación. La inmensa mayoría de la humanidad no nos entiende y no podemos tampoco pedirle que nos entienda; tiene sus propios terrores y no puede, realmente, comprender los nuestros, aun cuando quisiera; mucho menos comartirlos. (Arenas 1992a, 330)

> [In exile, Lázaro has been the only link to my past, the only witness to my past life in Cuba . . . And for Cubans, who, like us, . . . Suffering has marked us forever, and only with people who have gone through a similar experience can we perhaps find some level of understanding. Most people are unable to understand us nor should we expect them to; they have their own terrors and, even if they wanted to, cannot really fathom ours, much less share them.] (Arenas 1993a, 308, trans. Koch)

The experience of trauma and overlapping marginalities, then, brings about these more fixed identity politics. Throughout the interview, two important poles of approaching Arenas are demarcated. Salgado's underlying assumption is that shared origins facilitate interpretation, while Hurley recognizes that, although he had not always held the interpretive keys offered by experience, he did immediately understand what makes Arenas's writing great literature. Where Salgado's view of Arenas manifests an investment in identity politics, Hurley's reveals an attachment to the sorts of universalisms that sustain the vocation of translation.

The film's critical success might cast doubt on the notion that the translation of Arenas for international communities can present difficulties. For instance, Benigno Sánchez-Eppler discusses the difficulties that Arenas might pose for a specific North American community, a topic that, as demonstrated in Salgado's and Hurley's discussion, elicits different reactions. While the controversy that Arenas's works stirred up within Cuba is known, the more subtle problems that they can cause outside of the nation are less obvious but equally relevant. Sánchez-Eppler states that Arenas's text "also proves quite capable of grating against the supposedly more enlightened sensibilities of his possibly homophile contemporary U.S. urban readership with the documentation of sexual practices with animals and vegetables that are regarded as relatively commonplace in his rural setting" (Sánchez-Eppler 1996, 392). Contextual translation is an important dimension of understanding the global Arenas. For example, the autobiographer, from the position of the United States, is perplexed when he must fix a name to the homoeroticism of the Cuba of his youth: "No sé como llamar a aquellos jóvenes cubanos de entonces; no sé si bugarrones o bisexuales. Lo cierto es que tenían sus novias y sus mujeres" (Arenas 1992a, 132) "I do not know what to call the young Cuban men of those days, whether homosexuals who played the male role or bisexuals. The truth is that they had girl-friends or wives" (Arenas 1993a, 107, trans. Koch).

Sánchez-Eppler highlights well the role of specificity in sexual identities and the difficulty of translating gay experience and terminology from one context to another:

> When a story like the one Arenas tells to record his sexual contact with his uncle crosses the many borders he has crossed, such a story, together with the nature of the event it represents, is exposed to a transnational and transcultural multiplicity of value judgments very hard to control. But whatever the outcome of the unexpected and unmanageable readers' responses, the image has affected—transnationally—the unassailable straightness of the serious and ostensibly hetero-macho Cuban male, as much as it has brought to the U.S.-gay debates on intergenerational homosexuality one Cuban rural modality of the issue. (Sánchez-Eppler 1996, 392–93)

While mainstream suburban audiences may be startled momentarily by Schnabel's film, "urban homophiles" in the United States would likely not be severely shaken by its protagonist's actions. Rather than assault their horizons of expectations, the film creates a reified public that is at least now on the lookout for this writer. One might ask whether Schnabel heeds Sánchez-Eppler's (1996, 394) caution to avoid complete identification between the autobiographer or protagonist and the reader:

> on the North American front, the substantial gay and gay-affirming U.S. post-Stonewall readerships for whom his Cubanness will signify all sorts of indexes of otherness; in the Latin American rearguard, the substantially left-wing intelligentsia of post-Boom readers with their residual romantic attachments to Castro; and in the Cuban heartland of the island and Miami, all the politically irreconcilable parties who may agree only in their homophobia, plus the full census of queer Cubans both at home and abroad . . . readers would do well to retain or develop some awareness of the difference between the contexts operable in the moment and site of the narrated scene—1950s rural Cuba—and the moment and site of narration—late 1980s New York and its gay enclaves.

Amazon.com's suggestions for my future purchases, after having bought the DVD of *Before Night Falls*, include *Billy Elliot, Coming Out, The Pledge* (with Benicio del Toro), and *You Can Count on Me*. This selection of foreign and independent films suggests that, on the level of consumerism, the gap between Arenas and the "reader" that Sánchez-Eppler highlights above has been narrowed.

All this hype in the "world" brings the figure of Arenas back home to Cuba, albeit transformed. He has become, in some ways, more powerful because he is now far from anonymous, and he is no longer anonymous because he has been subdued abroad. It is of utmost importance to note that Cuba, more than three decades ago, got rid of the Unidades Militares de Ayuda a la Producción (UMAP), and it has made efforts to interpellate homosexuals as revolutionary subjects.[25] However, a culture of fear based on the following notions, that are brilliantly summarized by Emilio Bejel (2001), is hard to wipe out:

> Homosexuality is a corrupt and immoral practice; homosexuals must be forced to do hard agricultural labor so that the redeeming qualities of the rural atmosphere could cure their ills; homosexuals, being weak and therefore different from the base of macho Cuban culture, are perfect targets for recruitment by the enemy (American capitalism mainly); homosexuals are a threat to the nation because they corrupt children and young men and thus impede the formation of the "new man"; homosexuality constitutes an inversion of the "natural" gender roles and therefore breaks the basic laws of nature; and finally, homosexuality is the result of the distortions of capitalism, from which it may be concluded that socialism could now eradicate this social problem just as it could eradicate prostitution, drug addiction, and other ills and vices. (Bejel 2001, 101–02)

Cuban cultural workers, though they do not move directly through the commodity circuits of Amazon.com, do form part of the "world," and Schnabel's film has brought Arenas's name back to them, in a public manner, this time with the obligation that distance brings; that is, to write about him in response to the international attention. The film's trajectory, then, is not so different from that of Arenas's novels, such as *El mundo alucinante*, which was first published abroad and then later reentered the national realm in a samizdat manner. The samizdat circulation has meant that at different times, it was extremely difficult to find Arenas's books. In the late 1970s, according to Carlos Victoria (1996, 37), "even though *El mundo alucinante* had been published in Mexico several years before, it was impossible to find a copy of it in

Cuba." As was discussed in chapter 2, since between two thousand and three thousand copies of *Celestino* were published in Cuba in 1967, that novel's fate has been somewhat different.

Even under these precarious circumstances, Arenas's texts are not only read but he is "alive" in the cultural memory of many Cubans, much of which cannot be precisely documented, though it is suggested by the following list. Arenas's short story "El cometa Halley" was published in a 1999 Letras Cubanas anthology and republished on the Cuban Intranet in 2001 in *La Jiribilla*. Victor Fowler Calzada has highlighted Arenas's production in a number of critical pieces. Lourdes González Herrero, of the chapter of the Unión Nacional de Escritores y Artistas de Cuba (UNEAC, the national writers and artists union) in Holguín, published the poem "El único extranjero," in which a brief but not trivial citation of Arenas appears. The verse, "Al despedirse acuerda tirarnos una foto, y lo hicimos—dijo él a lo de Arenas" (When you say goodbye remember to take a picture, and we did," he said in the manner of Arenas), is significant in that it hints at the place in the Cuban imaginary of this once official ghost (González Herrero 1999, 27). In 2001, the young artists association Hermanos Saíz of Holguín, where Arenas lived for many years, convoked its third Celestino contest, in honor of Arenas's first novel. The film has also spurred attention on the conditions in which Reinaldo Arenas's real-life elderly mother, Oneira Fuentes Rodríguez, had been living in Holguín. She had not been included in her son's will, a will from which even those who had been included have not benefited on account of legal disputes. However, recently, the rumor mill had it that his mother was given a house. This detail likely is an exaggeration, a consequence of one of the most outstanding aspects of this recent tentative reincorporation: the publication of "Donde las arenas son más diáfanas" (2003) in the Cuban newspaper *Caimán barbudo*, in which Gabriel Pérez interviews Fuentes on the topics of Holguín, her son's stories, authorial rights, her son's will, and her impressions of the film. At the conclusion of the article, subtitled, "Reinaldo Arenas: el enfant más terrible," Fuentes is asked how she would like to say goodbye to her sons' readers. She says: "Deseándoles mucha felicidad. Y, que aunque sea algo tarde, les agradezco que hayan reconocido la obra de Reinaldo aquí. Y que se quede en la memoria de los holguineros . . . Les agradezco que lo admitan y les deseo muchas felicidades" (Desiring them much happiness. And, although it was somewhat late, I am grateful that they have recognized Reinaldo's work here. And that he remains in the memory of Holguineros . . . I am grateful that they admit him and I desire them much happiness). This almost prayer-like passage illustrates the more uncanny effects of Schnabel's film. Like many other elements of culture in Cuban society, this "aparecido," far from having disappeared, persistently resonates.

One of the most overt gestures toward a recuperation of Arenas after the film has been made on *La Jiribilla*, a Web site under the auspices of the Communist Youth Union's newspaper *Juventud Rebelde*.[26] To understand the process by which this previously banished personage has reentered the intellectual terrain, it is necessary to reference the first issue. According to *Juventud Rebelde*, the purpose of the journal is "profundizar en aquellos aspectos de la vida artística y literaria del país que muchas veces son manipulados o desconocidos fuera de Cuba" (to go deeper into those aspects of the artistic and literary life of the nation that are often manipulated or unknown outside of Cuba) (Rodríguez 2001). The population of Cuba is a little more than 11 million and access to the Internet is limited. It was estimated in 2001 that as many as ten people use each of the 3,625 computers with Internet access in Cuba (*Pioneer News* 2001). Furthermore, much of this access is designated for correspondence only for particular Web sites within the Cuban Intranet. In December 2003, there was a crackdown on unauthorized Internet usage from home called Resolution 180/2003. It only allowed those paying in dollars for their phone service such free access. Governmental policies related to the Internet are in flux, but continue to be a necessary component for evaluating how culture is generated and communicated. Available on the Cuban Intranet, *La Jiribilla*'s feature on Arenas in its very first issue in May 2001 is a limited, yet important change. It suggests that the film compelled official Cuban discourse to speak—albeit in a medium destined primarily, but not exclusively, for those living outside of the country—about this writer who continues to be a thorn in its side. Pedro de la Hoz's (2001) commentary on the site presents the scope of its treatment:

> Todo ello está diseñado a remarcar la idea de que el caso Reinaldo Arenas no es único, sino simboliza el calvario de un pueblo . . . Un espectador medianamente informado de la realidad cubana, aunque no comparta los presupuestos ideológicos de la Revolución, sabe prefectamente que esas imágenes pavorosas, remedo de las fantasias de Orwell, son insustentables.

> [All "in Schnabel's film" is designed to stress the idea that the Reinaldo Arenas case is not unique, but rather symbolizes the calvary of a

people . . . A modestly informed spectator of Cuban reality, even
though he or she may not share the ideological assumptions of the
revolution, knows perfectly that these horrific images, an imitation of
Orwell's fantasies, are unsustainable.]

De la Hoz's irritation with the film's magnification of the individual
tragedy of the writer is also inherent to the autobiographical genre, in
which the individual's life stands metaphorically for those of the
many. De la Hoz relates what I have presented as the filmic Arenas's
diminished aura to the film's making an individual story of one writer
into a national history of the revolution. Furthermore, in *La Jiribilla*,
the division of *nosotros* and *ustedes* demarcates distinct communities
of interpreters. The conclusion of another of that same issue's articles,
written by Enrique Ubieta Gómez, confirms this stance: "Quizás algún
lector extranjero se confunda, pero los cubanos saben discernir la
retórica del odio." (A foreign reader may make the mistake, but
Cubans will be able to distinguish rhetoric from hatred.)

A short sidebar that runs alongside both de la Hoz's article and
Ubieta Gómez's, under the heading "Notas al Fascismo Corriente"
[Notes on current fascism] and the title "Neutralidad Culposa"
[Culpable neutrality], reports the "furious attacks" of Cuban exile and
poet Belkis Cuza Malé on island Cuban writer Amir Valle, who "ha
defendido desde el boletín . . . una posición de respeto a los cubanos
'de dentro' y a los 'de afuera' " (has defended . . . a position of respect
toward Cubans from "inside" and "outside"). These polemics recall
the "Padilla affair" alluded to in Schnabel's film in the confession of a
fictitious character named Heberto Zorilla Ochoa. Although, likely in
the style of a "mischievous boy," *La Jiribilla* refers to Cuza Malé as an
émigré "more or less linked to literature." She is largely recognized for
being the former wife of the late poet Heberto Padilla who was jailed
by the Cuban Department of Security in 1971 for his literature that
was deemed counterrevolutionary, and who was freed after an intense
international campaign. Via the "frames" of the Web, the juxtaposition of this text alongside the de la Hoz and Ubieta Gómez essays
signals the strained nature of *La Jiribilla*'s recuperation of Arenas.

Another article on the Web site, Jon Hillson's "The Sexual Politics of
Reinaldo Arenas: Fact, Fiction and the Real Record of the Cuban
Revolution" (2001) (which the site offers in both English and in
Spanish translation), speaks of the "stylized, sanitized confection that
Arenas becomes." Although there are some similarities among my own
and Hillson's and de la Hoz's concerns, our rhetoric, conceptualization

of art's function, and more general conclusions are radically different. As these articles and the concomitant frames illustrate, the categories of *nosotros* and *ustedes* are not imagined, but the frames of *La Jiribilla* also illustrate that they may no longer be as clearly defined as they were in the past.

Schnabel's *Before Night Falls* takes Arenas to be a vestige of a dying world, one whose dreams reflected at once false and repressive ideologies and the belief in the transcendence of art. Keeping in mind this narrative, it is important to recall the several collections of essays about Arenas that resemble more closely eulogies testifying to the writer's immense being, illustrated with photographs of the writer with his friends. They connect the critics to their object of investigation, and bring readers up close to the faces of Arenas. In short, while forging particular "fables of intimacy," they have sustained the figure and ensure that he stands in for them. However, in the Arenian vein of continually questioning the manner by which affiliations are established and in that of cosmopolitan feeling, the salvation articulated by the film and its director should also be challenged. The narrative, in turn, prompts an evaluation of memory and reminds us of the need to resuscitate what has been less than forgotten. *Before Night Falls'* failure to adequately represent the negotiations that Arenas continually made among multiple affiliations sometimes in awkward and clumsy manners brings out the question of competing versions of cosmopolitanisms—one that tends to even out differences in order to insert another into a presentable and consumable scheme and one that allows difference to render itself as different. Nevertheless, to beg a single film to address a writer's multiple affiliations is likely asking too much.

Schnabel's "allegories of vocation" may recall Martha Nussbaum's configuration of cosmopolitanism as a series of concentric circles that agitate the public's sensibilities only enough for the new artistic object to be appropriated with excitement. This film, more immediately than Arenas's writing, does participate in mass culture. We must continue studying the movement and echoes of this film in places that are socially distant from the place of origin. The value that lies in such an investigation corresponds to a practice of cosmopolitanism that neither collapses into a facile universalism, nor asserts itself as the paradigm for universal cultural critique.

5

Uncomfortable Homes

Since the meaning of cultural products depends not only on the context in which they were created, but also on those in which they travel, it is important to attempt to do the impossible, that is, to assess them from multiple perspectives simultaneously. For instance, what could be viewed as containment in one place and time—a representation of Reinaldo Arenas during a particularly reactionary period in the United States ends up creating more of a burden in another context, Castro's post-Soviet Cuba. As discrepant cosmopolitanisms acknowledge their relation to the maneuverings of the market economy, they are able to address the enclosures and strictures on which disciplines are constructed. This chapter considers the echoes of the institutionalization of critique within the institutionalization of madness. Following the paradigms of intellectual and artistic figuration set forth in the previous chapters, we can begin to analyze unusual sites of conformation and contestation. Our focus throughout this book shifts from intellectual self-fashioning in itself to the interpretation of these authorial maneuvers in diverse contexts. It increasingly considers the significance of diverse visual cultures on the literary realm. The episode before us manifests the ethical parameters of cosmopolitanism, of embracing the flexibility that such a position assumes, as a way of coming to terms with certain disciplinary limitations. The visual and textual rendering of insane asylums suggests peculiar overlappings of nationalism and globalization. The intricacy of contemporary trade associations and agreements makes difficult the intellectual process of identifying the "monster" that José Martí and José Enrique Rodó, among many others, have associated with the United States. As our previous encounters with both Arenas and Eltit have demonstrated, enunciating a singular way out from beneath mutating and oppressive forces is even more so.

The way in which globalization and the disintegration of steadfast ideologies claim subjectivity and citizenry is a topic of investigation in Eltit's more recent novels. Unlike her earlier ones, in her most recent *Mano de obra* (2002a) there is no principal writer/artist figure through which other characters may envision hope. The question of how to construe agency in a world in which oppression is no longer incarnate in the body of an authoritarian leader—Augusto Pinochet—but rather distributed throughout society in insidious ways is in the forefront. The force of the market is totalizing—the worker of a *super* (market) is converted into its products through his labor—labor from which customers are blinded, but which supervisors incessantly observe. At the same time that the desires of the worker are nullified and supplanted by those of the supervisor, *Mano de obra* suggests that the global market is the principal driving force. However, interruption to rapid consumption does not take place on the level of aesthetic difficulty, as it had in the previously analyzed texts of Eltit. A negative review by a Chilean critic touches upon this point. In "Perdida en el supermercado" (Lost in the supermarket), Álvaro Bisama declares:

> Diamela Eltit ha terminado por transformarse en la Marcela Serrano de los intelectuales y alumnos de literatura. Una especie de autora top cuyo éxito no se mide en libros vendidos sino en los trabajos escritos con su obra como tema . . . la Eltit es una marca que se lleva para demostrar precisamente, que no se llevan marcas; sosteniendo el mito de que a la autora más avant garde de Chile se le comenta más que se la lee. (Bisama 2002)

> [Diamela Eltit has ended up becoming the Marcela Serrano of the intellectuals and literature students. A kind of top author whose success is not measured in books sold but rather in works written in which her work is a theme . . . Eltit is a brand that is worn to show precisely that you don't wear brands; sustaining the myth that the most avant-garde author in Chile is commented upon more than read.]

The aesthetic paradox of all this, he continues, lies in the fact that "mientras más difícil es la obra de Diamela Eltit, más atractivo literario tiene. Eso hace que *Mano de obra*, su última novela sea, por ende, un texto poco interesante" (the more difficult Diamela Eltit's work is, the more literarily attractive it is. This means that *Mano de obra*, her last novel, is not very interesting) (Bisama 2002). Rivera Westerberg jumps into this discussion, by asserting that Eltit is "profundamente chilena" (deeply Chilean) (Westerberg 2003). Against Bisama's claims, she evidences none other than the fact that Casa de las Américas dedicated its "Semana del Autor" to her (Westerberg 2003). National value is acquired through a cosmopolitan institution, other than the conglomerate of publishing houses in Spain. To the extent that Bisama asserts that Eltit has become a sort of brand name of marginality, customary links between originality and textual content, on the one hand, and authenticity and international reception, on the other, still need to be investigated, but not without recalling the current Chilean context of fierce commodification of even the most significant and political cultural objects. As Sophia A. McClennen (2001) delineates, the "big business" aspects of publishing in Chile, with the Spanish Planeta at the fore, are crucial to the creation of a true national movement.

As did the success of Schnabel's film impact the reissuing of Arenas's novels by Tusquets in Spain and Penguin in the United States, the critical success of Eltit's novels has meant that they too have been picked up by Seix Barral in Spain, one of the principal forces behind the cosmopolitan promotion of Latin American letters in the 1960s. Using a medium that is less challenging to readers than her previous novels, *Mano de obra* narrates the physical, ideological, and spiritual disintegration of subjectivity by neoliberalism. The novel's self aware-ness toward a local–global dynamic elucidates our discussion on the selling power of Eltit for "theory" as well on the role that her own cri-tique of neoliberalism plays with respect to the academic market. While it does not convey a means to overcome the more degrading consequences of living in today's world overrun by capitalism, it constructs an archive through which to recall other periods in which subjects often collectively resisted. The novel's chapter headlines refer-ence important resistance efforts in Chilean history, situating them geographically and temporally. In the present sociopolitical climate in which the disposability of objects is esteemed, Eltit projects what we may call the "stains of hope" inherited by the past—instances of those broken ideological dreams that still merit remembering.

Where Did the *Marlboro King Size* Go?

First, through chapter and section titles, *Mano de obra* remembers a history of workers' solidarity and revolt. The first section title— "Iquique, 1911"—recalls the massacre of more than 2,000 miners in the school of Santa María de Iquique in 1907 who have been commemorated in a song made popular by a folk group called Quilapayun, originally written by Luis Advis, in 1970, when the Unidad

Popular came to power. That important year also serves as the basis for the title of the second half of the novel—"Puro Chile, Santiago, 1970"—that cites the national anthem. Each of the chapter titles in the first section coincides with the names of workers' newspapers from the first few decades of the twentieth century, but the extent to which workers are subjugated is captured by the protagonist's complete lack of utterances. "No odio a la turba, no tengo fuerzas ni deseos, ni más voz que la que está dentro de mi cabeza" (I don't hate the mob. I don't have any energy or desire, nothing more than the voice that is within my head) (Eltit 2002a, 59). The most intimate detail about this character that is revealed in the first section is the pain that he endures on account of job-related ailments, a metaphor for overall societal harm afflicted on docile bodies by the nation in cahoots with the market. Unlike in *Lumpérica*, where the author-figure and the lumpen meet in the city square, an emblem of national monuments and rebellion, in *Mano de obra*, the margins sustain central commerce. More than through an artist/intellectual figure's travel to the margins, this novel's principal tactic of critique involves immersion in historical and subversive documents.

While the descriptive techniques utilized by Eltit echo those used in *Lumpérica* and *Por la patria*, the worker who is unable to exteriorize his voice can also be associated with El Mudito (the little Mute) of José Donoso's *El obsceno pájaro de la noche* (1970). In the words of Adriana Valdés, the little mute is "un ser desesperadamente excluido de sus propias fantasías" (1996, 103) (a being desperately excluded from his own fantasies). Parallels can be drawn with the figure of the *imbunche*—a child whose orifices are all sewn up by a witch in Chilean myth—that is later revamped by Donoso in the fictional representation of Chile's class system, provincialism, as well as global capitalism. The act of wrapping objects reflects the intensity with which characters are engulfed by forces larger than themselves in both Eltit's text and Donoso's masterpiece. "Envuelto en la nebulosidad de mis adversas condiciones, el único recurso que me resta es implorarle a esta (última) manzana que, por piedad, me devuelva mi salud perdida" (Enwrapped in the nebulousness of my adverse conditions, the only recourse that is left to me is to beg this last apple for pity, that it returns my lost health) (Eltit 2002a, 59). *Mano de obra*'s protagonist is not only enwrapped, but he also wraps. Because wrapping is his principal duty at the market, he invests a great deal of time in practicing this activity even at home, and under the observation of his housemates.

Gabriel, mucho más que iracundo, ensayaba, en las noches, múltiples maneras de envolver. Desplegaba una capacidad manual que nos maravillaba cuando lo observábamos en su absorto empeño por consolidar sus paquetes imaginarios. Unos envoltorios con los que buscaba incrementar su precisión en el súper. Sus manos lo conducían hasta una delicadeza difícil de concebir. Pero su cara, su expresión, la comisura de su boca denunciaban esa parte de su carácter que odiábamos y que nos mantenía en estado de alerta, pues por ese hilo casi invisible de saliva depositado en su torcida comisura, se deslizaba un sentimiento fóbico a las colas, a los supervisores, a las borracheras, a los uniformes y a las casetas de los guardias. Fóbico a los clientes, a los paquetes. Fóbico a sí mismo. (Eltit 2002a, 136)

[Gabriel, much more than angered, rehearsed, at night, multiple ways of packing. He revealed a manual capacity that made us marvel when we watched him in this absorbed exertion consolidating his imaginary packages. Some packages with which he sought to increase his precision in the supermarket. His hands drove him to a delicateness that is difficult to imagine. But his face, his expression, the corner of his mouth denounced the part of his character that we hated and that kept us in a state of alert—through an almost invisible drop of saliva deposited in the crooked corner of his mouth was revealed his phobia to lines, to supervisors, to drunkenness, to uniforms and to guardhouses. Phobic of clients, packages. Phobic of himself.]

The saliva that dribbles out from the corner of Gabriel's mouth also implies that which will not be contained. The disdain that Gabriel's housemates and coworkers feel toward this inkling of irrationality suggests its potential as threat, and as such, we may come to see the subversive potential within irrationality. There is just something about Gabriel's face that betrays the manner with which he ingratiates his boss and exposes the remains of his reactions to the systemic oppression.

A similar dynamic of wrapping is true for *El obsceno pájaro de la noche* where the lower-class characters reinvent their worlds through repackaging the leftovers of the upper social classes. This formulaic wrapping, associated with contamination and the demarcation and blurring of spatial categories, pervades Donoso's monstrosity of non-realistic representation. La Rinconada, one of the two macroplaces in the novel, houses those abnormal creatures known as monsters. There they are no longer the exceptions—it is a world that is created by the aristocrat Don Jerónimo de Azcoitía to correspond to his Boy: "Mandó sacar de las casas de la Rinconada todos los muebles, tapices, libros y cuadros que aludieran al mundo de afuera: que nada creara en su hijo la añoranaza por lo que jamás iba a conocer" (Donoso 1970, 240). (He ordered all the furniture, tapestries, books and paintings that suggested the outside world taken out of the houses at La Rinconada; nothing was to stir a longing in his son for what he was never to know.) (Donoso 1979, 187, trans. St. Martin and Mades.) Recreation and consumption is everything in this barrage in which there is "Nada de porques ni cuandos, de afueras, de adentros, de después, de partir, de llegar, nada de sistemas ni de generalizaciones" (Donoso 1970, 254). (No whys, whens, outsides, insides, befores, afters; no arriving or leaving, no systems or generalizations . . . Boy must live in an enchanted present, in the limbo of accident, of the particular circumstance, in the isolation of the object and the moment without a key.) (Donoso 1979, 197–98, trans. St. Martin and Mades.) Donoso's severe critique of the values of the Chilean bourgeoisie and their provincial aspirations toward cosmopolitanism culminates in the garb of one of the monsters—polo shirts with emblems of Marilyn Monroe and Ché Guevara. The old systems in place convert all of these recently dead humans into T-shirts so few years after their deaths. Donoso's fiction replicates the world of the *imbunche* in a grandiose and almost liberating manner. This fiction is not only closed off from the outside, but is also a product of creative grafting that, however dystopic, is home to a beautiful monstrosity.

Cultural asphyxiation can be the result of an excess of mandates and an excess of capital. Donoso's characters suffer the effects of rumors and hearsay, as well as from phobias that they are not sufficiently worldly. Like the characters in *De sobremesa*, they imagine that products from elsewhere are better than those from close to home, because the world is something abstract, out there. What is left out of a verbal exchange between two of the monstrous characters in the English translation of *El obsceno* condenses and dilutes the novel's depiction of consumerism. I do not believe that the omissions in the English translation's central chapter, chapter 15, can be entirely explained through theories of linguistic translation. Italicized brand names are entirely eliminated—no *Vogue*, no *Lapsang-Souchong*, no *Jasmine*, no *Marlboro King Size*. In fact, the paragraphs containing the first three items are entirely eliminated from the translation—a transformation that could be justified as the translator's attempt to improve the original by taking out less than urgent background if it were not for the fact that a paragraph containing *Marlboro King Size* also had been "tweaked." "Sirvió dos tazas de té y después de cruzar sus piernecitas rechonchas cogió un *Marlboro King Size* entre sus dedos arrugados como tornillos, esperando que su interlocutor se lo encendiera" (Donoso 1970, 257). In English: "She served two cups of tea and, after crossing her chunky little legs, took a long cigarette between fingers as wrinkled as screws, waiting for her companion to light it for her" (Donoso 1979, 199–200, trans. St. Martin and Mades). Whether the *Marlboro King Size* is extracted on account of taste or value or on account of a sort of trademark dispute is inconclusive. To examine the forces beyond the author's control puts us into a different frame beyond conventional reflection of literary models. As was the case in my analysis of Schnabel's biopic, loyalty toward the original is not what motivates my critique, but rather a concern for the ironic convergence between the fiction's focus on reification and its very fate within the English-language context.

What *El obsceno pájaro de la noche* and *Mano de obra* illustrate so clearly is the proximity of intellectual pursuits to other systems of control that ought to make critique a rather uncomfortable matter. As literary and cultural critics, the expectation is that we may speak of Donoso and Eltit in the same breath because they are apparently autonomous agents belonging to different generations from the same nation. Arenas and Eltit begin to raise eyebrows since the first is Cuban and is discussed principally by himself or in fewer cases in relation to other Cuban, homosexual or exilic writers. Eltit more frequently crosses disciplinary bounds, as suggested by Robert Neustadt's fascinating discussion of the multimedia nature of her oeuvre in relation to the art of Mexican-born Guillermo Gómez Peña and Chilean-born Alejandro Jodorowsky. Taking the lead from Donoso's and Eltit's characters, the act of recycling theoretical vocabulary or repackaging entails reading Eltit and Paz Errázuriz's photoessay on an insane asylum, *El infarto del alma* (1994) in light of another photoessay on the same general topic, which first appeared in Benetton's magazine *Colors* in 2002. In both *El obsceno pájaro de la noche* and *Mano de obra*, national identity is verified through the ability to purchase and/or acquire products, and if they are from elsewhere, they are ironically even more capable of providing characters comfort in their place and, to some extent, companies such as the multinational fashion house Benetton are responsible for this achievement. As such, Benetton is exceptional in creating a publication that does not explicitly advertise its own brand, yet the seemingly "quantifiableness" of others within its magazine *Colors* may remind us of the pageant of collectibles from all over the world that saturate José Fernández's salon in *De sobremesa*.

There is a discrepancy between Benetton's labor practices and its politically provocative advertising. Benetton has been involved in very real neocolonial encounters in the Patagonian region of Argentina, with respect to the appropriation of vast amounts of land previously occupied by the Mapuche Indians. On the same land that they now use as their wool farms, they constructed the Leleque museum, as a manner of paying tribute to those same people (Bartolone and Hacher 2002). Whether it is possible for particular projects to slip through the cracks of such an empire and assert something different is questionable. Benetton's advertising seems to reaffirm spectators' control of their surroundings and their ability to superficially traverse continents. However, as these worlds cohere, they also collide and make us aware of the current limits of disciplinary packaging. This process casts doubt on the divisions between consumerist and discrepant cosmopolitanisms.

Domestication

Sometimes moving within the insanity of the marketplace reveals contradictions that can serve as a powerful apparatus of cultural critique. The case of the translation of *El obsceno pájaro de la noche* is fascinating since it exaggerates the instability of meaning and the degree to which definitions of art are entwined by distinct economies. By investigating the currency of madness within zones of experience that are often considered disparate, we may gesture away from customary means of packaging thought. Even Diamela Eltit has criticized the Italian multinational company Benetton for the way it aestheticizes differences. As divergent as their goals may be, photojournalism and advertising evoke affect—whether formed out of fear, necessity, desire, and empathy, or a combination of them all. Although texts potentially can more directly elicit the proper moral reaction, photographs are not only responsible for conjuring feeling but they also depend on context. Still, one of the more preoccupying questions that emerged in the discussion of Schnabel's Arenas was the degree to which it promulgated an informed feeling beyond the nation or whether it simply replicated sameness. For discrepant cosmopolitanisms to operate as a critical category, the value of feeling beyond the nation needs to be especially inclusive. Artists, writers, musicians, and filmmakers are not the sole purveyors of ethical cosmopolitanisms. Supermarkets, advertising campaigns, and Internet sites all challenge our codes of cultural interpretation.

Without an absolute leader, Chileans began to look into how diverse Chilean institutions executed power and controlled citizens. One of these areas was the institutionalization of the insane. Also immersed in an international dialog on madness as metaphor, *El infarto del alma* (1994) by Diamela Eltit and Paz Errázuriz is a photoessay of the Philippe Pinel institution in the village of Putaendo, Chile, built in the 1940s for the purpose of housing tuberculosis patients that was later converted into a state hospital for the mentally ill and indigent when the epidemic ended. This project—like the photoessay entitled *Estrictamente no professional: Humanario* published in 1976, almost two decades before, by Sara Facio, Alicia D'Amico, and Julio Cortázar—is as situated within a particular context as it is immersed in broad national and international theoretical trends constitutive of post-structuralism and psychoanalysis. Facio's, D'Amico's, and Cortázar's faith in the ability to understand humanity, evident in the book's title, appears to be greater than the Chileans whose title reflects an attack that is not just on the soul but also on the concept of wholeness. With a vague echo of Rodó's antiprofessionalism and antispecialization, Cortázar's initial essay, "Estrictamente no profesional," emphasizes that there is a range of sanity, as there is of insanity, and those who bury themselves in one supposedly rational area are as insane as the interned. Some of the most pertinent questions that Cortázar asks are with respect to the "extraordinarily intelligent" Adolf Eichmann, the German largely responsible for the Nazi's "health" activities, as well as the tactics used by the Chilean junta to "*sanear mentalmente el país*" (sanitize mentally the country): "¿usted la pone del lado de la cordura?" (would you put it on the side of sanity?) (Cortázar 1976, n.p.). As we saw in *Mano de obra*, the only distinguishing factor between the sane and the insane is the "dripping saliva" with which the latter's expressions are depicted. The power of *Estrictamente no professional's* critique was intense on a political level, as it was published the same year as the military coup in Argentina. But the strictness elicited by Cortázar's title is timely in other ways as well. In those years of rebellion and commitment to ideology, *professionalism* stood for allegiances solely for the sake of upholding authority. It is also interesting that, unlike other works by this boom writer that circulate internationally, the significance of *Estrictamente no professional: Humanario* has hardly reverberated, even in the wake of *El infarto del alma*, within the North American academy.

In *El infarto del alma*, the social sciences and medicine are under scrutiny for the control that they together exert on patients for the state, but what the photoessay does not claim through these fields, it does through theory and literature. Involved in the workings of the Chilean Transition as much as in authoritarianism, *El infarto del alma* appears not to denounce any one ideology, but instead strives for decentering and lack of unified endings through its disjointed and multigeneric qualities. While we could see these tendencies as going against salability, they also are in line with the multidirectionality of the marketplace. Furthermore, the multiple discourses that Eltit utilizes to represent the asylum mimic, to an extent, the language of the interned. Eltit's and Errázuriz's account challenges the professional discourse of psychiatry and adheres to certain precepts of cultural theory. It exerts faith in feeling beyond one's own community. Like many of their predecessors, these artists link their expression to the insane, and their professional interests are satisfied by that bond.

"La Semana del Autor" commemorating Eltit at Havana's Casa de las Américas cannot be separated from Eltit's already constituted position within the field of Latin American and cultural studies in the United States, where her reputation rests on viewing her neo-avant-garde oeuvre as resistant to coercive and dominant structures. Eltit's election to the Modern Language Association as an honorary member in 2000 attests to the degree to which her work has been canonized. That critics frequently point to the fact that within Chile her work is not duly regarded because it is not sufficiently marketable as a commodity or as a political tool lends the Cuban encounter a distinct character. In "Traveling Theory," Edward Said reminds us that the movement of ideas and theories from one culture to another "is never unimpeded. It necessarily involves processes of representation and institutionalization different from those at the point of origin. This complicates any account of the transplantation, transference, circulation, and commerce of theories and ideas" (Said 1983, 196). How does *El infarto del alma*'s function transform when it moves from being a minoritarian cultural object in the context of the end of authoritarianism and neoliberalism to a celebrated artifact in the United States and Cuba?

At the core of this discussion are the identity and the role of the critic in the face of enduring processes of reification and globalization. By uniting geographically and historically disparate art objects— *Colors*'s *Madness* (2001–2002) and *El infarto del alma*—we can begin to engage the tenuous possibility of responding to cultural and political homogenization from within contemporary modes of commodification and of continuing to critique these processes using a specialized discourse and shocking images. In the case of *Colors*'s *Madness*, even describing it as artistic may be interrogated. Where are the artists? Where is the art? What is being sold? A cursory answer would lead us back to Eltit's *Lumpérica*—"commercial products" to a "desolate citizenry"? Susan Sontag emphasizes the degree to which the significance of photographic images changes according to the context in which they are displayed. "Socially concerned photographers assume that their work can convey some kind of stable meaning, can reveal truth. But partly because the photograph is, always, an object in a context, this meaning is bound to drain away; that is, the context which shapes whatever immediate—in particular, political—uses the photograph may have is inevitably succeeded by contexts in which such uses are weakened and become progressively less relevant" (Sontag 1990, 106). Because the Italian multinational fashion house Benetton publishes *Colors*, the magazine is frequently viewed as advertising, even though the actual logo cannot be located within it. The absence of the logo echoes the peculiar characterization of Eltit by Bisama, as a non-brand brand. What sort of agency we may attribute to *Colors* is clearly questionable. Nevertheless, the *Madness* issue attracted the attention of people outside the usual context in which it circulated. Most remarkable about the union of art, advertising, and humanitarianism is the fact that several of *Madness*'s images and text form part of the 2001 report of the World Health Organization. Adam Broomberg and Oliver Chanarin—the creative directors of the magazine between 2000 and 2002—have also held exhibitions of the photographs that appeared in *Colors*'s issues on asylums as well as on prisons. Furthermore, just a year after *Madness*, in 2003, specialists in photography and contemporary art books located in London and Venice, called Trolley, published a hardback book containing 300 color photos including many that appeared in the *Madness* issue. Some might say that Broomberg's and Chanarin's documentation of 12 different communities called *Ghetto* compensates for its colorful stylization with a thoughtful analysis of their selection process. They do emphasize the "making-up" process, or rather the rationale behind their technique, as well as their journey and the obstacles they faced in achieving their final product. The questions concerning authority and replication are most fascinating, as *Ghetto*'s cover is the same as the one on *Colors*'s issue 47 on *Madness*, but the transformation of contexts and instances of auto-citation do not stop there.

Madness documents the institutionalization of mental illness around the world, but dedicates 40 percent of the magazine to a singular hospital in Camagüey, Cuba. An illuminating detour took its team of creative directors and photographers to the Hospital Psiquiátrico René Vallejo, but not to the notoriously oppressive National Psychiatric Hospital in Havana. When the art directors and photographers of *Colors* initially proposed the project, they had intended to do an expose on the National Psychiatric Hospital in Havana, known as Mazorra. Before arriving in Cuba, they had been under the impression that they had secured the ability to do so with the institution's director, Eduardo Ordáz, who is infamous for having controlled it with an iron grip since the beginning of the revolution. The Cuban government, however, interrupted *Colors* by threatening to close down the Benetton stores if Mazorra remained the focus. With the exception of this ultimate detail that was revealed to me in an interview with Chanarin, all is spelled out in *Ghetto*, but not in *Madness*. Because Benetton was among the first companies to take advantage of the 1991 legal allowance for joint ventures, at least symbolically, the implications of such a shutdown would have been immense.[1] In this way, it is important to see that the plan was diverted not only by the officials, but also by Benetton's own financial motivation. Controlled by the national ministry of health, Camagüey's hospital is considered to be more representative of the Cuban mental health system, definitively under the auspices of the National Ministry of Health and described as more progressive—a detail that becomes especially fascinating in relation to the magazine's overall depiction of global politics. The degree to which the hospital in the province is progressive is certainly questioned by the magazine, but never as conspicuously as it is in *Ghetto* where the limits that were placed on Broomberg's and Chanarin's representation by the officials are noted in detail.

> Every image was vetted by the hospital director.
> Much was out of bounds . . . Any mention of the Cuban law of *peligrosidad* (dangerousness), which was often used to intern homosexuals and other citizens judged to be "in manifest contradiction with the norms of socialist morality." There were details we couldn't photograph; things we heard but could not write. This still applies. (Broomberg and Chanarin 2003, 80)

While *Colors*'s *Madness* holds back some key elements of the selection process, Chanarin and Broomberg feature them in their introduction to the section on this asylum, but as we shall see, their scrutiny does not stop there, but rather reaches their own tactics of representation.

El infarto del alma touches on similar points, but, for Eltit and Errázuriz, no such restrictions apply—their access is granted from the text's start due to Errázuriz's previous experiences with the place. She had photographed at the facility on a number of occasions.

El infarto del alma, by now a staple within studies of Latin Americanism, was coauthored by two highly esteemed neo-avant-garde Chilean artists. At least on the level of production, the threat to *El infarto del alma*'s autonomy is less immediately evident; historically, geographically, and artistically grounded, it involves fewer and less obscured detours. The book's theme—the mad in love—and its fragmented style, as Gareth Williams has suggested, possess commonalities with André Breton's *L'amour fou* (*Mad Love*) and while *El infarto del alma* claims to be inundated by that famous homage to love published in 1937, Williams marks a grand difference between the two saying that the latter does not promise "redemptive revelation" (Williams 2002, 294). "It is the negative exposure . . . of French surrealism's liberational quest for the positive love of the irrational and for the pure creations of the mind" (Williams 2002, 294). What we may extract from this inheritance is that, indeed, *El infarto* is involved in an international discourse on "madness," even as it is inserted into a very particular history uniquely analyzed by Williams. For instance, the overwhelming whiteness surrounding the frames of the photographs and the script reminds readers of the whitewashing of Chilean society during the Transition to democracy.

El infarto del alma and *Madness*, two seemingly isolated pieces, reveal distinct treatments of familiar and national cohesiveness. As they highlight the dehumanization of both authoritarian states and the marketplace, they oblige us into the almost vertiginous discomfort of multiple subject positions. Looking at these "accidents of critique," recalling the surrealists' emphasis on shock and chance, within an amalgam of art and advertising also allows us to address unique angles of traveling avant-garde art objects and accompanying theory. In considering *Colors*'s *Madness* as an "accident of critique," what must be kept in mind is that if *Colors* were to have succeeded in documenting the notorious hospital in Havana, and not the more progressive Camagüey hospital, a more typical portrayal of Cuba as anachronistic and authoritarian would have resulted. Benetton would have appeared as a metonymy for the marketplace as a champion of human rights.

With an edgy avant-garde photographic and bilingual narrative expose on life in mental institutions around the world, but especially in contemporary Cuba, the 2002 *Madness* reconstitutes identity and commodifies difference in a manner that departs from the more expected representations of Cuba of the "Special Period" encountered on the Internet, in film, in music videos, and in all sorts of fashion, travel, and cigar magazines. This difference, however, may be overshadowed by the controversial context in which the text appears. The horizons of expectations for the distinct photoessays are disparate. *El infarto del alma*, along with *El padre mío*, is frequently placed on the other side of an axis from the *testimonio*, and as such, there is an obligation to address them as provocation. *Colors's Madness*, produced by the multinational corporation Benetton, and Eltit and Errázuriz's *El infarto del alma*, published by Francisco Zegers, a small company focusing on theoretical works in Santiago, respond to distinct readerships as well as historical and geographical frameworks—differences that may be seen to impede any comparative account. However, they both transform the genre of the *testimonio*, and in so doing, compromise the fads of markets with their marketing of madness.[2] The fact that the magazine belongs to a corporation whose contradictory politics epitomize the ethical projections of the neoliberal world, a principal object of Errázuriz's and Eltit's critique, makes *Madness* appear in the form of an imprecise parody of *El infarto del alma*. A closer reading of the texts, however, reveals that the effects of their tactics of transgression and containment sometimes approximate each other.[3] In the past five years, Errázuriz's and Eltit's critique of the politics of the Chilean Transition into democracy has begun to find another home, albeit provisional, in the North American academy. It is a marketplace of its own that, in part, cannot be viewed separately from the globalizing one. It too relies on micropolitics and the aestheticization of difference for its categorization of identity and disciplines. Programs in ethnic and area studies emerged in the aftermath of the U.S. government's more and more sophisticated means to control others. *Mano de obra* represents through fiction many of the theoretical premises that Eltit asserts in a 2001 interview with Michael Lazzara at Princeton.

Claro, porque el mercado que es un sistema inteligente, no tiene ni estética ni ética. Entonces, hay ciertos textos reductores en donde todo, al final es susceptible a hacerse mercado, incluso el dolor, la violencia, el hambre, etcetera. Estoy pensando en Benetton, en la campaña de Benetton que organizó las ventas de sus ropas con lo más dramatico de la sociedad contemporánea. Y una de sus imágenes más promocionadas era un enfermo de SIDA en agonía, una fotografía de esa persona prácticamente muriéndose de SIDA. Y esa fotografía última, digamos, se usaba para vender ropa Benetton. Entonces, el mercado toma esas figuras, las repone y las destruye. Destruye su dramatismo, y destruye el asombro que nos pueden producir. (Eltit 2001, 11)

[Of course, because the market is an intelligent system. It does not have aesthetics or ethics. Then, there are certain reductive texts in which all, in the end, is susceptible to becoming market, including pain, violence, hunger, etcetera. I am thinking about Benetton, about the Benetton campaign in which the sale of clothing was tied to the most dramatic aspects of contemporary society. And one of its most promoted images was a sick person with AIDS in agony, a photograph of this person practically dying of AIDS. And this last photograph let's say, was used to sell Benetton clothing. So the market takes these figures, replaces them, and destroys them. It destroys their dramatic quality, and it destroys the shock that they can produce for us.]

In part, due to these sorts of advertising campaigns, well characterized by Eltit, Benetton has stores in 120 countries around the world and has an annual turnover of 1.9 billion euros, net of retail sales ("United Colors of Benetton: Who We Are").

The blurring of journalistic and fashion photography characteristic of Benetton's very visible campaigns has made them difficult to ignore. The above is not the only opinion that Eltit expressed on the topic. In the past few years, she has become more and more of a public intellectual, while still refusing to give in to the notion that literature must transmit messages. Published in December 2000, Eltit's contribution to a multi-authored article published in Buenos Aires's *Clarin* periodical, "2001: El desafío y la esperanza" (2000b), conveys outrage over Benetton's model of shock advertising. Eltit asserts that wherein this company's gestures of selling catostrophes are composed of shock without poetics, there is another kind that is invested in hope and political passion—a "sueño romántico" (romantic dream). Keeping the immensity of Benetton's multinationalism in mind, to what extent can we read the company-sponsored journal as a critique—in the sense of separating or exposing the truth in ideology—from within a globalizing narrative that firmly rests on a particular ordering of who we are, the economically and therefore socially liberated, and who they are, the more challenged, constrained, and confined.

Like Nelly Richard's critical discussion of neo-avant-garde production carried out in prominent forums, such as *Margins and Institutions: Art in Chile since 1973* (1986), *La Revista de Crítica Cultural*, and presentations on cultural critique in Latin America at numerous North

American universities and international conferences, her description of the way in which *El infarto del alma* circulated in the Transition's markets and cultural fairs is crucial to understanding the position Eltit's projects have come to occupy in Latin Americanism. *El infarto del alma* performed a fascinating symbolic function, described by Richard: "la austeridad y severidad críticas de una visualidad que usa metáfora *en negativo* de la relación foto/álbum/familia para desestructurar la ilusión de un grupo social reunido por la solidaridad de sus miembros" (the critical austerity and severity of a visuality that uses the metaphor *in negative* of the photo/album/family relationship in order to deconstruct the illusion of a social group reunited for the solidarity of its members) (Richard 1986, 253). Like Eltit's other neo-avant-garde projects, *El infarto del alma* critiques the politics of the state and patriarchy by focusing on the margins and transgressive conceptualizations of family. However, whereas *El padre mío* links a schizophrenic vagabond, referred to as "el padre mío," to the author's own transgressive artistic voice, and *Por la patria* turns its attention on an incestuous family that the dictatorship's roundups of *lumpen*, leftists, and homosexuals attempt to break into confessions of their having betrayed the nation, *El infarto del alma* creates a family out of the delusions of the sanatorium's patients. The linguistic dimensions that not only congeal, but also disrupt this social group are located in Eltit's text: When she accompanied Errázuriz to this legendary institution, Errázuriz had already visited it so many times that the hospital administration barely checked her when she entered with Eltit and the patients shouted "Tia Paz" upon her arrival. To a degree, the patients' familiar salutations embody the maintenance of Chilean society's social strata dramatized in *El obsceno pájaro de la noche*—younger generations and lower classes are impelled to reinforce their difference idiomatically through constructions of familiar address. Some of the modes of address are particularly haunting: Although Eltit is first startled by the way in which a woman older than she pleas for her attention saying "mamita" into her ear, she becomes accustomed to her elder's code. Through this intimacy, she acquires authorization from within the asylum in a manner that corresponds to the feminist intellectual voice acquired through "el padre mío." The interns of that marginal space, then, continue to occupy her own brain, after her departure but like the interned, she too is involved in a collaboration that seeks to link both text and image. Errázuriz and Eltit configure themselves as coconspirators whose complicity with each other mirrors the complicity among the amorous interns.

Unlike the black and white photos of amorous heterosexual couples in *El infarto del alma*, the photographs of individuals and couples in the Cuban section of *Colors*'s *Madness* are primarily in the faded greens and blues that, by now, have become the palette of this tropical and washed-out paradise, but they roughly correspond with those that are frequently used in mental institutions to appease patients. The irony of this overlapping comes out in the photograph of the pastel green–tiled wall with four wall hangings above of tropical scenery: including two lovebirds and the sea (figure 5.1). Several patients in love are interspersed throughout the magazine's different locations, but most of them appear in Camagüey, and most of the couple shots appear together on the same two-page spread (figures 5.2 and 5.3). Because they are oddly in a mix of street and asylum clothes and in front of a light blue curtain, they give the impression of having been photographed at a mediocre portrait studio. The astounding degree of decontextualization makes it seems as if the couples were captured in their dream lives. The pairs are quite diverse in height and race and it is difficult to pin down their whereabouts. The aestheticization represents the absurdity of a situation more than the beauty of these subjects. It is difficult to imagine cosmopolitan designers, artists, shoppers, and the likes glancing at the portraits without a degree of awe or condescension because they seem to recall the "tawdriness" of strip malls, rather than the staid quality of aristocratic parlors or even the dirty reality of the down and out. This contrasts tremendously with *El infarto del alma* where the couples are definitively shot on the grounds of the asylum, making it clear that their experience of each other has a context in the present and in the past as well (figure 5.4).

In addition to *Madness*'s cover, a self-portrait of Mario, 38 of 93 pages are devoted to the patients of the Camagüey hospital. In contrast, other locations of distinct residences for the mentally ill in Bouaké, Ivory Coast, Aversa, Italy, Gheel, Belgium, Los Angeles, USA, Valona, Albania, Sidney, Australia, Cape Town, South Africa, and Curitiba, Brazil receive much less attention. There are also some allusions to homosocial bonds and homosexual pairings. While the bigness and lack of movement in many of these portraits could be interpreted as containment, it could also be seen as dignifying. These photos were taken with a large-format camera and tripod that give them an air of nineteenth-century portraiture. There is little pretense of spontaneity. Concerning this decision, Broomberg explains, "All we're doing is giving people warning, letting the subjects represent themselves instead of pretending to catch 'the defining moment'

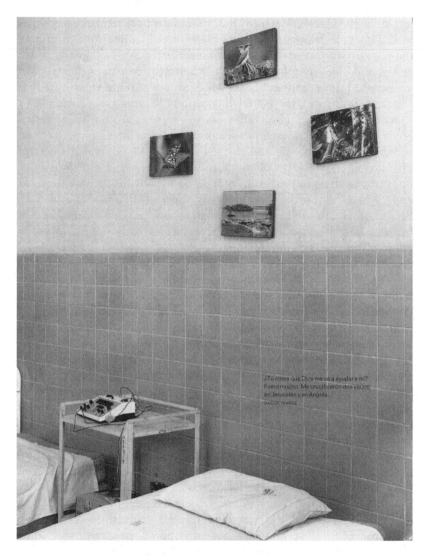

Figure 5.1

that speaks the unwitting truth. The point is we're being self-conscious about our intervention, about the fact that it is a mediated truth" ("Artthrob" 2004). It would be difficult to ignore Broomberg's self-critical tone, even though at that time, he was employed by a multi-national company that was at the forefront of disseminating the

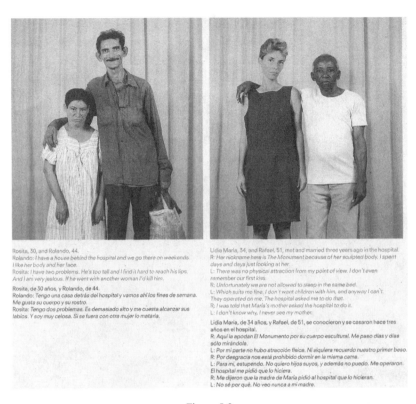

Rosita, 30, and Rolando, 44.
Rolando: *I have a house behind the hospital and we go there on weekends. I like her body and her face.*
Rosita: *I have two problems. He's too tall and I find it hard to reach his lips. And I am very jealous. If he went with another woman I'd kill him.*

Rosita, de 30 años, y Rolando, de 44.
Rolando: *Tengo una casa detrás del hospital y vamos ahí los fines de semana. Me gusta su cuerpo y su rostro.*
Rosita: *Tengo dos problemas. Es demasiado alto y me cuesta alcanzar sus labios. Y soy muy celosa. Si se fuera con otra mujer la mataría.*

Lidia María, 34, and Rafael, 51, met and married three years ago in the hospital.
R: *Her nickname here is The Monument because of her sculpted body. I spent days and days just looking at her.*
L: *There was no physical attraction from my point of view. I don't even remember our first kiss.*
R: *Unfortunately we are not allowed to sleep in the same bed.*
L: *Which suits me fine. I don't want children with him, and anyway I can't. They operated on me. The hospital asked me to do that.*
R: *I was told that María's mother asked the hospital to do it.*
L: *I don't know why, I never see my mother.*

Lidia María, de 34 años, y Rafael, de 51, se conocieron y se casaron hace tres años en el hospital.
R: *Aquí la apodan El Monumento por su cuerpo escultural. Me paso días y días sólo mirándola.*
L: *Por mi parte no hubo atracción física. Ni siquiera recuerdo nuestro primer beso.*
R: *Por desgracia nos está prohibido dormir en la misma cama.*
L: *Para mí, estupendo. No quiero hijos suyos, y además no puedo. Me operaron. El hospital me pidió que lo hiciera.*
R: *Me dijeron que la madre de María pidió al hospital que lo hicieran.*
L: *No sé por qué. No veo nunca a mi madre.*

Figure 5.2

marketability of ethnic diversity in 1980s. Adam Broomberg's and Oliver Chanarin's photographs are accompanied by relatively sustained interviews with the patients, a tactic that, corresponding to the magazine's "new millennial philosophy," embraces communities rather than the older form of disjointed images and maxims that resembled advertising. The most fascinating photos, on both an aesthetic and political level, are the self-portraits, especially, since on the cover, the patient named Mario gives the camera his back (figure 5.5). This implication of resistance to being observed is complicated; unlike the control over her secrets that Rigoberta used to possess, the placement of this color photograph on the cover of Benetton's magazine is seductive. Purchasers acquire something that is difficult to possess. The abundance of italicized words supposedly corresponding to direct speech give readers the impression that they have first-hand access to a largely inaccessible world. Nevertheless, such a "direct discourse"

María del Carmen (aka Chuchi), 54, and Otto, 58.
O: Chuchi and I met here in 1982. She was drinking water and I asked her to share it with me. We started talking. We first kissed under that mango tree. That is where our relationship began.
M: I can't remember that. It was 19 years ago.
O: The government gave me a house and we moved into it together. We come here during the day and work. Since we are both ill we have decided not to have children.
M: I am infertile. I was operated on. Otto and I decided together—it was our decision.

María del Carmen (alias Chuchi), de 54 años, y Otto, de 58.
O: Chuchi y yo nos conocimos aquí en 1982. Estaba bebiendo agua y le pedí que la compartiera conmigo. Comenzamos a charlar. Nos besamos por primera vez debajo de ese mango. Así comenzó nuestra relación.
M: No lo recuerdo. Fue hace 19 años.
O: El Gobierno me dio una casa y nos mudamos a ella los dos juntos. Venimos aquí de día y trabajamos. Como estamos ambos enfermos, hemos decidido no tener hijos.
M: Soy estéril. Me operaron. Otto y yo lo decidimos juntos; fue una decisión personal.

Mayra, 24, and Rolando, 23, met at the hospital.
M: When I met Rolando I was really beautiful with long hair, slim, beautiful teeth.
R: I kissed her the day we met. She was something to look at. Really magnificent. I fell deeply in love. The rest came later. If only we could sleep together just one night in the same bed. Unfortunately it's against the rules.
M: Like most of the women in this place I was operated on. The relatives want us to be infertile. I am afraid of having a child because it may starve. How can I feed a child?

Mayra, de 24 años, y Rolando, de 23, se conocieron en el hospital.
M: Cuando conocí a Rolando, yo era hermosa, con el pelo largo, delgada, los dientes preciosos.
R: La besé el día que nos conocimos. Era impresionante. Realmente magnífica. Me enamoré profundamente. El resto vino después. Ojalá pudiéramos dormir en la misma cama aunque sólo fuera una noche. Por desgracia, va contra las reglas.
M: Como la mayoría de las mujeres de aquí, estoy operada. Los familiares quieren que seamos estériles. Me da miedo tener un hijo porque podría morir de hambre. ¿Cómo voy a alimentar a un hijo?

Figure 5.3

Figure 5.4

Figure 5.5

frequently appears framed within a strong narrative whose conclusion has already been well consolidated. Whereas the technique of framing the images with a black line surrounded by white, the unconventional formatting of the text that exhibits varying degrees of white pages, the emboldened words, and few passages in quotation marks within the text all emphasize the element of *El infarto del alma*'s construction, the more conventional format and the manner in which the patients' words are always italicized in *Madness* underscore a singular route toward making sense of the other. However, because of this apparent facility, we ought not underestimate the sort of appeals that *Colors'* *Madness* makes to audiences. Here in the framed testimony of one of Camagüey's patients named Raquel (that appears in the text side by side in Spanish and in English), the degree to which the United States' problematic relation to Cuba is constitutive of national and familiar identity is evident (figure 5.6).

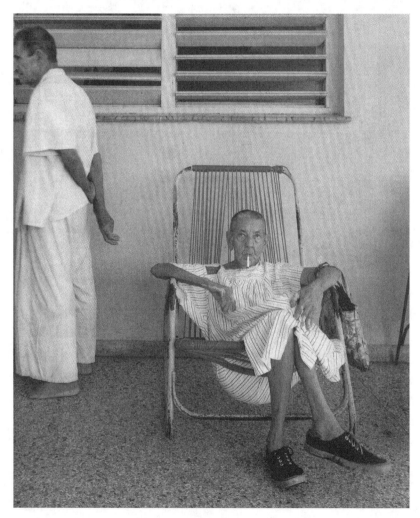

Figure 5.6

Pegué a mi hijo, sabes, y no había hecho nada malo.

Solloza tanto que es turbador. Tienes la sensación de que deberías consolarla, pero Raquel deja de llorar inopinadamente. Se inclina hacia delante, sonriendo, y asume una voz diferente, más infantil, conspiradora. *La niña que cuidaba en Cuba está ahora en California y me manda ropa que guardo en casa de mi hijo ¿Te apetecería ir a visitarla?* Más lágrimas. *Cuba es mi país. ¿Cómo voy a dejar un lugar tan bello?* Deja de llorar de nuevo y, con seductora satisfacción, dice: *Voy a ser bisabuela dentro de poco.*

Diez minutos después de la entrevista la vemos balancearse en una mecedora. Nos sonrió con complicidad y nos manda un beso. (*Madness* 2001–2002, 14–15)[4]

[I slapped my son, you know, and he'd never done anything wrong.

She's sobbing so much it's unnerving. You feel you should comfort her, but she turns off the tears by herself. She leans in, smiling, and takes on a different voice. It's more childlike, more conspiratorial.

You know, the girl I used to babysit for is in California now, and she sends me clothes that I keep in my son's house. Would you like to visit her? More tears. Cuba is my country. How can I leave such a beautiful place?

She stops crying again and with flirtatious pride, says: *You know, I'm going to be a great-grandmother soon.*

Ten minutes after the interview we see her moving backwards and forwards on a rocking chair. She smiles at us with complicity and blows us a kiss.]

Particularly fascinating for this study of cosmopolitanisms are the words "consolar" (comfort) and "complicidad" (complicity). The need for redemption is built into this passage, as is the suggestion that the concept of "redemption" is short sighted on account of its evangelical premise that rocks the other into submission. Raquel's own dynamics and capacity to convince are not annulled in this passage. The "after" of the interview betrays the pose of complicity that the sometimes sobbing Raquel, insistent that "she goes mad when people call her a whore," has conveyed to them with her seduction. The final framing of Raquel on the rocking chair recalls the unsteady relation to the outside of her confined space. Although confined, Raquel is profoundly grounded in Cuba and it is from this paradoxically unstable yet identifiable position that *Colors* suggest we interpret her seduction. In this instance, her performance conforms to those of other personages who knowingly play the role of "native informants"; she is not only proud and seemingly steadfast, but also needy. The national character of this insane subject is strangely affirmed by the international register.

In Raquel's speech, the absence of the many Cubans who have left is perceivable, but more generally, in the series of visual images, so is a larger societal and international duress. In this photo album, we, like Benetton's interlocutors, are introduced to Raquel, who is doubly confined, old, and conspiratorial; she rejects the label of whore, yet holds on to the narrative of the nation that is promoted in the "Special Period in Times of Peace." The narrative of national identity or *cubanidad* has been premised within official discourse as that form of solidarity, both prior to, but also conditioned by solidarity with the revolution. *Cubanidad* enables Cubans to survive the catastrophic material effects of the disintegration of the Soviet Union.[5] The aesthetic ramifications of this survival mechanism are visible in distinct media, since in recent years, Cuba's place within the imaginary of sexual tourism has been revamped. It can involve a seductive pleading and hustling called *jineterismo* that recalls the subtle methods of Wendy Guerra's Olga. *Jineterismo* is conscious of confinement and of the particular privilege that this singular sort of confinement entails. Even the government bureau of tourism has shaped its advertising campaigns according to this imperative. In the case of Raquel, the projection of this character is extraordinarily complex, since the changes within her discourse extend to a game whose referents are outside of the mental institution, in the very nation: she confesses, then cries, her voice becomes infantile, she mentions something very powerful (exiting the country, she cries again, she affirms her nationality, and then—within the frame of categories constitutive of adversity—she seduces). The power of these extended words to lead us to think of *Madness* as a commodity and as what Richard calls a "metaphor in negative" of the national photo album of the Special Period is immense.

The "after," the "ten minutes after the interview" in *El infarto del alma* is more intricate on account of a demanding combination of photography and self-conscious framing devices—windows within and a black line around the photos—that emphasize the extratextual framings of sanity, madness, and fragmented prose. In a manner similar to *Mano de obra*, *El infarto del alma* superimposes a new plot over a historical archive. It elaborates the symbolics of the disease tuberculosis for the nineteenth- and early part of the twentieth century. For these contemporary artists, Putaendo represents the last token to the Romantics for whom tuberculosis was associated with love and unproductive bodies—all that which challenged the salaried worker of industrialism. Eltit suggests in fairly direct prose that love links the former institution to the latter asylum that, as illustrated by the photographs, the state is unable to take away.

Even though, as previously suggested, the visual framing devices as well as the varied font and formatting slow down facile consumption or comprehension of the other, another aspect of the text gestures toward the merging with the marginal subjects. Unlike scientific approaches implemented by repressive institutions to comprehend and control sociological problems, depending on a clearly demarcated self and other, the artists attempt to form part of the alternative community at the same time that they signal the impossibility of doing so. Alongside the photographs of insane couples are complex narrative voices whose diversity, at first, appears to be organized with chapter-like titles, such as "Te escribo," "Diario de viaje (viernes 7 de agosto 1992)," ultra-brief but illogical documentations of disparity entitled "La falta," almost catch-like allusions to French post-Structuralism such as "El otro, mi otro" (figure 5.7), the Romantic cliché, "El sueño imposible," referring to the impossible dream of Juana, a patient and girlfriend of José, that was recorded by Errázuriz in January 1990, the follow-up "Juana La Loca" that precedes a one-page portrait of Juana in which the narrator speculates about her origins in the Valparaíso refuge and her symbolic connection to the mad ancient queen of Spain, and finally simply "Escribo." That several of these titles and subtitles are utilized more than once emphasizes the degree to which the psychotic voices penetrate the text's structure. While Beckett explained *El padre mio*, throughout the 75 unnumbered pages of diverse and complex narrative voices of *El infarto del alma*, Eltit ties her artistic predecessors Andre Breton and Arthur Rimbaud to brief conversations between the visitors and asylum dwellers that are set off from the rest of the text in quotation marks. In contrast to hospital-like numbers that inextricably link a patient to an ailment or freak show-like photographs with quantifiable colonialist objectives, the ambiguity of the names and gazes universalize their disparate situations, without appealing to the impulse to form empathic ties to individuals' stories and faces. The neo-avant-garde approach toward documenting patients' transgressive affiliations with one another highlights the policies of consumption that led to the purchasing power of Chile's citizens determining their social worth. The more symbolic "after" to the concealed expose involves a subtle process of contradictory reinstitutionalization in which *Cosmopolitanisms and Latin America* partakes. At the same time, the backward and forward movement between present

EL OTRO, MI OTRO

El sujeto parece prisionero de lo que es una repetición cuando busca en su tránsito al otro, que se aparece o desaparece ante su vista bajo distintas formas, a lo largo de lo que será toda su vida. El otro, continente de su múltiple paradójica sentimentalidad y de la modalidad de su sobrevivencia, se va a expresar también en la diversidad de sentimientos y búsquedas que posee el sujeto, sea el deseo, sea el poder, sea Dios.

En todas las distintas expresiones apasionadas yace el otro, que a la vez que lo conforta lo amenaza, cuando pone en peligro la estabilidad de su frágil unidad que, sin embargo, requiere tercamente traspasar su propio umbral para perderse en la disolución de su poder, de su propia imagen, de su miedo. A la manera de una carrera incesante marcada por la desigualdad, los afectos caen sobre la otra figura en la que se depositan los signos simbólicos y materiales de un anhelo cuyas fronteras presentan límites difusos.

Ahí está la madre. Acecha encogida en el contraluz de su propio vientre dilatado. Ahí está la madre, con sus dientes afilados de amor, preparándose para hacer -a costa de sus prolijas dentelladas- a un ser que cumpla con su imagen y semejanza, que no será su imagen y semejanza sino el deseo abstracto de sí. A dentelladas, la madre intenta reparar su parte ominosa que la devela, que la revela como un fracaso ante ella misma. Pero la madre no deja de afirmar, en esas horas, que sólo permitirá que en su interior se reproduzca y se condense la perfección que la va a reivindicar. Ella piensa en su vientre y ve cómo se expande y cómo crece y cómo asciende y promete que sus sufrimientos le serán recompensados. La madre está en un violento y solitario estado de expansión corporal.

El otro se levanta como fantasía de un deseo siamés en el que lo idéntico se completa con el requisito de lo

Figure 5.7

and past, Cuba and Chile is meant to shake up the politics of that reception.

The very "soul" of the photoessay pertains to the continuity of place that goes beyond the state's shifting demands for housing and controlling its marginal citizens. Beholden to the strained compatibility of love and disease, especially tuberculosis, within the Romantic imagination, Eltit and Errázuriz document the remnants of this passion within a society of Transition whose initial leadership under Patricio Aylwin barely altered the neoliberal economic policies, which had been previously conceptualized, in part, as "shock treatment," during Pinochet's dictatorship. Much of Eltit's baroque fiction and essays attempts to resist the effects of the policies of consumption that led to the purchasing power of Chile's citizens becoming the principal factor determining their social worth. In *El infarto del alma*, Eltit takes the affection that continues to exist among patients in the state mental institution to be a form of resistance (figures 5.8 and 5.9). That female mental patients, who have been sterilized, sometimes delude themselves into thinking they are able to reproduce, is symbolic of the government's not entirely successful attempt to detain not only the soul, but also to prevent the reproduction of ideologies threatening to its legitimacy. The ethical ramifications of Eltit's aestheticization of

Figure 5.8

Figure 5.9

these figures in the face of the humiliation they suffer at the hands of the government is a question that several critics including Jean Franco, Julio Ramos, Nelly Richard, Robert Neustadt, and Mary Beth Tierney-Tello have all contemplated. For Neustadt, Eltit's confusion of critique within a system of representational discourse creates a " 'tangle of conflicting intentions' [that] reveals an understanding of the political and the aesthetic as inextricably related both to each other, and significantly to narrative" (Neustadt 1999, 28). Julio Ramos's extraordinary close reading of *El infarto del alma* is even more decisive with respect to his interpretation of the ethical implications: "el reverso mismo de la lógica instrumental y de la economía acumulativa . . . en una práctica alterna de intercambios" (Ramos 2000, paragraph 11) (the very reverse of instrumental logic and accumulative economy. . . . in an alternate practice of exchanges), and Tierney-Tello wrestles with the texts as commodity, first suggesting that:

> one reader's dignification is another's commodification. But such commodification is perhaps inevitable. Eltit's intervention seems to accept commodification as a fact of late-twentieth-century cultural life, choosing to transform it into a contestatory practice. Indeed, Eltit's project seems to demand that, since this text is to become a cultural

commodity anyway, its exchange value should be top dollar, in order to thoroughly disrupt the elite-popular paradigm. (Tierney-Tello 1999, 92)

She then asserts that Eltit's texts propose "solidarity through the aesthetic" (Tierney-Tello 1999, 92). I have been inclined to think that Eltit is most ethical when she foregrounds the "cosmetic" process of "making-up the world" by which truths are shaped, as occurred in *Por la patria*, "Nomadic Bodies," and in *Lumpérica*, to a lesser degree.

Although the confessions and photographs within *Colors* tend to follow a more traditional and almost case-like pattern of documentation, the patients, and not the authorities, reveal their ages to the interlocutor. Similarly, the discrepancy between the World Health Organization's current classification of mental disease and the patients' own conceptualization of their condition using an outdated code of theirs is brought to the surface immediately with the interlocutor's question: "¿Sabe de qué sufre?" "Do you know what you're suffering from" and the patient's response "295.3" (*Madness* 2001–2002, 4). Then comes the interlocutor's explanation: "295. 3 is the number once assigned to paranoid schizophrenia by the World Health Organization in its Classification of Mental Disease and Behaviors. Now it's F20.0, but for Julio the old number is still the one that makes sense of his illness" (*Madness* 2001–2002, 4). While *Madness* cautiously articulates some questions of positionality, as well as the tentative and often oppressive facets of "globalism," it imposes linguistic standards that are far from the local argot: "*Cuando la fotografiasteis, Silvia se fue corriendo a ver a mi novia y le mostró la fotografia, diciendole: Me han fotografiado porque soy negra, y a ti no*" (emphasis in original) (When you took Silvia's picture, she went straight to my girlfriend and showed it to her. She said: They took my picture because I'm black—but they didn't take yours" (*Madness* 2001–2002, 20). Where the dimension of framing of that cultural object is exposed, the mechanism that converts the Cuban Spanish of the witnesses into peninsular Spanish is suppressed within italics denoting standardization and accessibility. The unlikely use of the *vosotros* form, second person (informal) plural, along with the unusual and infrequently articulated verbs and structures reflects the continued expectation of intralingual translation and stylization.

While the ethical questions concerning the photographic representation of the interns who are on antipsychotics do not appear, they are present in what I am calling the diary of *Madness*—*Ghetto* actually remarks: "Patients who are heavily medicated will do almost anything they are told in front of a camera. Some have never been photographed before—would they understand the cultural and chemical process of taking their image? Towards the end of our stay in Camaguey, it seemed a better idea to devise a system whereby the patients could photograph themselves. By squeezing the ball on the end of a long release cable they could take their photograph when and how they chose" (Broomberg and Chanarin 2003, 81). The pharmaceuticals enter Eltit's text in a similar fashion. She inquires about how to translate the "visualidad muda de esas figures deformadas por los fármacos" "the mute visuality of these figures deformed by pharmaceuticals" (Eltit 1994, n.n.). To a degree, the subjective account of ages recalls the way in which Eltit yields to the multiple models of temporality that function within the insane asylum; nonetheless, *Madness* mounts a stylized and particular version of life abroad whose imprecision is questionable on grounds that a transforming Cuban linguistic reality disappears. However, when it apparently randomly cites Roberto Fernández Retamar, as a Cuban poet only, and not also as a renowned critic and director of *Casa de las Américas*, cracks within systems of ordering begin to be exposed. "Dichosos los normales, esos seres extraños" (Happy the normal—those strange beings) in the same typography used to identify the patients' names, is placed in the light blue of the tropical sky, above a photograph of an asylum couple (*Madness* 2001–2002, 35). Like the slip in the translation, whether this visual montage is intended as some sort of transgression of officialdom or is an unintentional collapse is difficult to know. If we are to surmise that it is the product of ignorance and discard of patrimony does that mean that its power to visually suggest something else with regard to the Cuban context is null? It is fascinating that Roberto Fernández Retamar frequently rests on that divide, as a transgressive "marginal," for the U.S. academy and as a powerful and centered revolutionary in Cuba.

Other dimensions of a more material, less celestial, Cuban reality are also present. The magazine's ethical position seems to be apparent in the discussion of the decreasing population of the Camagüey Hospital, that is the result of "pilot projects that have sought to look into the relationship between madness and sanity . . . and not whether the mentally ill can be reintegrated into the community" (*Madness* 2001–2002, 4). The fact that the precedent of this program of reintegration revolves around a doctor, Franco Basaglia, who in the 1970s, in Trieste, Italy "started the fight to close mental hospitals" is made evident, only after examining the photographs of the Ivory Coast

(*Madness* 2001–2002, 50). The Italy represented in the photographs is not the Italy of those innovators. It is instead the South, in Adversa, near Naples, that is not "under the jurisdiction of the Ministry of Health," but rather under that of a more local jurisdiction not reached by those sorts of pilot projects (*Madness* 2001–2002, 50). Those in Cuba in recent years, in fact, actually grew out of frequent collaborations with Italy. Moreover, the Benetton Foundation has collaborated with the Centro Studi, Ricerca e Formazione in Salute Mentale on renovations on the site of Basaglia's renowned transformation of the Trieste mental institution. More specifically, the Centro Studi, Ricerca e Formazione in Salute Mentale (CSR) of the Friuli Venezia Giulia region organized a conference, sponsored by the Pan-American Health Organization and the Italian Cooperation, which brought about the 1995 Carta de la Habana aiming to reorient care from psychiatric hospitals to the community. Furthermore, the CSR organized the participation of the Cuban Official delegation of Cienfuegos in the international meeting in Trieste in 1998 called "Franco Basaglia: The Possible Community." Following this event, the Cuban Ministry of Health "declared its will to disseminate the experience under way in Cienfuegos all over the country" ("World Health Organization Mental Health Unit"). The Fondazione Benetton Studi Ricerche, whose president is Luciano Benetton, in fact, has collaborated with the CSR on renovations on the site of Basaglia's renowned transformation of the Trieste mental institution ("Fondazione Benetton Studi Ricerche").[6]

In this way, we form a different understanding of *Colors*'s interest, and also of Cuba, as a nation that is somewhat more unified than Italy. This unique Caribbean nation also appears to be more successfully supported than those parts of Italy that, to borrow *Colors*'s phraseology from a 1996 expose on a Cuban village, are "in the middle of nowhere" (Balmaseda 1996). *Madness* then signals ruptures in the globalizing world's narratives of advancement. The Cuban intern's "295.3" suggests that the country is left behind. This notion becomes even more nuanced when considered beside the south of Italy. Now, let us recall not only Raquel's statement, but also that of Yuriel who suggests "*La mujer más bella del mundo es la esposa de Fidel*" (emphasis in original) (The most beautiful woman in the world is Fidel's wife) (*Madness* 2001–2002, 32) and that of Pedro who reveals "*Quise suicidarme dos veces, las dos veces con un Sputnik, una navaja rusa*" (emphasis in original) (I tried to commit suicide twice, both times with a Sputnik, a Russian knife) (*Madness* 2001–2002, 10)—all taken beside the representation of Italy. So phantasmagorical is the concept of Fidel's wife that Yuriel's statement becomes paradigmatic of decades of authoritarian rule that speak through the discourse of the categorically insane. On a similar note, among the many allusions to the "Special Period" within the text, Pedro's confused mention of Sputnik confounds temporal periods. Immediately, *Madness*'s readers recall the Cold War's races in outer space. Together, *Madness*'s statements reveal an almost parodic faith in *cubanidad*, that is both conditioned by the system and beyond its limits. Their words and images now ("after") displayed in the 2001 report of the World Health Organization's website reveal a subtle portrayal of loyalty, dependence, and oppression whose own efforts at translation and concealment in themselves reveal the fissures and limits of developmental theory and globalization as well as the possibility of "accidents of critique."

That the women of René Vallejo, like those of Putaendo convey consternation over their ability to reproduce also signals the extent to which the weight of controlling madness falls on these female bodies in comparative contexts. As a counterpoint to the institution's deputy director who states "Nuestra política es la contracepción o la esterilización, con el permiso de los familiares" (Our policy is contraception or sterilization—with relatives' permission) (*Madness* 2001–2002, 26), María del Carmen (alias Chuchí) explains "Soy estéril. Me operaron. Otto y yo lo decidimos juntos; fue una decisión personal" (I am infertile. I was operated on. Otto and I decided together—it was our decision) (*Madness* 2001–2002, 29). However, another patient Mayra reveals that external forces helped to guide her in the decision to become sterile. "Como la mayoría de las mujeres de aquí, estoy operada. Los familiares quieren que seamos estériles. Me da miedo tener un hijo porque podría morir de hambre. ¿Cómo voy a alimentar a un hijo?" (Like most of the women in this place I was operated on. The relatives want us to be infertile. I am afraid of having a child because it may starve. How can I feed a child?) (*Madness* 2001–2002, 29).

It is difficult to read this statement without thinking of the United States over 40-year embargo of the island nation as well as Bush's continued efforts at constricting it further. In response to the more general question outside of how an isolated Cuba is going to feed its children, the government, as Elisa Facio's research has pointed out, in recent years, has pushed toward diversifying tourism through an emphasis on Cuba's contributions in the medical, ecological, historical, recreational, and cultural spheres (Facio 2000, 69). Nevertheless, the images of intrigue, of sexual, and yet, still somehow naïve and deprived youth, palm trees, and old American automobiles driven by fading *salseros* have not entirely been dispelled, the more popular encounters with this tropical island illustrate. In the face of both Cuba's diversification of tourism that showcases its access to medical care and facilities, and the images of Cuba that those on its apparent outside have come to expect, *Madness* renders a more complicated portrait of local and global space.

More than any other contemporaneous project of globalization or multiculturalism, this initial 1989 tagline—"Ein magazin qui parle about el resto del mondo"—evoked that common language invented approximately a century before in the hopes to resolve global problems: Esperanto. In that new "hope," shadowing the disintegration of the Soviet Union and the reunification of Germany, grand narratives of liberation are transformed, as the very process of reification is presented through parody, all in the manner typical of neoliberal economies of exchange in which inequities are sustained. In fact, since the fiftieth anniversary issue, 41, little of the first incarnation of *Colors* remains. Replacing the old tagline is "A Magazine about the Rest of the World"; its singularity is perhaps less pretentious, more direct in its manner of directing the reader toward particular goals. Since its fiftieth anniversary, the expressed intent of *Colors* is on community, with the goal of transforming the previous fast and flashy slogan-like and disruptive material into a more sustained and interactive engagement in a single place ("*Colors*: What We Say").[7] The reference to the fiftieth anniversary issue when emphasizing the evolution of Benetton's advertising as opposed to the year 2000 designated by the Christian calendar is a reflection of how difficult it is to locate that outside reference within the company's plentiful primarily on-line explanations of their diverse advertising, cultural, and humanitarian projects, of which the company's 2001 collaboration with the United Nations on volunteerism is most notable (*Colors* 46—Volunteers). For instance, in the final pages of *Colors*, as in the archive of its website ("*Colors*: Archives"), all of the covers with their corresponding issue numbers are perusable. It is as if *Colors* has restructured the calendar according to their publication.

Although such appalling inwardness in the context of advertising has fallen under attack for "containment," several issues of *Colors* along with its perennial section called Yellow Pages located in the back, right before the masthead, directing readers to additional information, do suggest that there is an outside to the magazine's enclosed world of shocking photos and maxims where solutions to the problems may be encountered by if not activist, at least, activated readers. Catherine David's "Benetton effect" that associates specularization with paralysis of judgment would reject this differentiation. Paralleling Eltit's characterization of Benetton, David suggests that its advertising "reinforces the mounting spectacularization and instrumentalization of 'contemporary art' by the culture industry, where art is used for social regulation or indeed control, through the aestheticization of information or through forms of debate that paralyze any act of judgment in the immediacy of raw seduction or emotion" (David 1997, paragraph 2). Henry A. Giroux similarly affirms that Benetton's representations of dying AIDS patients and terrorist car bombings, among others, were not the alternative form of corporate communication promoted by the company, and instead encouraged the implementation of more radical pedagogical instruments that took advantage of public culture as a place of contestation. Somewhat less singularly oppositional than Giroux, Senna Tinic attempts to see how advertising may go beyond presenting images that convince consumers of desires hitherto unknown to them, conceiving Benetton's advertising campaign as providing, in postmodern fashion, enough space for multiple, contestatory, and contained readings.

The fact that the magazine is not circulated in many of the countries represented in its pages supports my suggestion that *Colors* may be read as an imprecise parody. However, that lack of circulation is a complicated matter. In a correspondence with the art director of the *Madness* issue, Olivier Chanarin told me that indeed *Colors* tried to deliver by courier these magazines to the Camagüey hospital, but their attempts were unsuccessful. Furthermore, the clerks at the Benetton store in Old Havana informed me in July 2003 that, although for approximately one and a half years, they had not stocked the *Colors* magazine in the store, previously, they had distributed it.[8]

If we turn our attention simultaneously on two commodities—that of Cuba supposedly opened, and the almost faddish function of the *testimonio*, even the *anti-testimonio*, within the discipline of Latin Americanism with the United States—we may revise slowly and cautiously our understanding of *Colors*. The extra-visual politics of Benetton are disgraceful. Nevertheless, although the shock value of many of Benetton's advertising campaigns' aesthetics depends on rapid forgetting and lack of attention to concrete referents, it is a mistake to equate them with mere decontextualization and erasure. What happens when defamiliarization meets neoliberal marketing strategies is really a question that may be asked of both *El infarto de alma* and *Colors*'s *Madness* issue.[9] With the difficult economic conditions facing the publishing industry in Latin America, as a whole, Eltit's and Errázuriz's project hardly traverse distinct communities of readers. By now, it has figured much more prominently in cultural studies outside of Chile, primarily in the United States, wherein the *testimonio*'s centrality has made Eltit's anti-testimonial and neo-avant-garde approach the symbol of literary and minoritarian art, distant from the more penetrable voices of the masses. While to claim that this text was destined for consumption by a small circle of U.S. academics is both useless and difficult to prove, it is important to recognize the constraints on the circulation of such a "minoritarian" book. That similar questions regarding self and other, or cultural object and recipient, can be posed of both the Chilean neo-avant-garde artistic project and *Colors*' *Madness* signals the importance of examining the intersections of critique and commodity in the least expected places.

*   *   *

While we may expect only consumerist versions of cosmopolitanism, we also discover politically significant testimonies concerning the cultural pressures entailed by migration, race, oppression, and economic sanctions. The experimental and more obviously political texts presented their own series of contradictions and entanglements. Delineating the common ground between a a discipline (a method of knowing) and reified knowledge (what is conventionally assumed) may help illuminate discrepant cosmopolitanisms that transform and even overcome existing disciplinary expectations and boundaries of knowledge. Cosmopolitans are those who perceive the world as their home even when these worlds profoundly contradict the comforts of conventional attachments and structures of belonging. How those specific histories of places connect to other circumstances and contexts is part of a rhetoric that travels, migrates, and perhaps even transcends the rigid and lapidary strictures of a singular place.

The ethics of reading that draws from this back and forth, this relationship in active and critical motion, forms the foundations of a knowledge that derives from a place whose place is no less than the worldly idea of cosmopolitanism that is in many ways the *aporia* of our times. Cosmopolitanism allows us to consider the complicities of reading as well as the situation and situatedness of critical activity. It establishes a relationship between the compromises involved in cultural criticism and the situation of postcolonial studies in the world. Proximity and distance are unsettled, unstable, and incalculable categories that shift the ground beneath our feet; different shades are refracted through a different prism of understanding.

Only a fragment of an art object remains the same when it travels; the autonomy and aesthetic semblance of a work of art in Santiago assumes a different form in New York. What remains of it is a complex relationship that is as much about place as it is about the predicament of its activity and movement. It is a movement that demands that we constantly reassess our disciplinary aims, our critical strategies, and interpretative methods in order to grasp it through space and from place to place. To say, for example that the manner in which Arenas was victimized by the repressive dimensions of the Cuban Revolution was also punctuated by the imperialistic efforts during those same years does not ameliorate repression. A cosmopolitan approach elucidates how histories of involvement are articulated by authors; it suggests how critics may interact with authors' visions of themselves in the world. Cosmopolitanism is, in many ways, a strategic perspective that remaps, reinvisions, and reinvents the pathways over and through which culture travels. It recontextualizes, problematizes, and challenges our own understanding of our relationships and our attachments. It even figures a minatory complicity with them. The form and velocity of the Internet and the slick advertising of corporations such as Benetton emerge as components of these remappings. Our disciplinary affiliations, our experiences, and our search for knowledge all function together, as a repertoire for the narratives of self-fashioning that we construct in a process of analysis and critical activity. The Internet and Benetton emerged in this book as components of these remappings. This back and forth strategy entails listening to what, for example, Eltit may have inherited from Walter Benjamin and poststructuralism. It establishes a dialog between her premises and our position vis-à-vis the vast field of cosmopolitan studies. Indeed, what is remarkable about Eltit's characters, on the most complex intersubjective sphere, is the manner in which they do not inhabit solely the local sphere; they seek out alternate geographies, but not, through actual travel outside of the nation. Instead, an attitude and ethos of abjection pervades her writing. Her protagonists are marginal; many of them have been debilitated and disabled by authoritarianism and a patriarchal logic that is conditioned by their position as peripheral subjects in the world.

Cosmopolitanism is composed of multiple directions and multifarious perspectives, Writers are positioned not only in relation to their families (through their filiations), but through their vocations and their very relationship to the world and its secularity. While Arenas and Eltit are not the typical subjects of cosmopolitics in Latin America, their improbability allows us to envision their functions geopolitically, spatially, and globally, instead of in the provincial, confined, and national spaces in which they have been conventionally interpreted. Indeed cosmopolitanism extends beyond the movement between North and South America; such a movement also involves other places, some which we have visualized in this book, Ancient Greece, nineteenth as well as twentieth-century France, the Soviet Union, Southern Italy, Spain. Nineteenth-century cosmopolitanisms establish the conditions of artistic production beyond place. It includes the relationship between author and critic, writer and audience, and critics and the very institutions they inhabit.

The tropes of humility and localness also weave a continuous thread. As Arenas and Eltit humble themselves within interviews and essays, those gestures of humility are elaborated globally. Frequently they mask the authors' varied affiliations with distant places and different cultures. This masking is instrumental to how critics read and interpret their works as part of a process of sustaining their own conceptions of their activity and, at the same time, obscuring their own mobility or lack thereof. Unlikely homes and discomfort are converted into critical strategies of reading the self and other.

Notes

Chapter 1   Cosmopolitanisms between the Americas

1. It is impossible to speak of the spatial dimensions of this institution without referencing Juan Carlos Quintero Herencia's book (2002) *Fulguración de espacio: Letras e imaginario institucional de la Revolución Cubana (1960–1971)*. It brilliantly theorizes the discursive modalities of the revolution through an analysis of this institution and its cultural magazine, setting up the dynamics of "us" and "them" about which I speak in chapter 4 in relation to another Cuban cultural magazine called *La Jiribilla*. In this case, the spatial dimensions are complicated by the fact that it began exclusively as an online journal.
2. As of November 8, 2004, although not prohibited to hold, the dollar was no longer accepted in Cuban shops, only locally printed convertible pesos.
3. Repeating an unfortunate and oft-committed error, I fail to address Brazilian literary and cultural studies. There is an increasing body of theory on *cosmopolitanism* produced in that context, for which Jorge Schwartz's work (1983) may be considered as fundamental.
4. See Milton Friedman's *Milton Friedman en Chile: Bases para un desarrollo económico* (1983).
5. Chris Perriam's work (2003) analyzes representations of masculinity within Spanish cinema, as well as different international and domestic ingredients that contribute to the stardom of Spanish actors. While Perriam deals principally with Spanish cinema, his discussion of Javier Bardem's stardom could easily influence a broader discussion of the commodification of Reinaldo Arenas.
6. Unless otherwise noted, translations from Spanish are my own.
7. The most important texts for the present argument by these authors are Timothy Brennan's *Salman Rushdie and the Third World* (1989) and *At Home in the World: Cosmopolitanism Now* (1997), Bruce Robbins's *Secular Vocations: Intellectuals, Professionalism, Culture, Feeling Global* (1993), as well as his edited collection with Pheng Cheah *Cosmopolitics: Thinking and Feeling beyond the Nation* (1998), also Amanda Anderson's *The Powers of Distance: Cosmopolitanism and the Cultivation of Detachment* (2001).
8. See especially the special issue of *Theory, Culture and Society* 7(2–3) (1990) called *Global Culture, Nationalism, Globalization and Modernity*, also published

as a book edited by Mike Featherstone; see also special issue of *Theory, Culture and Society* 19(1–2) (2002) called *Cosmopolis*. See *Boston Review* (1994). Martha Nussbaum et al.'s lead essay appeared in the October/November issue. A distinct version is gathered with other essays on the topic in Martha Nussbaum et al., ed., *For Love of Country: Debating the Limits of Patriotism* (1996). The journal *Public Culture* published a volume in 2000 called "Millenial Quartet" on alternative modernities, globalization, millennial capitalism and the culture of neoliberalism, and cosmopolitanism. The issue 12(3) on cosmopolitanism, edited by Homi K. Bhabha, Carol A. Breckenridge, Dipesh Chakrabarty, and Sheldon Pollock was also published in 2002 as a book by Duke University Press.

9. My premise is in the vein of Pheng Cheah and Bruce Robbins, *Cosmopolitics: Thinking and Feeling beyond the Nation* (1998) and Sheldon Pollock, Homi Bhabha, Carol Breckenridge, and Dipesh Chakrabarty's *Public Culture*'s millennial issue on cosmopolitanism.

10. *Criollo* refers to a person born in America of European descent. Naomi Lindstrom aptly notes the variety of the term's connotations, as well as its overall significance. "Criollo could designate exceptional sharpness of wit, a talent for mockery, an informal style of interaction, or an attitude of resentment toward crown and church authorities. Whatever it designated, the spread of the term signaled an awareness that those born in the New World, regardless of ancestry or citizenship, were developing a certain autonomy of outlook that preceded outright calls for the end of colonial rule" (1998, 18). Regarding the background of the concept *criollismo*, Pérez Firmat states: "Although the temporal limits of criollismo are imprecise (criollism is still practiced today), there is fairly widespread agreement on the aesthetic program of this tendency. As the word suggests, works of this persuasion attempted, arguably for the first time, to capture the specificity of American nature and culture. Thus, criollist literature is characterized by its attention to native landscapes, regional dialects, rustic characters, and autochthonous themes" (1989, 8).

11. For more on the Padilla case, see Lourdes Casal, *El caso Padilla*, containing official documentation of the background to the case that includes Padilla's valorization of Guillermo Cabrera Infante's oeuvre and position, as well as his confession, and the important denunciation from an intellectual community. Several memoirs also address this case, including Heberto Padilla's *La mala memoria* (1989), Guillermo Cabrera Infante's, *Mea Cuba* (1992), Manuel Díaz Martínez's, "El caso Padilla: crimen y castigo (Recuerdos de un condenado)," and Jorge Edwards's *Persona non grata*. Scott Johnson's *The Case of the Cuban Poet Heberto Padilla* (1977) is inspired by Casal's text. In fact, it not only contains several of the same documents in English, but also contextualizes the case around Padilla's relations to two texts, both published in France in 1970, that were critical of the Cuban Revolution, one by the Czechoslovakian K.S. Karol, *Les guérilleros au pouvoir*, and another by the French René Dumont, *Cuba, est-il socialiste?* Also, in *Reinaldo Arenas: The Pentagonía* (1994), Francisco Soto discusses the impact of these books on the political climate of the 1970s in Cuba.

12. In his essay "Calibán revisitado" ("Caliban Revisited") published originally in *Casa de las Américas* in 1986 and republished in *Todo Caliban* in 2003, Fernández Retamar revises his approach by explicitly contextualizing his essay in the polemical framework of the early 1970s. See Horacio Machin (2000), "Roberto Fernández Retamar, profesional de la utopia," for a discussion of Fernández Retamar's self-fashioning and the symbolic importance of this critic within the discipline of cultural studies and Latin Americanism in the United States.

13. See Casal (1971), Documento No. 17, the second letter from European and Latin American intellectuals to Fidel Castro, 123–24. For an English translation of letter, published in *The New York Times*, see Scott Johnson (1977, 12–13).

14. Since 1992 when renowned Cuban exiled writer Guillermo Cabrera Infante made public in *Mea Cuba* that he had received an anonymous facsimile of Carpentier's birth certificate, revealing the author's birthplace to be Lausanne, Switzerland, a datum that Carpentier had never mentioned, there has been increasing debate over the author's origins (386). Brennan's phrase upon describing Carpentier—"despite his cosmopolitan credentials"—suggests something about the writer's socialization (Brennan 1997, 306).

15. See Aníbal González Pérez (1983) on this subject:

> Nos referimos, por supuesto, a los hechos (que nunca pasan por alto los manuales de historia literaria de este período) de la guerra hispano-cubano-norteamericana de 1898 y la toma del istmos de Panamá por los Estados Unidos, en 1903. Ambos sucesos estremecieron a la *élite* hispanoamericana, y encauzaron la tendencia autoanalítica que ya apuntaba en los escritos modernistas, hacia la vieja cuestión (planteada por los románticos hispanoamericanos en el "americanismo" literario) acerca de la existencia y la vigencia de un "ser" hispanoamericano. Así como en Francia la crisis político-militar del caso Dreyfus incitó a los franceses (en el desagradable contexto del antisemitismo) a reevaluar su "espíritu nacional," la doble conmoción del 98 y de la política norteamericana del "big stick" reanimó en los hispanoamericanos un sentimiento que tal vez no cabría llamar "nacionalista," sino "panhispánico" o incluso, como querían muchos modernistas (ansiosos de que no se perdiera el vínculo espiritual con Francia), "panlatino." (128)

> [We are referring, of course, to the facts (that the manuals of literary history of this period never overlook) of the Hispanic-Cuban-North American War of 1898 and the taking of the Panama isthmus by the United States, in 1903. Both events shook up the Spanish American elite and channeled the self-analytical tendency, that the *modernista* writings already suggested, toward the old question (outlined by the Spanish American romantics in literary "Americanism") regarding the existence and the presence of a Spanish American being. As in France where the political military crisis of the Dreyfus case incited the French (in the unpleasant context of anti-Semitism) to reevaluate their

"national spirit," the double commotion of '98 and the North American "big stick" policy revived in Spanish Americans the feeling that perhaps would not be suitable to call "nationalist," but rather "pan-Hispanic" or even, as many *modernistas* wished (anxious of not losing their spiritual link with France), "pan Latin."]

16. This explanation is provided by the editor of *De sobremesa*, Héctor Orjuela, in a footnote.

17. While Robbins does not mention the Stoics, their worldview is important to keep in mind with regard to the original meaning of "cosmos." For them, cosmopolitanism was an ontic condition based on the following rational principles. Making an epochal move from polytheism to monotheism, the Stoics appropriated the principal anthropomorphic god of the Greeks, Zeus, and imagined him to be a more abstract deity—divine principle. Such a divine principle manifests itself in phenomena, thus creating a web of universal interconnectedness of beings. This universal interconnectedness has its ethical implications as depicted in the Stoics's concept of cosmopolitanism. Copleston explains "an ethical basis for the Stoic Cosmopolitanism was found in the fundamental instinct or tendency of self-preservation or self-love. In the first place, of course, this instinctive tendency to self-preservation shows itself in the form of self-love, i.e. the individual's self-love. But it extends beyond self-love in the narrow sense to embrace all that belongs to the individual, family, friends, fellow-citizens and, finally, the whole of humanity" (1985, 400). While it is natural to love those closest more, the ideal is to "love all men as we love ourselves" (1985, 400). Thus, it is useful to recall the compatibility of the natural link and the ethical consequences when thinking of the recent variants of cosmopolitanism purporting to be more modest and less normative.

18. In the context of this discussion, it is interesting to note that, beginning in 1894, Silva was associated with the Caracas magazine *Cosmópolis*.

19. See Jorge Schwartz's *Vanguarda e cosmopolitismo na década de 20* (1983), Gloria Videla de Rivero's "El simultaneísmo cubista-creacionista entre cosmopolitismo, autorreferencialidad y trascendencia" (Cubist-creacionist simultaneism among cosmopolitanism, autoreferentiality, and transcendence) (1989), and Mihai Grünfeld's "Cosmopolitismo modernista y vanguardista: una identidad latinoamericana divergente" (1989) for more on this topic.

20. Camille Fojas (2004) is similarly engaged with the topic of cosmopolitanism and Rodó. While our attention to details is different, I would agree with her conclusion that "the rhetoric of *Ariel* is insufferable and its classical boys-only model is tiresomely narrow . . . In the end, it retains the most useful model of cosmopolitanism, one forgotten in the relentless drive to be modern. America is urged to rethink the problem of hospitality manifest in immigration policy, rights of guests and workers, rights of the queer and the outcast, and of all manner of difference from the norms of men-at-work nationalism."

21. Many Latin American intellectuals, since Rodó, have often invoked Arielism to characterize their function in society. However, beginning with Georg Lamming's *The Pleasures of Exile* (1960), intellectuals have often appropriated the Caliban figure as the symbol for the Latin American situation. This symbol

finds its culmination in Roberto Fernández Retamar's essay "Caliban" (1971) in which the Cuban critic commends Rodó for his identification of the Northern enemy, but rejects his overall plan that favors a Europeanized intellectual.

22. Like José Martí, Rodó uses America here to refer to our America, this being Latin America.

23. See Maarten Van Delden (1990) "The Banquets of Civilization: The Idea of Ancient Greece in Rodó, Reyes and Fuentes" for a fascinating discussion of the "metaphorical association of youth with classical Greece" (305).

24. Martha C. Nussbaum's envisioning of concentric circles has been one of the models of cosmopolitanism most denigrated for what many see as its over-looking of particulars. See Nussbaum's "Patriotism and Cosmopolitanism," *For Love of Country* (1996), in addition to Robbins's description of this debates in *Feeling Global: Internationalism in Distress* (1999, 147–70). Also see Michael Bérubé's "Citizens of the World, Unite! Martha Nussbaum's Campaign to Cultivate Humanity" (1997) for more on these debates.

25. I have in mind Sylvia Molly's brief analysis of posing and physicality in Ariel. "This is an essay that shuns the visual with passion, an essay in which only one voice is heard, that of the master Próspero, speaking for the last time to an undifferentiated group of male students. Not only do these students lack voice . . . but they remarkably lack bodies and lack gestures . . ." (1998, 150).

26. In an unpublished essay, entitled "Acculturation or Evading Dangerous Intersections: Reading Richard Rodriguez in the Context of José Enrique Rodó's Ariel," that I delivered at the American Comparative Literature Association conference in 1997, I compare the writer Richard Rodriguez's response to and creation of his modern experience in *Days of Obligation: An Argument with My Mexican Father* (1992) and *Hunger of Memory: The Education of Richard Rodríguez: An Autobiography* (1982) with Rodó's *Ariel* (1994/1900). I postulate that both writers are privileging the universality that can be achieved by a liberal education, the value of natural selection, and the importance of acculturation. My comparison also hinges on the fact that Rodriguez was, like Rodó, a child of immigrants (in his case, to the United States of the twentieth century, and not to the Uruguay of the previous one) and that he writes and succeeds in a space in which the diversity of ethnicities is at least superficially valued, and education is implicated in a complex social and political system. Nevertheless, for Rodriguez, like Rodó, a liberal education is conceived as an entity that is detached from those mechanisms and as capable of bringing the best qualified into positions of power.

27. Arenas repeatedly emphasizes the role of exile in Cuban literary history. See his "La literatura cubana en el exilio" (1995b) for a brief discussion of this theme as well as a listing of the contemporary figures with which he was most fascinated. Lilliane Hasson's in-depth interview with Arenas also deals with this theme (Arenas 1992b, 58).

Chapter 2   A *Guajiro's* Cosmos

1. Guerra's title is somewhat deceptive, since Olga is a common name in Spanish, which entered the Cuban context long before the island's relations with the Soviet Union.

2. Néstor Almendros was born in Spain and became an exile in Cuba after the Spanish Civil War. He later left Cuba for France.

3. There is a growing body of research on the experiences of homosexuals with the Cuban Revolution. See Argüelles and Rich (1984), Bejel (2001), Leiner (1994), Lumsden (1995), Quiroga (2000), and Young (1981). Rafael Ocasio (2002) contextualizes in detail Arenas's life within the sociopolitical climate of the 1960s and 1970s.

4. Enrico Mario Santí's "The Life and Times of Reinaldo Arenas" (1984) and Rafael Ocasio's "Gays and the Cuban Revolution" (2002) provides a rich source of biographical information on this arrest.

5. In an interview with Liliane Hasson (1992b, 42), Arenas relates that it was the Cirilio Villaverde prize of 1964, not 1965. The number of copies seems to differ depending on the source, therefore I have inserted "between." See Santí (1984, 230), Soto (1994), Senegal (1992), and Smorkaloff (1997) for a discussion of the delay and print run.

6. See section entitled "La biblioteca" or "The Library."

7. See Fidel Castro, *Política cultural de la revolución cubana: documentos* (1977, 17). The refrain is reiterated as "Dentro de la Revolución: todo; contra la Revolución ningún derecho" (Within the Revolution: everything; against the Revolution, no right).

8. See Guillermo Cabrera Infante's *Mea Cuba* (1992) and Heberto Padilla's *La mala memoria* (1989).

9. Barquet names Antonio Benítez Rojo's *Los inquilinos* (1976) and José Soler Puig's *El pan dormido* (1975) as the grand exceptions to this uniform methodological approach (1994, 38).

10. In *La mala memoria*, Padilla describes his arrest and experience in a hospital from where he saw the broadcast of the "Primer Congreso Nacional de Educación y Cultura" (April 23–30, 1971), that was not only published in *La Gaceta de Cuba* (March–April 1971), but also in *Casa de las Américas*, Year XI, no. 65–66 (March–June 1971). The latter publication appeared alongside Padilla's confession. For an English translation, see Scott Johnson, *The Case of the Cuban Poet Heberto Padilla: Introduction, Selections and Translations* (1977).

11. See Ernesto Guevara, "El socialismo y el hombre en Cuba" (1973). See Brad Epps, "Proper Conduct: Reinaldo Arenas, Fidel Castro, and the Politics of Homosexuality" (1995) as well as Lee Edelman, "Tearooms and Sympathy, or, The Epistemology of the Water Closet" (1992) for a discussion of the linking between homosexuality and communism in the United States of the 1950s.

12. Using the revolutionary figure David and the homosexual Diego of *Fresa y chocolate* as a paradigmatic relation, Arnaldo Cruz-Malavé's excellent article "Lecciones de cubanía" (1998) complicates the relation between homosexuality and the nation by focusing on the homosexual subject's interruption of the *hombre nuevo*. This process entails the homosexual's introducing the Revolutionary to a cultural and Epicurean continuity that makes manifest the distance or breach between the self and the imposed tradition of the *hombre nuevo*, and results in an overall questioning of whether the homosexual

assimilates the heterosexist discourse only, or whether the heterosexist one also does the homosexual discourse.

13. The HIV positive were mandatorily quarantined until 1994. Although an infraction on individual rights, this fact cannot be understood only within this context, but rather in that of distinct philosophies of how to treat this new disease. See Marvin Leiner, *Sexual Politics in Cuba: Machismo, Homosexuality, and AIDS* (1994), for historical data regarding homosexuals in the revolution and the treatment of AIDS sufferers.

14. See Leon Grinberg and Rebeca Grinberg, *Psychoanalytic Perspectives on Migration and Exile* (1989) for a thorough investigation of the many phenomena that affect exiles and their old and new communities.

15. Indeed, it was in 1964, according to Francisco Soto, when Arenas was working on drafts of *Celestino* that he met the maestro famous for this "curso délfico" (*Reinaldo Arenas* xvii).

16. Although Foucault announces countermemory in "Nietzsche, Genealogy, History," published in *Language, Counter-Memory, Practice: Selected Essays and Interviews* (1977), he does not provide as clear and direct an explanation of the term as do Mari Carmen Ramírez (1999) or even Svetlana Boym in *The Future of Nostalgia* (2001).

17. You will note that the implicit link between Bakhtin and Julia Kristeva that I have made has its own history. "With her compatriot, Tzevétan Todorov, Kristeva was among the first to introduce Bakhtin's work to a Western audience" (Moi 1986, 34). Her work in the late 1960s and early 1970s dialogues with Bakhtin. Especially important for her is the subversive word in the tradition of carnival.

18. Paul Julian Smith is similarly intrigued by Arenas's intense counter-surveillance of the system. Referring to *Antes que anochezca*, Smith states, "if sex and writing are authentic activities which tolerate no prohibition, they are also insidiously affected by the state censorship which would keep them under wraps. On Castro's entry into Havana, it is the splendid hair and beards of the Revolutionaries that attract Arenas's amorous attention (p.68) . . . On the paradise of the Isla de los Pinos, the 'erotic fury' of five thousand military recruits is in direct proportion to their Revolution-inspired repression (p.119)" (1996, 75).

19. Those searching for a means to depart the island customarily go to embassies, seeking asylum. The most notorious instance of this situation is the crowding of Cubans into the Venezuelan and especially Peruvian embassies in 1979, preceding the Mariel boatlift. See María Cristina García, *Havana USA* (1996) for a detailed account of this event.

20. Sylvia Molloy's interpretation of the meaning of "allobiography" is slightly distinct from its coinage that she also cites, that is Richard A. Butler's *The Difficult Art of Autobiography* (1968). I am using Molloy's variation of the term here, rather than Butler's that points out a deficiency. Allobiographies, for him, are what happens to texts if they are not sufficiently self-centered; they are no longer "real" biographies (19).

21. *Los imprescindibles* (The Essential) *Fray Servando Teresa de Mier*, in addition to containing his works, provides an informative prologue on the friar's

life and writings, a bibliography, and chronology connecting Servando's life and the histories of the colony (Mexico) and Spain. The friar's famous Guadalupan Sermon of December 1794 proposed that the Virgin of Guadalupe did not appear to Juan Diego, but rather centuries before the Spaniards' arrival, to Saint Thomas, the apostle, who is represented in the indigenous divinity Quetzalcoatl. The logical conclusion of this sermon would be that Spain has no legitimate claim on the New World, given that the conquest was justified by the need to suppress idolatry and replace it with Christianity. Adriana Méndez Rodenas's *Gender and Nationalism in Colonial Cuba: The Travels of Santa Cruz y Montalvo, Condesa de Merlin* (1998) is an excellent analysis of La Condesa's position in Cuba's literary history as well as a general source of information on this author.

22. See the letter to Delfín Pratts Pupo dated July 24, 1973, as well as the editor's note explaining his pseudonym, both in *La necesidad de libertad* (1986).

23. It is interesting to note that in *El color del verano* the celebration of carnival helps to initiate time travel.

24. See Roberto González Echevarría's introduction (1993a) to *De dónde son los cantantes* regarding Sarduy's early years in Paris.

25. See Lilianne Hasson, "¿Y en Francia Qué?" (2002) Also see Canaparo (2000), the section entitled L'Affaire du Seuil.

26. I have omitted a few words from Hurley's translation that link it to the previous passage.

27. See the notes "Sobre la obra" (About the Work) presenting *La loma del angel* (1987), in which Arenas describes literary creation as an act of betrayal.

28. Lezama Lima also links Francisco de Miranda to Fray Servando and Rodríguez, in the discussion of "El romanticismo y el hecho americano" (Romanticism and the American deed) in *La expresión americana* (1993/1957).

29. Arenas sometimes supported himself constructing *barbacoas*.

30. In an interview with Aleida Anselma Rodríguez, Arenas suggests

> Yo he leído siempre con respeto a Carpentier y creo que *El siglo de las luces* es una gran novela, pero siempre he pensado que la narrativa de Carpentier no parte de un fin poético, o sea, no parte de un fin inspirado, sino de un plan preconcebido a través de documentos, de un cálculo y eso me hace siempre verla como una cosa un poco muerta, como una armazón muy bien hecha, pero más bien una cosa arquitectónica, no literaria. (Arenas 1981a, 53)

> [I've always read respectfully Carpentier and I believe that *El siglo de las luces* is a great novel, but I've always thought that Carpentier's prose does not merge forth from a poetic end, or rather, from an inspired end, but rather from a preconceived plan through documents, from a calculatedness and this makes me always see it as a little bit dead, like a very well made framework, but architectonically-so, not literary-wise.]

31. "La belleza bajo un sistema dictatorial es siempre disidente, porque toda dictadura es de por sí antiestética, grotesca" (Arenas 1992a, 113) (Under a

dictatorship beauty is always a dissident force, because a dictatorship is itself unaesthetic, grotesque) (Arenas 1993a, 87).

32. These days for the privileged in richer countries, these terms would luckily no longer adequately describe the illness and its consequences.

Chapter 3   Just a Vieja de Barrio

A segment of chapter 3 appeared in *Chasqui*, November 2000. It was published as "Wordly" Conjuctions and Disjunctions: On Cosmopolitanism and Nomadism in Diamela Eltit's *Por La patria* (1986) and El padre mío (1989)."

1. Throughout Richard's critiques, she highly regards art with an ability to discourage compassion or solidarity. For example, in "Bordes, diseminación, postmodernismo: una metáfora latinoamericana de fin de siglo" (1994) she interprets Eltit's *El padre mío* as dissuading solidarity formation and questioning identity politics on all levels.

2. The topic of critical distance is a persistent concern of critics on postmodernity. Fredric Jameson's "Postmodernism, or the Cultural Logic of Late Capitalism" (1984) bemoans the collapse of depth models, or hermeneutic models of the inside and outside, and warns of the superficiality of postmodernism. A concomitant issue evolves around postmodernism and ethics, one of particular importance for critiquing Eltit's work under dictatorship. Post-structuralist theory celebrated the collapse of an outside, the possibility of an ethical imperative being imposed on a narrative, since that system was perceived as a product of oppressive Enlightenment values of universal subjects. However, literature's re-engagement with ethics became obvious around the 1987 discovery that the deconstructionist Paul de Man was involved in anti-Semitic writing in the 1930s. This year is symbolic; for, in his chapter on Ethics in the book *Critical Terms for Literary Study* (1995), Geoffrey Galt Harpham dates critics' renewed preoccupation with ethics several years prior to that event.

3. I have in mind here the following instances in which an other penetrates the poetics of modernist authors. Vagrants and prostitutes play an important role in Baudelaire's depiction of Paris and modernity in *Les Fleurs du Mal (The Flowers of Evil)*. The outskirts and their dwellers are central to Borges's mythicized Buenos Aires in *Fervor de Buenos Aires* (Fervor of Buenos Aires) published in 1923. Finally, the vagrant/tramp Emmanuèle is of inordinate importance in Cortázar's *Rayuela (Hopscotch)* since their encounter forces the protagonist Oliveira to realize that desire and the abject are intertwined.

4. With respect to this inclusion of the body and especially, on the body's orifices throughout *Lumpérica*, Eltit's aesthetic, like Arenas's, also relates to a Bakhtin's grotesque realism.

5. In "On Ethnographic Self-Fashioning: Conrad and Malinowksi," Clifford treats two of Malinowski's works, *A Diary in the Strict Sense of the Term* (1967) and *Argonauts of the Western Pacific* (1922), explaining that the diary is a "polyphonic text" which "forces us to grapple with the complexities of such encounters and to treat all accounts based on fieldwork as partial constructions" (1988, 97).

6. There are several critical pieces that help to elucidate Eltit's role as intellectual/ describer and her relationship to the described. See Malverde Disselkoen (1991), Richard (1998), and Neustadt (1995a, 1995b, 1997, 1999).

7. Although Clifford revised his ideas on cosmopolitanism in "On Ethnographic Self-Fashioning," in a review of Edward Said's *Orientalism*, he criticizes Said for a similar type of homogenization that he labels cosmopolitanism. See James Clifford's review of Edward W. Said, *Orientalism*, republished in Clifford (1988).

8. *Sudaca*, a term used by Spaniards to denigrate *sudamericanos* or South Americans, is recovered by Eltit in *El cuarto mundo* to signify a more cohesive and powerful difference, that is the result of identifying with Latin America.

9. See Chapter 1 for an explanation of this difficult-to-translate phrase.

10. For more on the linguistic systems in Eltit, consult Norat (2002).

11. Gisela Norat's *Marginalities* spells out their specificities.

12. Although this fact is not mentioned in the translation, the 1997 foreword is nearly identical to an article entitled "Errante, errática" published in the multi-authored volume entitled *Una poética menor: La narrativa de Diamela Eltit* (1993) as well as in *Emergencias* (2000a). I shall quote from *Emergencias* and the foreword.

13. "Cuerpos nómadas," first published in Spanish in 1996, was republished in the collection *Emergencias*. It also appears in English as "Nomadic Bodies" in 1997.

14. On May 9, 1990, Supreme Decree No. 355 of the Ministry of the Interior was published in the *Diario Oficial*. Chilean President Patricio Alwyn appointed an eight-man commission to investigate the impact of Pinochet's violence, out of which emerged *Informe de la Comisión Nacional de Verdad y Reconciliación* (1991) (*Report of the Chilean National Commission on Truth and Reconciliation* 1993).

15. The English foreword is more lengthy and explanatory than the original Spanish essay.

16. I cannot help but be reminded of Donna J. Haraway's "A Cyborg Manifesto: Science, Technology, and Socialist-Feminism in the Late Twentieth Century" (1991) in Franco's usage of the phrase "body machine." Haraway's analysis of organic and cyborg intellectuals enriches the present discussion of the inter-subjective experience in Eltit.

> American radical feminists . . . have profoundly affected our political imaginations—and perhaps restricted too much what we allow as a friendly body and political language. They insist on the organic, opposing it to the technological. But their symbolic systems and the related positions of ecofeminism and feminist paganism, replete with organicisms, can only be understood in Sandoval's terms as oppositional ideologies fitting the late twentieth century. They would simply bewilder anyone not preoccupied with the machines and consciousness of late capitalism. In that sense they are part of the cyborg world. But there are also great riches for feminists in explicitly embracing the possibilities inherent in the breakdown of clean distinctions between organism and machine and similar distinctions structuring

the Western self. It is the simultaneity of breakdowns that cracks the matrices of domination and opens geometric possibilities. What might be learned from personal and political "technological" pollution? I look briefly at two overlapping groups of texts for their insight into the construction of a potentially helpful cyborg myth: constructions of women of color and monstrous selves in feminist science fiction (Haraway 1991, 174).

While it would be fallacious to transfer directly Haraway's myth to the Latin American context without taking into account another tradition of feminist thought and experience of modernity, Haraway's myth does salute "pollution" and the blending of subject/object positions as weapons to the potentially disrupt patriarchy.

17. In the Spanish text of *Lumpérica*, the principal character is named L. Iluminada. The English translation refers to that same character as E. Luminata. In my discussions of this character, I will be utilizing the former.

18. Gisela Norat (2002) points to diverse implications of the electric light of a giant neon sign, linking it to sacred and pornographic messages.

19. In "Incisive Incisions: (Re)Articulating The Discursive Body," Robert Neustadt analyzes the body and text, united in the process of cutting. His depiction of *Lumpérica*, like the Ensayo General, as "a non-linear series of *cortes* that perpetually revises itself while reconfiguring the image of L. Iluminada in the plaza" (1995a, 54) is of particular interest for the present discussion on conjunctions and disjunctions.

20. On pretended continuity, Foucault states: "History becomes 'effective' to the degree that it introduces discontinuity into our very being—as it divides our emotions, dramatizes our instincts, multiplies our body and sets it against itself. 'Effective' history deprives the self of the reassuring stability of life and nature, and it will not permit itself to be transported by a voiceless obstinacy toward a millennial ending. It will uproot its traditional foundations and relentlessly disrupt its pretended continuity. This is because knowledge is not made for understanding; it is made for cutting" (1977, 154). Also see Guillermo García-Corales, "La desconstrucción del poder en *Lumpérica*" (1993), for a Foucauldian reading of *Lumpérica*.

21. Sylvia Tafra (1998) utilizes Julia Kristeva's terminology to describe the subject-in-process as well as play in Eltit's texts, especially *Lumpérica* and *Por la patria*.

22. In an interview with Fernando Burgos and M.J. Fenwick, Eltit characterizes the novel in this manner:

> Es una novela bastante literaria. Está engranada más que en la vida real en una literatura que hay que hacer. (1995, 348)
>
> [It is quite a literary novel. It is enmeshed in literature that must be made more than in real life.]

23. Think of "Mi situación personal engloba toda la realidad de un pueblo" (Menchú 1983, 21). "My personal experience is the reality of a whole people"

(Menchú 1984, trans. Ann Wright, 1), one of the first resolutions in *Me llamo Rigoberta Menchú y así me nació la conciencia*, perhaps the most publicized and controversial *testimono*.

24. In "Speaking Out Together: Testimonials of Latin American Women" Lynda Marín emphasizes how in testimonies of women, "The narrator speaks her story to an actual person, another woman. The audience is never an abstraction. Therefore, Doris Sommer says, the narrative voice sometimes slips into the second person, and as a result each reader becomes the 'you' that addresses the interviewer" (65).

Chapter 4   Face to Screen

A segment of chapter 4 appeared in *Nepantla: Views from South* (4.2) 2003. It was published as "Global Arenas: Narrative and Filmic Translations of Identity."

1. In Ana María Simo and Reinaldo García Ramos's response to B. Ruby Rich and Lourdes Argüelles's interpretation of the United States' condemnation of homophobia in Cuba as overblown and based on its focusing only on exceptional periods of crisis, Simo and García Ramos suggest that, in fact, the actual system of Castro's government is built around such baiting imperialism against this marginal group.

2. One of Rodríguez Monegal's most important tributes to Arenas appears in *Mundo Nuevo* in 1968 alongside a fragment of *Celestino antes del alba*. That publication of *Celestino* has its own story, part of which is found in *La necesidad de libertad* where two letters that Arenas wrote to Rodríguez Monegal are reprinted.

3. See Irene Rostagno's *Searching for Recognition: The Promotion of Latin American Literature in the United States* (1997, 89–143).

4. The CD-Rom by Claudio Canaparo, *The Manufacture of an Author*, also contains a copy of Arenas's CV and a vast quantity of data regarding the U.S. academy's interest in Arenas.

5. That, as Esterrich comments, "Arenas vivió un exilio fuera de los círculos latinoamericanos y, en efecto, fuera de la principal colonia cubana estadounidense" (Arenas lived as an exile outside of the Latin American circles and, in effect, out of the principal Cuban United States colony) (16), is important for understanding Arenas's eccentricities.

6. See Robert Richmond Ellis's "The Gay Lifewriting of Reinaldo Arenas: *Antes que anochezca*" for an excellent analysis of the conflicting aspects in Arenas's writing on homosexuality.

7. One of the earliest multithematic books containing several essays on Arenas is Jean Beranger, Jean Cazemajou, Jean-Michel Lacroix, and Pierre Spriet (eds.), *Multilinguisme et multiculturalisme en Amerique du Nord: Temps, mythe et histoire*. 1989. Several critics discuss Arenas's oeuvre implementing Bakhtin's theories. One collection, however, discusses Arenas among many other writers in relation to Bakhtin. See Ana Beatriz Flores de Franco, *Voces e ideologies:*

Estudios bajtinianos (1996). For a discussion of many of the critical collections of Arenas's work linked to their point of origin and affiliations with other critical writings, see Canaparo (2000).

8. I am referring to a site at entheogen.com/books.html, which no longer exists as "Books about Entheogens and the Psychedelic Experience" and calvin.usc.edu/~trimmer/famous_names.html.

9. This list is not beyond debate. Irene Rostagno does not even include Carpentier in the second category of boom membership (1997, 90).

10. Andreas Huyssen's "Adorno in Reverse: From Hollywood to Richard Wagner" (2002) helps to account for Theodor Adorno's hesitations with his own theory of the *culture industry*, which are frequently ignored by critics. That "in capitalist society high art is always already permeated by the textures of that mass culture from which it seeks autonomy" (43) is important to bear in mind when considering Schnabel's film and self-positioning.

11. See Naremore (2000) regarding writing about adaptation as translation: "Most writing on adaptation as translation, even when it assumes a tone of quasi-scientific objectivity, betrays certain unexamined ideological concerns because it deals of necessity with sexually charged materials and cannot avoid a gendered language associated with the notion of 'fidelity' " (8).

12. Since the DVD is divided into easy-to-reference "chapters," I have borrowed this term.

13. By 1993, Andrew Hurley had translated three of the five novels of the *pentagonía*: *Farewell to the Sea* (1986), *Singing from the Well* (1987), and *The Palace of the White Skunks* (1990). In 1994, *The Assault* was first published by the Viking, and in 2000, the fourth book of the series, *The Color of Summer*, was released.

14. In an interview, Hurley (1995, 44) suggests that the visibility of Arenas in the United States suffered from his not having had a worthy "padrino."

15. The transnational desirability of the local homosexual body is acutely documented by José Quiroga in *Tropics of Desire: Interventions from Queer Latino America* (2000, 12) through a focus on a photographic essay by Benno Thoma (Holland) wherein the state's rejection of the homosexual is converted into the "homosexual body desired by capitalism" (2000, 12). The cover image of Quiroga's book is also taken from Thoma's collection.

16. Arenas's published corpus includes three volumes of poetry, *El central* (1981b), *Voluntad de vivir manifestándose* (1989), *Leprosorio: Trilogía poética* (1990a).

17. Weiss (2001, 84) relates an interesting anecdote linking Schnabel's artistic expression, independence, and Hollywood: "Now when he insisted to me that the $8 million he spent in Mexico shooting 'Before Night Falls' was equivalent to $21 million spent in the States, I sensed the calculation. He was letting studio heads know that he wasn't just an indie guy; he could handle a big budget."

18. See Quiroga (2000, 12) for more on Arenas's outspokenness about the state's repressive treatment of Piñera.

19. Salah D. Hassan (2002, 6) briefly discusses Schnabel's representation of Piñera and Lezama Lima in his introduction to a volume called *"Origins" of Postmodern Cuba*.

20. With respect to the portrayal of the Cuban artist's sexuality, my opinion differs especially from that of Michael Bronski (2001, 56), who asserts that Schnabel and Cunningham O'Keefe brought "Arenas's complex memoir to life without any compromise," and this means they do not "downplay the importance Arenas places on sexuality." Bronski critiques mainstream audiences for their inability to conceive of (homo)sexuality in art as anything but pornographic, but sees *Before Night Falls* as exceptional in its ability to break through this dichotomy.

21. The significance of the mother in Arenas's production is impossible to miss. In fact, the directness of the link in this scene of the film brings to mind one of the most negative reviews that *Antes que anochezca* has received (Pereira 1992, 56): "You don't have to lay this autobiography down on Freud's couch to see that she is the key to explaining the *caso* Arenas—beyond the social commotion that the country has lived in these past three decades."

22. Most of Arenas's books were published in Spanish after he came to the United States.

23. The music reproduces this language split. As composer Carter Burwell explains on the DVD commentary track (chapter 25), "Cuban music mostly played the external events of his life and the score ended up playing the internal events."

24. See Navarro (2001) for a discussion of memory and forgetting in the revolutionary context.

25. It is usually agreed upon that UMAPs, having lasted two to three years, were closed between 1967 and 1968.

26. The journal's definition of *jiribilla* is: "un cubanismo. Se dice de la persona (generalmente un niño) bastante intranquila" (a Cubanism. It is said of a restless person [generally a child]). A more precise reference to José Lezama Lima's essay "Lectura" is encountered on the cover of the first issue of the paper version of the periodical, which as of May 2003, contained a selection of its articles available on the website, in addition to other exceptional pieces, two times each month.

Chapter 5   Uncomfortable Homes

A segment of chapter 5 appeared in New Centennial Review (4.2) (2004). It was published as "Partraitures of Institutionalization."

1. See Massimo Bongiovanni (1993) for one of the earliest journalistic accounts of the joint venture.

2. Adam Broomberg and Oliver Chanarin are the magazine's creative directors and are responsible for much of this issue #47.

3. See Henry A. Giroux (1994) for a discussion of Benetton's advertising tactics of containment.

4. From now on, this issue of *Colors* will be referred to as *Madness* in this chapter and in the Works Cited.

5. For a discussion on the implications of this concept in the current period, see Ariana Hernández-Reguant's "Radio Taino and the Cuban Quest for

Identi . . . *Qué*." Hernández-Reguant's article will be published by Duke University Press in December 2005 in collection entitled *Cultural Agency in the Americas*, edited by Doris Sommer.

6. The URL for the foundation's site has a side bar for "workshops." Once, workshops has been selected, go to "Workshop San Giovanni, Trieste." There is no separate URL for that site. Another important project can be located from the Research sidebar. It leads to information on "Groundwork for an atlas of psychiatric hospitals."

7. This site no longer exists.

8. In a correspondence on November 14, 2002, Olivier Chanarin told me that indeed *Colors* has tried to deliver by courier these magazines to the Camagüey hospital.

9. For an interesting discussion of Brechtian techniques, see Neustadt (1999, 45–46).

Bibliography

Abreu, Juan. 1998. *A la sombra del mar: Jornadas cubanas con Reinaldo Arenas*. Barcelona: Casiopea.

Aching, Gerard. 1997. *The Politics of Spanish American Modernismo: By Exquisite Design*. New York: Cambridge University Press.

Achugar, Hugo. 1998. "Leones, cazadores e historiadores. A propósito de las políticas de la memoria y del conocimiento." In Santiago Castro-Gómez and Eduardo Mendieta (eds.), *Teorías sin disciplina. Latinoamericanismo, poscolonialidad y globalizatión en debate*. Mexico City: University of San Francisco Press. 271–85.

Ahmad, Aijaz. 1987. "Jameson's Rhetoric of Otherness and the 'National Allegory.'" *Social Text* 17: 3–25.

Almendros, Néstor and Orlando Jiménez Leal, directors. 1984. *Mauvaise conduite*. Losange et Antenne 2.

Anderson, Amanda. 1998. "Cosmopolitanism, Universalism, and the Divided Legacies of Modernity." In Pheng Cheah and Bruce Robbins (eds.), *Cosmopolitics: Thinking and Feeling beyond the Nation*. Minneapolis: University of Minnesota Press. 265–89.

———. 2001. *The Powers of Distance: Cosmopolitanism and the Cultivation of Detachment*. Princeton, NJ: Princeton University Press.

Arenas, Reinaldo. 1967. *Celestino antes del alba*. Havana: Unión.

———. 1971. *Hallucinations: Being an Account of the Life and Adventures of Friar Servando Teresa de Mier*. Translated by Gordon Brotherston. New York: Harper & Row.

———. 1981a. "Reinaldo Arenas: Entrevista en La Habana." Interview by Aleida Anselma Rodríguez. *Prismal/Cabral: Revista de Literatura Hispánica/Caderno Afro Brasileiro Asiático Lusitano* 6: 50–59.

———. 1981b. *El central*. Barcelona: Seix Barral.

———. 1982a. *Cantando en el pozo*. Barcelona: Argos Vergara.

———. 1982b. "Dangerous Manuscripts: A Conversation with Reinaldo Arenas." Interview by Franz-Olivier Giesbert. *Encounter* 58(1): 60–67.

———. 1982c. "Donde no hay furia y desgarro, no hay literatura: Entrevista con Reinaldo Arenas." Interview by Rita Virginia Molinero. *Quimera* 17: 19–23.

———. 1982d [1969]. *El mundo alucinante (Una novela de aventuras)*. Caracas: Monte Avila.

Arenas, Reinaldo. 1983. "Reinaldo Arenas y su mundo alucinante. Una Entrevista." Interview by Mónica Morley and Enrico Mario Santí. *Hispania* 66: 114–18.

———. 1986a. *Necesidad de libertad: Mariel: testimonios de un intelectual disidente*. Mexico City: Kosmos.

———. 1986b. *Farewell to the Sea*. Translated by Andrew Hurley. New York: Viking.

———. 1987. *La loma del ángel*. Barcelona: Dador.

———. 1988[7]. *Singing from the Well*. Translated by Andrew Hurley. New York: Penguin.

———. 1989. *Voluntad de vivir manifestándose*. Madrid: Betaña.

———. 1990a. *Leprosorio: Trilogía Poética*. Madrid: Betaña.

———. 1990b. *The Palace of the White Skunks*. Translated by Andrew Hurley. New York: Viking.

———. 1991. *El color del verano*. Miami: Universal.

———. 1992a. *Antes que anochezca*. Barcelona: Tusquets.

———. 1992b. "Memorias de un exiliado. Entrevista con Reinaldo Arenas." Interview by Lilliane Hasson. In Ottmar Ette (ed.), *La escritura de la memoria*. Frankfurt am Main: Vervuert Verlag. 35–63.

———. 1993a. *Before Night Falls*. Translated by Dolores Koch. New York: Viking.

———. 1993b. "Verdades de ayer y verdades de hoy: Entrevista de Danubio Torres Fierro con Reinaldo Arenas." Interview by Danubio Torres Fierro. *Vuelta* 195: 49–52.

———. 1994. *The Ill-Fated Peregrinations of Fray Servando*. Translated by Andrew Hurley. New York: Penguin.

———. 1995a. "Viaje a la Habana." In *Viaje a la Habana (Novela en tres viajes)*. Miami: Universal. 93–153.

———. 1995b. "La literatura cubana en el exilio." *Puente Libre: Revista de Cultura* 2(5–6): 107–11.

———. 1995c [1994]. *The Assault*. New York: Penguin.

———. 1999. "El cometa Halley." In Alberto Garrandés (ed.), *Aire de luz: Cuentos cubanos del siglo XX*. Havana: Letras Cubanas. 261–74.

———. 2000. *The Color of Summer*. Translated by Andrew Hurley. New York: Penguin.

Argüelles, Lourdes and B. Ruby Rich. 1984. "Homosexuality, Homophobia, and Revolution: Notes toward an Understanding of the Cuban Lesbian and Gay Male Experience, Part I." *Signs: Journal of Women in Culture and Culture and Society* 9(4): 683–99.

"Artthrob." http://www.artthrob.co.za/03apr/listings_gauteng.html (accessed January 24, 2004).

Bakhtin, Mikhail. 1984. *Rabelais and His World*. Translated by Hélène Iswolsky. Bloomington: Indiana University Press.

Balmaseda, Liz. 1996. "Benetton Exploits Cuban Town in an Ugly Fashion," *Miami Herald*, August 3, sec. B, p. 1.

Barquet, Jesús J. 1994. "Rebeldía e irreverencia de Reinaldo Arenas." In Reinaldo Sánchez (ed.), *Reinaldo Arenas: Recuerdo y presencia*. Miami: Universal. 27–38.

Barrios de Chungara, Domitila 1978. In Moema Viezzer (ed.), *Si me permiten hablar: Testimonio de Domitila una mujer de las minas de Bolivia*. Mexico City: Siglo XXI.

Bartolone, Pauline and Sebastian Hacher. 2003. "Benetton on Mapuche Territory." http://www.mapuche.nl/english/benetton251103.htm (accessed August 1, 2005).

Baudelaire, Charles. 1964. *The Painter of Modern Life*. Translated by Jonathan Mayne. London: Phaidon.

———. 1972 [1961]. *Les fleurs du mal*. Paris: Gallimard.

Bejel, Emilio. 1996. "*Antes que anochezca*: autobiografía de un disidente cubano homosexual." *Hispamérica* 25.74 (1996): 29–45.

———. 2001. *Gay Cuban Nation*. Chicago, IL: University of Chicago Press.

Benjamin, Walter. 1969a [1968]. "On Some Motifs in Baudelaire." Translated by Harry Zohn. In Hannah Arendt (ed.), *Illuminations: Essays and Reflections*. New York: Schocken. 155–200.

———.1969b [1968]. "The Work of Art in the Age of Mechanical Reproduction." Translated by Harry Zohn. In Hannah Arendt (ed.), *Illuminations: Essays and Reflections*. New York: Schocken. 217–53.

Benetton. 2001–2002. *Colors: Madness* 47. Creative Directors Adam Broomberg and Oliver Chanarin (December–January).

Benítez Rojo, Antonio. 1976. *Los inquilinos*. Havana: Arte y Literatura.

Bérubé, Michael. 1997. "Citizens of the World, Unite! Martha Nussbaum's Campaign to Cultivate Humanity." *Lingua Franca* (September): 54–61.

Bhabha, Homi K. 1996. "Unsatisfied: Notes on Vernacular Cosmopolitanism." In Laura García-Moreno and Peter C. Pfeiffer (eds.), *Text and Nation: Cross-Disciplinary Essays on Cultural and National Identities*. Columbia, SC: Camden House. 191–207.

Birringer, Johannes, director. 1996. *Lovers' Fragments/Fragmentos de enamorados: A Video Dance Poem*. Columbus, OH: AlienNation Company.

———. 1998. "Information Pack" *North by South: Before Night Falls: Distances: A Digital Dance-Film/Music Concert*. Columbus, OH: AlienNation Company.

Bisama, Alvaro. 2002. "Perdida en el supermercado." *La Tercera Guía*. http://guia.tercera/cl /2002/07/26/literatura 1.htm (accessed March 20, 2004; site no longer accessible).

Blanco-Fombona, Rufino. 1908. "Notículas: ¿Qué es el rastacuerismo?" *Letras y Letrados de Hispano-América*. París: Sociedad de ediciones literarias y artísticas. 298–301.

Bongiovanni, Massimo. 1993. "United Colors of Capitalism; Benetton sbarca a Cuba ma solo per turisti." *Il Sole 24 Ore* 24 January, p. 1.

Borges, Jorge Luis. 1969 [1923]. *Fervor de Buenos Aires*. Buenos Aires: Emece.

Boym, Svetlana. 2001. *The Future of Nostalgia*. New York: Basic Books.

Brennan, Timothy. 1989. *Salman Rushdie and the Third World: Myths of the Nation*. New York: St. Martin's Press.

———. 1997. *At Home in the World: Cosmopolitanism Now*. Cambridge, MA: Harvard University Press.

———. 2002. "Cosmo-Theory." *South Atlantic Quarterly* 100(3): 659–89.

Breton, André. 1966 [1937]. *L'amour fou*. Paris: Gallimard.

Bronski, Michael. 2001. "Reel Politick: Before Night Falls." *Z Magazine* (April): 56–60.

Broomberg, Adam and Oliver Chanarin. 2003. *Ghetto.* London: Trolley.

Brunner, José Joaquin. 1990. "Preguntas a José Joaquin Brunner." *Revista de Crítica Cultural* 1: 20–25.

Bruss, Elizabeth. 1980. "Eye for I: Making and Unmaking Autobiography in Film." In James Olney (ed.), *Autobiographical: Essays Theoretical and Critical.* Princeton, NJ: Princeton University Press. 207–309.

Butler, Richard A. 1968. *The Difficult Art of Autobiography.* Oxford: Clarendon Press.

Cabrera Infante, Guillermo. 1992. *Mea Cuba.* Barcelona: Plaza and Janes.

Campa, Román de la. 1999. *Latinamericanism.* Minneapolis: University of Minnesota Press.

Canaparo, Claudio. 2000. *The Manufacture of an Author. Reinaldo Arenas's literary world, his readers and other contemporaries.* London: King's College London/Centre for Latin American Cultural Studies. (Book: 31pp. + CD-ROM: 764pp.)

Cánovas, Rodrigo. 1990. "Apuntes sobre la novela *Por la patria* (1986), de Diamela Eltit." *Acta Literaria* 15: 147–60.

Carpentier, Alejo. 1949. *El reino de este mundo.* Mexico City: Ibero Americana de Publicaciones.

Casa de las Américas Bulletin. 2002. "Semana de autor: Diamela Eltit," Edited by Jorge Fornet. November 12–15.

Casal, Lourdes, ed. 1971. *El Caso Padilla: Literatura y Revolución en Cuba.* Miami: Universal.

Castells, Ricardo. 1995. "Retamar's 'The Tempest' in a Cafetera." *Cuban Studies* 25: 165–82.

Castro, Fidel. 1977. *Política cultural de la revolución cubana.* Havana: Ciencias Sociales.

Castro-Gómez, Santiago and Eduardo Mendieta, eds. 1998. *Teorías sin disciplina. Latinoamericanismo, poscolonialidad y globalización en debate.* Mexico City: University of San Francisco Press.

"Centro Studi, Ricerca e Formazione in Salute Mentale (CSR) Friuli Venezia Giulia Region-Italy." http://www.triestesalutementale.it/allegati/Scheda1999.pdf (accessed January 24, 2004).

Cheah, Pheng and Bruce Robbins, eds. 1998. *Cosmopolitics: Thinking and Feeling beyond the Nation.* Minneapolis: University of Minnesota Press.

Christ, Ronald. 1997. "Translator's Afterword." In Eltit, *E. Luminata.* Santa Fe: Lumen. 205–34.

Cimet, Esther. 1973. "¿Cosmopolita?: ensayo sobre la cultura moderna en América Latina de Jean Franco." *Comunidad* 8(42): 234–38.

Clifford, James. 1988. "On Ethnographic Self-Fashioning: Conrad and Malinowski." *The Predicament of Culture: Twentieth-Century Ethnography, Literature, and Art.* Cambridge, MA: Harvard University Press.

———. 1997 [1992]. "Traveling Cultures." *Routes: Travel and Translation in the Late Twentieth Century.* Cambridge, MA: Harvard University Press.

————. 1998. "Mixed Feelings." In Pheng Cheah and Bruce Robbins (eds.), *Cosmopolitics: Thinking and Feeling beyond the Nation*. Minneapolis: University of Minnesota Press. 362–70.

Cobo-Borda, Juan Gustavo. 1988. "Silva, bogatano universal." In Juan Gustavo Coba Borda (ed.), *José Asunción Silva, Bogotano Universal*. Bogotá: Biblioteca de Bogotá. 29–123.

"*Colors*: Archives." http://www.benetton.com/colors/archive/archive.html (accessed January 24, 2004).

"*Colors*: Press." http://www.benetton.com/food/press/pressinfo/colors/ (accessed January 24, 2004).

"*Colors*: What We Say." http://www.benetton.com/wws/aboutmake/colors/index.html (accessed January 24, 2004).

"*Colors* 46—Volunteers." www.benetton.com/colorspress46/colors46.pdf (accessed December 30, 2004).

Copleston, Frederick. 1985. *A History of Philosophy*. 3 vols. Garden City, NY: Image Books.

Corral, Wilfrido H. 1999. "Ángel Rama y Reinaldo Arenas en Estados Unidos: intelectuales especularios y la cultura crítica de hoy." *Cuadernos Americanos* 78: 168–205.

Cortázar, Julio. 1976. In Julio Cortázar Silvia D'Amico, and Sara Facio. *Estrictamente no professional*. *Humanario*. Buenos Aires: La Azotea.

Cruz-Malavé, Arnaldo. 1998. "Lecciones de cubanía: Identidad nacional y errancia." *Revista de Crítica Cultural* 17: 58–67.

Darío, Rubén. 1971 [1905]. *Cantos de vida y esperanza*. Madrid: Espasa Calpa.

————. 1981 [1898]. "El triunfo de Calibán." In Raymundo Ramos (ed.), *El ensayo politico latinoamericano en la formación nacional*. Mexico City: ICAP. 225–28.

————. 1993 [1896]. "Palabras liminares," *Prosas profanas*. Mexico City: Espasa Calpe.

————. 1994 [1888]. *Azúl*. Prologue by Juan Valera. Mexico City: Espasa Calpe.

David, Catherine P. 1997. "Introduction to *documenta X* in the *Short Guide*." Press Info. *Universes in Universe/Documenta*. http://www.universes-in-universe.de/doc/e_press.htm (accessed January 24, 2004).

De Man, Paul. 1984. *The Rhetoric of Romanticism*. New York: Columbia University Press.

Derrida, Jacques. 2001. *On Cosmopolitanism and Forgiveness*. New York: Routledge.

Díaz Matínez, Manuel. 1997. "El caso Padilla: Crimen y Castigo (Recuerdos de un Condenado)", *Encuentrode la Cultura Cubana* 4/5: 88–96.

Diogenes of Laertius. 1972. *Lives, Teachings, and Sayings of Famous Philosophers*. Translated by R.D. Hicks. Cambridge, MA: Harvard University Press.

Donoso, José. 1970. *El obsceno pájaro de la noche*. Barcelona: Seix Barral.

————. 1972. *La historia personal del boom*. Barcelona: Anagrama.

————. 1979. *The Obscene Bird of Night*. Translated by Hardie St. Martin and Leonard Mades. Boston: Nonpareil Books.

Dorfman, Ariel. 1986. "Código político y código literario: el género testimonio en Chile hoy." In René Jara and Hernán Vidal (eds.), *Testimonio y literatura*.

Minneapolis: Society for the Study of Contemporary and Lusophone Revolutionary Literatures. 170–234.

Dorfman, Ariel. 1991. *Some Write to the Future: Essays on Contemporary Latin American Fiction*. Translated by George Shivers with the author. Durham, NC: Duke University Press.

Dunont, René, 1970. *Cuba, est-il Socialiste?* Rans: Editions du Seuil.

Edelman, Lee. 1992. "Tearooms and Sympathy, or, The Epistemology of the Water Closet." In Andrew Parker, Mary Russo, Doris Sommer, and Patricia Yaeger (eds.), *Nationalisms and Sexualities*. New York: Routledge. 263–84.

Edwards, Jorge. 1973. *Persuna non grata*. Barcelona: Barral.

Ellis, Robert Richmond. 1995. "The Gay Lifewriting of Reinaldo Arenas: *Antes que anochezca*." *a/b: Auto/Biography Studies* 10(1): 126–44.

Eltit, Diamela. 1983. *Lumpérica*. Santiago, Chile: Ornitorrinco.

———. 1985. "Acoplamiento incestuoso." Interview by A.M.F. *Revista Hoy* 421, August 12–18, 41.

———. 1986. *Por la patria*. Santiago, Chile: Ornitorrinco.

———.1988. *El cuarto mundo*. Santiago, Chile. Planeta.

———. 1989. *El padre mío*. Santiago, Chile: Francisco Zegers.

———. 1991. "Diamela Eltit: Escritos sobre un werpo." Interview by Juan Andrés Piña. In Juan Andrés Piña, (ed.), *Conversaciones con la narrativa chilena*, Santiago, Chile: Los Andes. 223–254.

———. 1992a. Interview by Sandra Garabano and Guillermo García-Corales. *Hispamérica* 62: 65–75.

———. 1992b. "On Literary Creation." In Raymond Leslie Williams (ed.), *The Novel in the Americas*. Niwot, CO: University Press of Colorado. 145–52.

———. 1993. "Errante, errática." In Juan Carlos Létora (ed.), *Una poética de literatura menor: La narrativa de Diamela Eltit*. Santiago, Chile: Cuarto Propio. 17–25.

——— and Paz Errázuriz. 1994. *El infarto del alma*. Santiago, Chile: Francisco Zegers.

———.1995. "L. Iluminada en sus ficciones: conversación con Diamela Eltit." Interview by Fernando Burgos and M.J. Fenwick. *Inti: revista de literatura hispánica* 40–41: 335–66.

———. 1997a. *E. Luminata*. Translated by Ronald Christ. Santa Fe: Lumen.

———. 1997b. "Nomadic Bodies." *Review: Latin American Literature and Arts* 54: 42–50.

——— . 2000a. *Emergencias*. Santiago, Chile: Planeta.

Eltit, Diamela, Nuria Amat, Carlos Monsivais, Clara Obligado, Andrés Rivera, and Álvaro Vargas Llosa. 2000b. "2001: El desafío y la esperanza." http://www.clarin.com/suplementos/zona/2000/12/31/z-00301.htm (accessed August 8, 2005).

———. 2001. *Diamela Eltit: Conversación en Princeton*. Interview by Michael Lazzara. http://www.princeton.edu/plasweb/publications/Cuadernos/cuaderno5_frontcover.pdf (accessed April 28, 2004).

———. 2002a. *Mano de obra*. Barcelona: Seix Barral.

———. 2002b. "Otro giro a la literatura." Interview by María Teresa Cárdenas. http://www.letras.s5.com/eltit080802.htm (accessed April 27, 2004).

Emery, Amy Fass. 1996. *The Anthropological Imagination in Latin American Literature*. Columbia, MS: University of Missouri Press.

Epps, Brad. 1995. "Proper Conduct: Reinaldo Arenas, Fidel Castro, and the Politics of Homosexuality." *Journal of the History of Sexuality* 6(1): 231–83.

———. 1996. *Significant Violence: Oppression and Resistance in the Narratives of Juan Goytisolo, 1970–1990*. Oxford: Clarendon Press.

Esterrich, Carmelo. 1994. "La trayectoria exílica de Reinaldo Arenas." Diss. University of Wisconsin-Madison.

Estévez, Abilio. 1995. "Between Nightfall and Vengeance: Remembering Reinaldo Arenas." In Ruth Behar (ed.), *Bridges to Cuba/Puentes a Cuba*. Ann Arbor: University of Michigan Press. 305–13.

Facio, Elisa. 2000. "Jineterismo during the Special Period." In John Cotman and Eloise Linger (eds.), *Cuban Transitions at the Millennium*. Largo, MD: International Development Options. 55–75.

Felman, Shoshana. 2003 [1985]. *Writing and Madness (Literature/Philosophy/ Psychoanalysis)*. Translated by Martha Noel Evans, Shoshana Felman, with the assistance of Brian Massumi. Appendix translated by Barbara Johnson. Palo Alto: Stanford University Press.

Fernández Retamar, Roberto. 1989. *Caliban and Other Essays*. Translated by Edward Baker. Minneapolis: University of Minnesota Press.

———. 2003. *Todo Calibán*. San Juan, Puerto Rico: Ediciones Callejón.

Flores de Franco, Ana Beatriz. 1996. *Voces e ideologías: Estudios bajtinianos*. Córdoba: Alción.

Fojas, Camilla, 2004. "Literary Cosmotopia and Nationalism in *Ariel*." *CLCWeb: Comparative Literature and Culture* 6(4) http://clcwebjournal.lib.purdue.edu/ clcweb04-4/fojas04.html (accessed January 23, 2005).

"Fondazione Benetton Studi Ricerche." http://www.fbsr.it/eng/ (accessed January 24, 2004).

Foucault, Michel. 1977. In Donald F. Bouchard (ed.), Bouchard and Sherry Simon (trans.), *Language, Counter-Memory, Practice: Selected Essays and Interviews by Michel Foucault*. Ithaca, NY: Cornell University Press.

Fowler Calzada, Víctor. 1992. "Arenas, el irreverente." *La Nuez: Revista Internacional de Arte y Literatura*: 22–23.

Franco, Jean. 1970 [1967]. *The Modern Culture of Latin America: Society and the Artist*. Revised edn. Baltimore, MD: Penguin

———. 1994. *An Introduction to Spanish-American Literature*. 3rd. edn. New York: Cambridge University Press.

———. 1995. "Jean Franco: un retrato." Interview with Diamela Eltit and Nelly Richard. *Revista de Crítica Cultural* 11: 18–21.

———. 2002. *The Decline and Fall of the Lettered City*. Cambridge, MA: Harvard University Press.

Friedman, Milton. 1983. *Milton Friedman en Chile: Bases para un desarrollo económico*. Santiago, Chile: Banco Central.

García, María Cristina. 1996. *Havana USA: Cuban Exiles and Cuban Americans in South Florida, 1959–1994*. Berkeley: University of California Press.

García Canclini, Néstor. 1992. *Culturas híbridas: estrategias para entrar y salir de la Modernidad*. Buenos Aires: Sudamericana.

García-Corales, Guillermo. 1993. "La deconstrucción del poder en *Lumpérica*." In Juan Carlos Létora (ed.), *Una poética de literatura menor: La narrativa de Diamela Eltit*. Santiago, Chile: Cuarto Propio. 111–25.

Giroux, Henry A. 1994. *Disturbing Pleasures*. New York: Routledge.

González Echevarría, Roberto. 1985. *The Voice of the Masters: Writing and Authority in Modern Latin American Literature*. Austin: University of Texas Press.

———. 1993a. Introduction. *De dónde son los cantantes*. By Severo Sarduy. Madrid: Cátedra.

González Echevarría, Roberto. 1993b. "An Outcast of the Island." Review of *Before Night Falls*. *New York Times Book Review* (October 24, 1993b): 33.

González Herrero, Lourdes. 1999. *Papeles de un naufragio* Holguin: Ediciones Holguin.

González Pérez, Aníbal. 1983. *La crónica modernista hispanoamericana*. Madrid: José Porrúa Turanzas.

Gramsci, Antonio. 1985. In David Forgacs and Geoffrey Nowell-Smith (eds.) and William Boelhower (trans.), *Selections from Cultural Writings*. Cambridge, MA: Harvard University Press.

Grinberg, Leon and Rebeca Grinberg. 1989. *Psychoanalytic Perspectives on Migration and Exile*. New Haven, CT: Yale University Press.

Grünfeld, Mihai G. 1989. "Cosmopolitismo modernista y vanguardista: una identidad latinoamerica divergente." *Revista Iberoamericana* 146–47: 33–41.

Guerra, Wendy. 2003. "Olga ya no es nombre ruso." *Encuentro de la cultura cubana* 26/27: 271–76.

Guevara, Ernesto. 1973. *El socialismo y el hombre en Cuba [por] Ernesto Che Guevara*. Montevideo: Ediciones Nativas Libro.

Gugelberger, Georg. 1996. *The Real Thing: Testimonial Discourse and Latin America*. Durham, NC: Duke University Press.

Gutiérrez Alea, Tomás and Juan Carlos Tabio, directors. 1995. *Fresa y chocolate*. Miramax.

Hall, Stuart. 1997. "The Local and the Global: Globalization and Ethnicity." In Anthony D. King (ed.), *Culture, Globalization and the World-System. Contemporary Conditions for the Representation of Identity*. Minneapolis: University of Minnesota Press. 19–39.

Haraway, Donna. 1991. *Symians, Cyborgs, and Women: The Reinvention of Nature*. New York: Routledge.

Harpham, Geoffrey Galt. 1995. "Ethics." In Frank Lentricchia and Thomas McLaughlin (eds.), *Critical Terms for Literary Study*, 2nd edn. Chicago, IL: University of Chicago Press. 387–405.

Hassan, Salah. 2002. "Origins of Postmodern Cuba." *CR: The New Centennial Review* 2(2): 1–17.

Hasson, Lilliane. 2002. "¿Y en Francia Qué?" http://www.hispanocubana. org/revistahc/paginas/revista8910/REVISTA12/articulos/enfrancia.html (accessed April 27, 2004).

Henríquez Ureña, Pedro. 1963 [1945]. *Literary Currents in Hispanic America*. New York: Russell and Russell.

Hernández-Reguant, Ariana. forthcoming. "Radio Taino and the Cuban Quest for Identi . . . Qué?" In Doris Sommer (ed.), "*Cultural Agency in the Americas*," Durham, NC: Duke University Press.

Hillson, Jon. 2001. "The Sexual Politics of Reinaldo Arenas: Fact, Fiction, and the Real Record of the Cuban Revolution." *La Jiribilla*. http://www.lajiribilla.cuba web.cu/2001/nro1mayo2001.html (accessed January 30, 2003).

Hochman, David. 2004. "In searching we trust." *The New York Times* (March 12, 2004). Accessed online.

Hoz, Pedro de la. 2001. "Antes que anochezca:¿Arte o panfleto?" *La Jiribilla*. http://www.lajiribilla.cubaweb.cu/2001/nro1mayo2001.html (accessed January 30, 2003).

Hurley, Andrew. 1995. "Del mar y sus ritmos: Arenas en inglés." Interview with César Salgado. *Apuntes posmodernos* 6(1): 40–49.

Huyssen, Andreas. 2002. "Adorno in Reverse: From Hollywood to Richard Wagner." In Nigel Gibson and Andrew Ruben (eds.), *Adorno: A Critical Reader*. Oxford: Blackwell. 29–56.

Ichaso, León and Orlando Jiménez-Leal, directors. 1979. *El super*. New Yorker Films.

Jameson, Fredric. 1984. "Postmodernism, or The Cultural Logic of Late Capitalism." *New Left Review* 146: 53–92.

———. 1986. "Third-World Literature in the Era of Multinational Capitalism." *Social Text* 15: 65–88.

———. 1991. *Postmodernism, or, The Cultural Logic of Late Capitalism*. Durham, North Carolina: Duke Up.

———. 1996. "On Literary and Cultural Import-Substitution in the Third World: The Case of Testimonio." In Georg Gugelberger (ed.), *The Real Thing: Testimonial Discourse and Latin America*. 172–91.

Jara, René and Hernán Vidal, eds. 1986. *Testimonio y literatura*. Minneapolis: Society for the Study of Contemporary and Lusophone Revolutionary Literatures.

Jofré, Manuel Alcides. 1986. *Literatura chilena en el exilio*. Santiago, Chile: Centro de Indagación y Expresión Cultural y Artística.

Johnson, Scott. 1977. *The Case of the Cuban Poet Heberto Padilla*. New York: Gordon Press.

Kadir, Djelal. 1993. *The Other Writing: Postcolonial Essays in Latin American Culture*. West Lafayette, IN: Purdue University Press.

Kant, Immanuel. 1983. *Perpetual Peace, and Other Essays on Politics, History, and Morals*. Translated by Ted Humphrey. Indianapolis, IN: Hackett Publishing Company.

Kaplan, Caren. 1996. *Questions of Travel: Postmodern Discourses of Displacement*. Durham, NC: Duke University Press.

Kard, K. S. 1970. *Les guérilleros au pouvoir: l' itinéraire politique de la révolution cubaine*. Paris: Robert Laffort.

Kristeva, Julia. 1982. *Powers of Horror: An Essay on Abjection*. Translated by Leon S. Roudiez. New York: Columbia University Press.

———. 1991. *Strangers to Ourselves*. Translated by Leon S. Roudiez. New York: Columbia University Press.

———. 1993. *Nations without Nationalisms*. Translated by Leon S. Roudiez. New York: Columbia University Press.

Lagos, María Inés. 1993. "Reflexiones sobre la representación del sujeto en dos textos de Diamela Eltit." In Juan Carlos Létora (ed.), *Una poética de literatura menor: La narrativa de Diamela Eltit*. Santiago, Chile: Cuarto Propio. 127–40.

Lamming, George. 1984 [1960]. *The Pleasures of Exile*. New York: Allison and Busby.

Lechte, John. 1990. *Julia Kristeva*. New York: Routledge.

Leiner, Marvin. 1994. *Sexual Politics in Cuba: Machismo, Homosexuals, and AIDS*. Boulder, CO: Westview Press.

Lezama, Lima, José. 1993 [1957]. *La expresión americana*. Mexico City: Fondo de Cultura Económica.

Lindstrom, Naomi. 1998. *The Social Conscience of Latin American Writing*. Austin: University of Texas Press.

Loss, Jacqueline. 2000. "Worldly Conjunctions and Disjunctions: On Cosmopolitanism and Nomadism in Diamela Eltit's *Por la patria* (1986) and *El padre mío* (1989)." *Chasqui: Revista de literatura latinoamericana* 29(2): 24–42.

Ludmer, Josefina, ed. 1994. *Las culturas de fin de siglo en América Latina*. Buenos Aires: Beatriz Viterbo Editora.

Lumsden, Ian. 1995. *Machos, Maricones, and Gays: Cuba and Homosexuality*. Philadelphia, PA: Temple University.

Machin, Horacio. 2000. "Roberto Fernández Retamar, profesional de la utopia." In Elzbieta Sklodowska and Ben A. Heller (eds.), *Roberto Fernández Retamar y los estudios lantionamericanos*. Pittsburgh, PA: Instituto Internacional de Literatura Iberoamericana. 155–81.

Malverde Disselkoen, Ivette. 1991. "Esquizofrenia y literatura: El discurso de padre e hija en *El padre mío* de Diamela Eltit." *Acta Literaria* 16: 69–76.

Manrique, Jaime. 1999. *Eminent Maricones: Arenas, Lorca, Puig, and Me (Living Out, Gay and Lesbian Autobiographies)*. Madison, WI: University of Wisconsin Press.

Marín, Lynda. 1991. "Speaking Out Together: Testimonials of Latin American Women." *Latin American Perspectives* 18(3): 51–68.

Martí, José. 1975 [1891]. "Nuestra América." In *Obras Completas* 6. Havana: Ciencias Sociales. 15–23.

———. *Ismaelillo*. 1977 [1882] Ángel Augier. Havana: Arte y Literatura.

McClennan, Sophia A. 2001. "Chilex: The Economy of Transnational Media Culture." *Cultural Logic* 3(2). http://eserver.org/clogic/3–1&2/mcclennen.html (accessed January 23, 2005).

McKillop, Alan D. 1965. "Local Attachment and Cosmopolitanism—The Eighteenth Century Pattern." In Frederick W. Hilles and Harold Bloom (eds.), *From Sensibility to Romanticism: Essays Presented to Frederick A. Pottle*. New York: Oxford University Press. 191–218.

Menchú, Rigoberta. 1984. In Elisabeth Burgos-Debray (ed.) and Ann Wright (trans.), *I, Rigoberta Menchú: An Indian Woman in Guatemala*. London: Verso.

Menchú, Rigoberta and Elizabeth Burgos-Derbray 1983. *Me llamo Rigoberta Menchú así me nació la conciencia*. Mexico City: Siglo Veintiuno.

Méndez Rodenas, Adriana. 1998. *Gender and Nationalism in Colonial Cuba: The Travels of Santa Cruz y Montalvo, Condesa de Merlin*. Nashville, TN: Vanderbilt University Press.

Mier Noriega y Guerra, José Servando Teresa de. 1997. *Los Imprescindibles: Fray Servando Teresa de Mier*. Prologue by Héctor Perea. Mexico City: Cal y Arena.

Mish, Frederick C., ed. 1985. *Webster's New Ninth Collegiate Dictionary.* Springfield, MA: Merriam-Webster.

Moi, Toril, ed. 1986. "Introduction." *The Kristeva Reader.* New York: Columbia University Press.

Molloy, Sylvia. 1991. *At Face Value: Autobiographical Writing in Spanish America.* New York: Cambridge University Press.

———. 1998. "The Politics of Posing." In Molloy and Robert McKee Irwin (eds.), *Hispanisms and Homosexualities.* Durham, NC: Duke University Press. 141–60.

Monguió, Luis. 1968. "De la problemática del modernismo; la crítica y el cosmopolitismo." In Homero Castillo (ed.), *Estudios críticos sobre el modernismo.* Madrid: Gredos. 254–66.

Moraña, Mabel. 1998. "El boom del subalterno." In Santiago Castro-Gómez and Eduardo Mendieta (eds.), *Teorías sin disciplina. Latinoamericanismo, poscolonialidad y globalización en debate.* Mexico City: University of San Francisco Press. 233–43.

Moreiras, Alberto. 1996. "The Aura of Testimonio." In Georg Gugelberger (ed.), *The Real Thing: Testimonial Discourse and Latin America.* Durham, NC: Duke University Press. 192–224.

———. 1998. "Irrupción y conservación en las guerras culturales." *Revista de Crítica Cultural* 17: 68–71.

———. 1999. *Tercer espacio: Literatura y duelo en América Latina.* Santiago, Chile: LOM Ediciones.

Morrison, Stephen M. "Sales of Arenas's Texts," personal e-mail to Jacqueline Loss, August 9, 2001.

Naremore, James. 2000. *Film Adaptation.* New Brunswick, NJ: Rutgers.

Narváez, Jorge. 1986. "El testimonio 1972–1982: Transformaciones en el sistema literario." In René Jara and Hernán Vidal (eds.), *Testimonio y literatura.* Minneapolis: Society for the Study of Contemporary and Lusophone Revolutionary Literatures. 235–80.

Navarro, Desiderio. 2001. "In Media Res Publicas: On Intellectuals and Social Criticism in the Cuban Public Sphere." *Nepantla: Views from South* 2(2): 355–71.

Negrín, María. 1997. "Reinaldo Arenas." In Verity Smith (ed.) and Ann Wright (trans.), *Encyclopedia of Latin American Literature.* Chicago, IL: Fitzroy Dearborn. 48–49.

Nethersole, Reingard. 2001. "Models of Globalization." *PMLA* 116: 638–49.

Neustadt, Robert Alan. 1995a. "Incisive Incisions: (Re)Articulating the Discursive Body in Diamela Eltit's *Lumpérica.*" *Cincinnati Romance Review* 14: 151–56.

———. 1995b. "Diamela Eltit: Clearing Space for Critical Performance." *Women and Performance: A Journal of Feminist Theory* 7(2)–8(1): 218–39.

———. 1997. "Diamela Eltit: Leyendo entre signos." In Magdalena Maíz and Luis H. Peña (eds.), *Modalidades de representación del sujeto auto/bio/gráfico femenino.* Mexico City: Colección Andamios. 55–69.

———. 1999. *(Con)Fusing Signs and Postmodern Positions Spanish American Performance, Experimental Writing, and the Critique of Political Confusion.* New York: Garland.

Nietzsche, Friedrich. 1974. *The Gay Science.* Translated by Walter Kaufmann. New York: Vintage.

Norat, Gisela. 2002. *Marginalities: Diamela Eltit and the Subversion of the Mainstream in Chile.* Newark, DE: University of Delaware Press.

Nordau, Max. 1993 [1892]. *Degeneration.* Introduction and translation by George L. Mosse. Lincoln, NE: University of Nebraska Press.

Nuez, Iván de la. 1999. "De la tempestad a la intemperie." In De la Nuez (ed.), *Paisajes después del muro.* Barcelona: Ediciones Península. 163–79.

Nussbaum, Martha C. 1996. *For Love of Country: Debating the Limits of Patriotism.* Boston, MA: Beacon Press.

Ocasio, Rafael. 2002. "Gays and the Cuban Revolution: The Case of Reinaldo Arenas." http://www.erin.utoronto.ca/~w3his454/Ocasio2002.pdf (accessed April 27, 2004).

Olivárez, Carlos. 1997. *Nueva narrativa chilena.* Santiago, Chile: LOM Ediciones.

Padilla, Heberto. 1989. *La mala memoria.* Barcelona: Plaza and Janés.

Paz, Octavio. 1964. "El caracol y la sirena." *Cuadrivio.* Mexico City: Joaquín Mortiz.

Pereira, Manuel. 1992. "Reinaldo antes del alba." *Quimera* 111: 54–58.

Pérez, Gabriel. 1993. "Donde las arenas son más diáfanas: Reinaldo Arenas: El enfant más terrible." *Caimán barbudo digital.* http://www.caimanbarbudo.cu/caiman318/paginas/reinaldo.htm (accessed December 30, 2004).

Pérez Firmat, Gustavo. 1989. *The Cuban Condition: Translation and Identity in Modern Cuban Literature.* New York: Cambridge University Press.

Perriam, Chris. 2003. *Stars and Masculinities in Spanish Cinema: From Banderas to Bardem.* New York: Oxford University Press.

Pioneer News. 2001. "Reinaldo Arenas: Star of Internet Journal's Review." http://www.thepioneer.com/international/june2_debut.htm (accessed August 14, 2005).

Pollock, Sheldon. 2000. "Cosmopolitanism and Vernacular in History." *Public Culture* 12(3): 591–627.

Pogge, Thomas Winfried *Menko.* 2002. *World Poverty and Human Rights: Cosmopolitan Responsibilities and Reforms.* Malden, MA: Blackwell.

Pratt, Mary Louise. 1992. *Imperial Eyes: Travel Writing and Transculturation.* New York: Routledge.

———. 1996. "Overwriting Pinochet: Undoing the Culture of Fear in Chile. (The Places of History: Regionalism Revisited in Latin America)." *Modern Language Quarterly* 57(2): 13pp. Online. Web Searchbank (accessed April 13, 1997).

Quintero Herencia, Juan Carlos. 2002. *Fulguración del espacio: Letras e imaginario institucional de la Revolución Cubana (1960–1971).* Rosario, Argentina: Beatriz Viterbo.

Quiroga, José. 2000. *Tropics of Desire: Interventions from Queer Latino America.* New York: New York University Press.

Ramírez, Liliana. 1995. "La autobiografía como desfiguración." *Texto y contexto* 28: 189–208.

Ramírez, Mari Carmen. 1999. *Cantos Parallelos: Visual Parody in Contemporary Argentinean Art.* Austin: Jack S. Blanton Museum of Art, University of Texas Press.

Ramos, Julio. 2000. "Dispositivos del amor y la locura." In María Ines Lagos (ed.), *Creación y resistencia: La narrativa de Diamela Eltit, 1983–1998.* Santiago,

Chile: Centro de Estudios de Genero y Cultura en America Latina, Facultad de Filosofia y Humanidades. Also available at *Nomadías* 2. Online. http://www.uchile.cl/facultades/filosofia/publicaciones/nomadias/n2/ramosj.html (accessed January 24, 2004).

Rauhe, Walter. 1994. "Sognando I Tropici- Viaggio nella Cuba di oggi diventata il regno del baratto; Il Che fa colore tra rum e salsa." *Il Sole 24 Ore* (April 10). Domenica Tempo Liberato 38.

Renan, Joseph Ernest. 1878. *Caliban, suite de La tempête, drame philosophique.* Paris: Calmann-Lévy.

Richard, Nelly. 1986. *Margins and Institutions: Art in Chile since 1973.* Melbourne: Art and Text.

———. 1989. *La estratificación de los márgenes: sobre arte, cultura y políticas.* Santiago, Chile: Francisco Zegers.

———. 1993. "Cultural Peripheries: Latin America and Postmodernist Decentering." *Boundary 2: The Postmodernism Debate in Latin America* 20(3): 156–61.

———. 1994. "Bordes, diseminación, postmodernismo: una metáfora latinoamericana de fin de siglo." In Josefina Ludmer (ed.), *Las culturas de fin de siglo en América Latina.* Buenos Aires: Beatriz Viterbo Editora. 240–48.

———. 1998a. "Intersectando Latinoamérica con el latinoamericanismo: discurso académico y crítica cultural." In Santiago Castro-Gómez and Eduardo Mendieta (eds.), *Teorías sin disciplina. Latinoamericanismo, poscolonialidad y globalización en debate.* Mexico City: University of San Francisco Press. 245–70.

———. 1998b. *Residuos y metáforas (Ensayos de crítica cultural sobre el Chile de la Transición).* Santiago, Chile: Cuarto Propio.

Riera, Miguel. 1992. "El mundo es alucinante." *Quimera* 111: 58–59.

Robbins, Bruce. 1993. *Secular Vocations: Intellectuals, Professionalism, Culture.* New York: Verso.

———. 1995. "The Weird Heights: On Cosmopolitanism, Feeling, and Power." *Differences: A Journal of Feminist Cultural Studies* 7(1): 23pp. Online. Academic Index (database on University of Texas system; accessed September 9, 1996).

———. 1998. "Introduction Part I: Actually Existing Cosmopolitanism." In Pheng Cheah and Bruce Robbins (eds.), *Cosmopolitics: Thinking and Feeling beyond the Nation.* Minneapolis: University of Minnesota Press. 1–20.

———. 1999. *Feeling Global: Internationalism in Distress.* New York: New York University Press.

Robert, Paul. 2001. *Le grand Robert de la langue française.* Paris: Dictonnaires Le Robert.

Rodó, José Enrique. 1917. *Cinco Ensayos: Montalvo.-Ariel.-Bolívar.-Rubén Darío.-liberalismo y jacobinismo.* Madrid: América.

———. 1988. *Ariel.* Translated by Margaret Sayers Peden. Austin: University of Texas Press.

———. 1994 [1900]. *Ariel.* Mexico City: Espasa-Calpe.

Rodríguez, Andrea. "Rescatan en Cuba a Reinaldo Arenas." *Reforma.com.* www.reforma.com/parseo/printpage?pagetoprint=./cultural/articulo (accessed July 21, 2001).

Rodriguez, Richard. 1982. *Hunger of Memory: The Education of Richard Rodriguez: An Autobiography.* Boston: D.R. Godine.

———. 1992. *Days of Obligation. An Argument with my Mexican Father.* New York: Viking.

Roig de Leuchsenring, Emilio. 1961. *El grupo minorista de intelectuales y artistas habaneros.* Havana: Cuadernos de Historia Habanera.

Rojas, Rafael. 1995. "The Cuban Difference." In Iván de la Nuez (ed.), *La isla posible.* Barcelona: Destino. 235–37.

Rosenblat, Ángel. 1960. *Buenas y malas palabras en el castellano de Venezuela.* Caracas: Ediciones Edime.

Rostagno, Irene. 1997. *Searching for Recognition: The Promotion of Latin American Literature in the United States.* Westport, CT: Greenwood Press.

Said, Edward W. 1983. *The World, the Text, and the Critic.* Cambridge, MA: Harvard University Press.

Salomon, Noël. 1978. "America Latina y el cosmopolitismo en algunos cuentos de *Azul.*" In Matyas Horanyi (ed.), *Actas del simposio internacional de estudios hispánicos: Budapest, 18–19 de agosto de 1976.* Budapest: La Academia de Ciencias de Hungría. 13–37.

———. 1979. "Cosmopolitanism and Internationalism in the History of Ideas in Latin America." *Cultures* 6(1): 83–108.

Sánchez, Reinaldo, ed. 1994. *Reinaldo Arenas: Recuerdo y presencia.* Miami: Universal.

Sánchez-Eppler, Benigno. 1994. "Call My Son Ismael: Exiled Paternity and the Father/Son Eroticism in Reinaldo Arenas." *Differences* 6(1): 66–97.

———.1996. "The Displacement of Cuban Homosexuality in the Fiction and Autobiography of Reinaldo Arenas." In Michael J. Shapiro and Hayward R. Alker (eds.), *Challenging Boundaries: Global Flows, Territorial Identities.* Minneapolis: University of Minnesota Press. 383–407.

Santa Cruz y Montalvo, Mercedes, Condesa de Merlin. 1974 [1844]. *Viaje a la Habana.* Havana: Arte y Literatura. Santí, Enrico Mario. 1984. "The Life and Times of Reinaldo Arenas." *Michigan Quarterly Review* 23: 227–36.

Santi, Erinque Mario. 1984. "The life and times of Ronaldo Arenas." *Michigan Quarterly Review* 23(2): 227–236.

Schlereth, Thomas J. 1977. *The Cosmopolitan Ideal in Enlightenment Thought: Its Form and Function in the Ideas of Franklin, Hume, and Voltaire, 1694–1790.* Notre Dame: University of Notre Dame Press.

Schnabel, Julian, director. 2000. *Before Night Falls.* AOL/Fine Line/Time Warner.

Schwartz, Jorge. 1983. *Vanguarda e cosmopolitismo.* São Paulo, Brazil: Perspectiva.

———. 1991. *Las vanguardias latinoamericanas: Textos programáticos y críticos.* Madrid: Cátedra.

Senegal, Humberto. 1992. "Reinaldo Arenas y Celestino antes del alba." *La Nuez: Revista Internacional de Arte y Literatura* 4(12): 6–8.

Shouse, Corey. 2000. "The Benetton Effect: The Testimonial Aesthetic and First-Third World Markets of Symbolic Goods." In Debra Castillo and Mary Jo Dudley (eds.), *Transforming Cultures in the America.* Ithaca, NY: Cornell University Press. 79–89.

Silva, José Asunción. 1968 [1925]. In Héctor Orjuela (ed.), *Obras completas Tomo 2 (De sobremesa)*. Buenos Aires: Plus Ultra.

Smith, Paul Julian. 1994. "The Language of Strawberry." *Sight and Sound* 12: 30–34.

———. 1996. *Vision Machines: Cinema, Literature and Sexuality in Spain and Cuba, 1983–93*. New York: Verso.

Smorkaloff, Pamela María. 1997. *Readers and Writers in Cuba: A Social History of Print Culture, 1830s–1990s*. New York: Garland Publishing.

Soler Puig, José. 1975. *El pan Dormido*. Havana: Uniōn, 1975.

Sommer, Doris. 1993. "Resisting the Heat: Menchú, Morrison, and Incompetent Readers." In Amy Kaplan and Donald E. Pease (eds.), *Cultures of United States Imperialism*. Durham, NC: Duke University Press. 407–33.

Sontag, Susan. 1990. *On Photography*. New York: Doubleday Anchor Books.

Soto, Francisco. 1994. *Reinaldo Arenas: The Pentagonía*. Gainesville: University Press of Florida.

Strausfeld, Michi. 2000a. *Cubanismo!: Junge Erzähler aus Kuba*. Frankfurt: Suhrkamp.

———. 2000b. *Nuevos narradores cubanos*. Madrid: Ediciones Siruela.

Tafra, Sylvia. 1998. *Diamela Eltit: El rito de pasaje como estrategia textual*. Santiago, Chile: RiL.

Tierney-Tello, Mary Beth. 1999. "Testimony, Ethics, and the Aesthetic in Diamela Eltit." *PMLA* 114: 78–96.

Tinic, Senna. 1997. "United Colors and United Meanings: Benetton and the Commodification of Social Issues," *Journal of Communication* 47(3): 3–25.

Toulmin, Stephen. 1990. *Cosmopolis: The Hidden Agenda of Modernity*. New York: Macmillan.

Trigo, Benigno. 1994. "La función crítica del discurso alienista en *De sobremesa* de José Asunción Silva." *Hispanic Journal* 15(1): 133–46.

Ubieta Gómez, Enrique. 2001. "Arenas y la noches: Notas sobre un libro de memorias." *La Jiribilla* www.lajiribilla.cubaweb.cu/2001/nro1mayo2001.html (accessed January 30, 2003).

Ugresic, Dubravka. 2003. "Alchemy." *Context: A Forum for Literary Arts and Culture* 13 online edition. http://www.centerforbookculture.org/context/no13/ugresic.html (accessed April 28, 2004).

"United Colors of Benetton: Who We Are: Overview." http://www.benettongroup.com/en/whoweare/overview.htm (accessed December 30, 2004).

Unruh, Vicky. 1994. *Latin American Vanguards: The Art of Contentious Encounters*. Berkeley: University of California Press.

Valdés, Adriana. 1996. *Composición de lugar*. Santiago, Chile: Editorial Universitaria.

Valera, Juan. 1994. "Carta-Prólogo de Juan Valera." In Rubén Darío (ed.), *Azúl*. Mexico City: Espasa Calpe. 9–26.

Van Delden, Maarten, 1990. "The Banquets of Civilization: The Idea of Ancient Greece in Rodó, Reyes and Fuentes." *Annals of Scholarship: An International Quarterly in the Humanities and Social Sciences* 7(3): 303–21.

Victoria, Carlos. 1996. "La catarata." *Apuntes postmodernos* 6(1): 36–38.

Videla de Rivero, Gloria. 1989. "El simultaneísmo cubista-creacionista entre cosmopolitismo, autorreferencialidad y trascendencia." *La Torre: Revista de La Universidad de Puerto Rico* 12: 565–86.

Villanueva-Collado. Alfredo. 1988. "Ideología y política; José Asunción Silva y la corrupción de la semilla histórica en *De sobremesa*." *Discurso literario* 6(1): 255–66.

———. 1991. "Gender Ideology and Spanish American Critical Practice: José Asuncion Silva's Case." In Julio Rodríguez-Luis and William Luis (eds.), *Translating Latin America: Culture as Text*. Binghamton: Center for Research in Translation. 113–25.

Weiss, Philip. 2001. "Big." *The New York Times Magazine* (March 25, 2001): 44+.

Wenders, Wim, director. 1999. *Buena Vista Social Club*. A Road Movies Production in association with Kintop Pictures, ARTE, and ICAIC.

West-Durán, Alan. 1997. *Tropics of History: Cuba Imagined*. Westport, CT: Bergin and Garvey.

Westerberg, Rivera. 2003. "Eltit ataca y es atacada desde la alienación del Consumismo." *Pieldeleopardo: Revista latinoamericana de cultura y política* 12 (March). http://old.pieldeleopardo.com/N12/ (accessed December 27, 2004).

Williams, Gareth. 2002. *The Other Side of the Popular: Neoliberalism and Subalternity in Latin America*. Durham, NC: Duke University Press.

"World Health Organization Mental Health Unit." http://whokosovo.exclusion. net/trieste.asp (accessed January 24, 2004).

"World Health Report 2001: Audio Clips." World Health Organization Mediacentre. http://www.who.int/multimedia/whr2001/photo.html (accessed January 24, 2004).

Young, Allen. 1981. *Gays under the Cuban Revolution*. San Francisco: Grey Fox Press.

Yúdice, George. 1993. "We are Not the World." *Social Text* 31–32: 202–16.

Index